Violence and Grace

Rethinking the Early Modern

Violence and Grace

Exceptional Life between Shakespeare and Modernity

Nichole E. Miller

Northwestern University Press
Evanston, Illinois

Northwestern University Press
www.nupress.northwestern.edu

Printed in the United States of America

10 9 8 7 6 5 4 3 2 1

ISBN 978-0-8101-3658-8 (paper)

The Library of Congress has cataloged the original, hardcover edition as follows:

Miller, Nichole E., author.
Violence and grace : exceptional life between Shakespeare and modernity / Nichole E. Miller.
pages cm. — (Rethinking the Early Modern)
ISBN 978-0-8101-3014-2 (cloth : alk. paper) — ISBN 978-0-8101-6808-4 (ebook)
1. English drama—Early modern and Elizabethan, 1500–1600—History and criticism. 2. Politics and literature—England—History—16th century. 3. Violence in literature. 4. Sex role in literature. 5. Political science—Philosophy—20th century. I. Title. II. Series: Rethinking the Early Modern.
PR658.P65M55 2014
822.309358—dc23

2014033199

CONTENTS

ACKNOWLEDGMENTS

"Acknowledgments" seems a wildly inadequate heading for what these paragraphs need to convey—partly because to "acknowledge" usually means to concede something or grant a point, perhaps grudgingly. Though this book concerns both violence and grace, I am happy to say that the acknowledgments are all about grace—the many gifts, tangible and intangible, bestowed by family, friends, mentors, colleagues, students, carers, institutions, and communities that have made it possible.

This book started as a dissertation at the University of California, Irvine, but really with two graduate seminars in winter 2001: Julia Reinhard Lupton's "Marlowe and Shakespeare" and Étienne Balibar's "Cruelty, Civility, Tragedy." Jacques Derrida's 2000–2004 lectures on "The Death Penalty" and "The Beast and the Sovereign" also planted many ideas, as I am realizing more than ever now that the lectures are appearing in print. Though various works by each are cited in the following pages, I wanted to note at the outset that those early lectures and seminars proved formative in ways I am still discovering—intellectually, pedagogically, ethically, politically. Julia later became the best of advisors, and remains a generous mentor and friend. One of the most innovative scholars and writers I have ever known, she is also a gracious advocate and builder of households and community. Victoria Silver's deep learning, unique modes of teaching, and loving support continue to sustain me. Her perspectives on genre, equity, and political philosophy inform my thinking in ways that (again) I'm still figuring out, though my debt to her is perhaps most evident in chapter 2. Jane Newman, my first mentor at Irvine and one of the first to sit down with me to read works by Agamben and Benjamin so crucial to this book, still answers last-minute e-mail queries about German quotations, and remains a staunch mentor and friend. I am also glad to thank Jayne Lewis and the late Richard Kroll for comments on a very early version of chapter 1, and Étienne Balibar for comments on a seminar paper on *Coriolanus* that remained very much in my mind while I was writing chapter 3 some five years later. In addition to those already mentioned, I am grateful to the faculties of the English, Comparative Literature, and Women's Studies Departments, past and present.

During my first years in California, Nicholas Dodge, Kerry Duff, and Jay Rollins became my extended family—I thank them again for being there in such vital ways. In California and afterward, fellow graduate students Matt Ancell, Kelly Corwin, Jason Denman, Anna Kornbluh, Debra Ligorski, Gene Navakas, Jennifer Rust, Melissa Sanchez, Walt Wadiak, Sarah Wheaton, and Catherine Winiarski talked through ideas, read and commented (often more than once) on all or part of many of these chapters, as well as on book, grant, and conference proposals. The dissertation wouldn't have been finished without Paul Dahlgren, Linda Greenberg, and Katherine Mack. Matt, Jason, Jen, Melissa, and Catherine continue to field reading requests, occasionally collaborate on conferences, and inspire me with their own work.

Coming to Temple in 2008 meant becoming part of two lively intellectual communities, my colleagues and students at the university and the members of the Philadelphia-area medieval and early modern Works in Progress (WIP) group. Kathy Biddick and Shannon Miller were, and are, wise shepherds, and have also become beloved friends. I wouldn't have made it through the first year here, let alone six, without their compassionate guidance. My colleagues in the English department and beyond have supported me in immeasurable ways—special thanks to those who have read drafts of everything from syllabi to chapters and book and grant proposals, and have taken the time to talk about them afterward. Shelley Brivic, Rachel Blau DuPlessis, Eli Goldblatt, Kate Henry, Joyce Joyce, Sue-Im Lee, Peter Logan, Steve Newman, Dan O'Hara, Paula Robison, James Salazar, Alan Singer, Larry Venuti, and Sue Wells have generously offered assistance and advice whenever I sought it. Kristina DeVoe, librarian extraordinaire, has ordered books, arranged sessions with Special Collections, and assisted with various queries and advice over the years. My students at all levels, but particularly graduate students in past seminars on "Shakespeare and Political Life" and "Shakespeare and Paul," provide a never-ending source of intellectual stimulation. Talissa Ford, Alex Gottesman, Brian Teare, Shannon Walters, and Gabe Wettach have been true friends.

A 2001 conversation with Walt Wadiak about the economy of the gift became yet another seed for chapter 3, and the dissertation version was nurtured by conversations and questions after job talks at Temple, Wayne State, Willamette, and Buffalo in early 2008; I thank my hosts for their hospitality as well as their stimulating interlocutorship. A much-revised version of this chapter appeared in *Criticism* in 2009. I am grateful to Arthur Marotti and Ken Jackson for suggesting I submit it, Jonathan Flatley for his comments and editorial expertise, and the no-longer anonymous reader for his feedback. Most of *Violence and Grace* consists of previously unpublished work, though in addition to the *Coriolanus* piece, a slightly different version of the prologue appeared in a special issue of *The Journal of Cultural and Religious Theory* on Arendt and Shakespeare in 2006, under the aegis of Julia Lupton. As part of the Temple Premodern Studies Symposium, I presented portions of chapter 1 as a talk in a 2009 colloquium, "On the Undeadness of the King's Two Bodies," sponsored by the Center for Humanities at Temple (CHAT). Thank you to Kathy Biddick and Shannon Miller for organizing the gathering, as well as to Graham Hammill, Ben Parrish, Eric Song, and Garrett Sullivan for their thoughtful questions and conversation. The final two chapters and introduction of *Violence and Grace* were written, and the remaining chapters heavily revised, thanks to support provided by a semester of junior study leave and a summer research stipend awarded by Temple's College of Liberal Arts, as well as the course release attached to a yearlong CHAT faculty fellowship. The CHAT fellowship stipend and two research grants-in-aids from Temple's College of Liberal Arts enabled me to travel to conferences and archives as well as to purchase research materials and illustrations for the book, and I am glad to acknowledge this institutional support.

Current and former WIPsters Alice Dailey, Jane Hedley, Matt Kozusko, Zack Lesser, Kristin Poole, Katherine Rowe, Lauren Shohet, Eric Song, Jamie Taylor, and Elly Truitt have workshopped drafts, answered random e-mail questions, and generally helped me navigate the writing of this book and the beginnings of two new research projects, as well as introducing me to some of the many resources for Renaissance studies in the region. Scholars I've met at conferences and talks over the years have provided yet another form of intellectual community. Seminars at the American Comparative Literature Association and the Shakespeare Association of America and panels at the Renaissance Society of America and the Group for Early Modern Cultural Studies provided initial, wider audiences for bits of every chapter in this book. I have been grateful and astounded by the generous feedback received from fellow participants and audience members. In particular, I would like to thank Curtis Perry for his extensive and helpful comments on sections of an early version of chapter 1 after he moderated our GEMCS panel in 2007; organizer Christopher Pye and participants James Kuzner and Ineke Murakami of the "Shakespeare and Sacrifice" SAA seminar in 2009 for asking astute questions and pushing me to think further about a chunk of chapter 3; Randall Martin for inviting me to contribute a paper to a 2010 RSA panel on "Shakespeare and Paul" that became the genesis for chapter 4, and Tommy Anderson for inviting me to contribute a paper to a 2011 SAA seminar on "Radical Romans and Shakespeare's Politics" that started me on the path to chapter 5. I would also like to thank Rick Barney, Linda Bree, Graham Hammill, Tom Lay, and Jerry Singerman for comments and advice on early drafts of my book proposal.

Henry Carrigan's interest in a one-off paper about *Philoctetes* and Job at a 2009 ACLA seminar on "Politics, Religion, and Literature" and an impromptu talk afterward about what was still, at that point, a mostly unrevised dissertation eventually (and most happily!) led me to Northwestern University Press, where Henry has proven a strong advocate and kindly guide. It gives me very great pleasure to publicly thank my two reviewers at Northwestern, who offered smart, sympathetic, and helpful readings. I am indebted to them for their suggestions, and also for their summaries of my argument and its stakes. They helped me to see my own book much more clearly than I had, and I hope it is stronger as a result. Gianna Mosser marshaled me through the contract process and assisted with early manuscript questions; subsequently, Anne Gendler has supervised and aided every aspect of its production. I owe Anne and her assistants many thanks just for laboring to turn the bug-ridden chapter 5 file into a workable document, and since then she has shepherded the manuscript through the production process, responding to my numerous quibbles and queries with patience, tact, and delightful flashes of humor. I am grateful to Mike Ashby for his diligent copyediting; to the proofreader, Mark Reschke, for catching errors I had missed; and to Steven Moore for his index (and his willingness to add to it at the last moment).

Finally, though, this book would not have come into being without the nurturance of my family (including and sometimes especially its furry members), who have loved and supported me through every struggle as well as sharing each joyous moment. So this book is for my family: past, present, and *à venir*.

Violence and Grace

INTRODUCTION

The Problem: Exceptional Life

Violence and Grace explores the interaction between Renaissance drama and the political thinkers of the first part of the twentieth century. Each chapter stages a dialogue between an early modern play (by Shakespeare, Marlowe, and Middleton) and a modern work of political philosophy (by Walter Benjamin, Carl Schmitt, Ernst Kantorowicz, Hannah Arendt, Simone Weil, and Max Weber) that draws on early modern drama to ground its own critique of modern statecraft. My primary goal is not only to demonstrate the ways the playwrights explore the febrile political tensions of the period, but also to show how their works illuminate modern political phenomena originating in medieval and Renaissance political theology. While the early modern works I analyze emphasize connections between domestic and state forms of violence, refusing any separation of public and private realms, the modern philosophers who appropriate and deploy such texts in their own works do not always remain attentive to this resistance. If the plays contain elements the philosophers occasionally disregard, then we need to reread modern political thinkers in the light of this productive excess. In examining characters suspended outside or above what Aristotle defines as the essentially "political" form of life as that of a man among men, a citizen among citizens, I am interested in the ways both early modern dramatists and modern political thinkers inflect the idea of "exception" when it comes to *life*, focusing on gender and sexuality as primary sites of this inflection.

Violence and Method

This book does not simply use modern theoretical texts to read early modern plays; nor, conversely, is it always explicitly about source study, formalist reading, or intellectual history, though all of these methodologies come into play. Rather, it traces radial synergies and analogies between modernity and early modernity, demonstrating how the plays can highlight what the philosophers leave out. While political theology names the juridical and philosophical lineage of modern states of exception, it does not always take its gendered origins and end points into account. Particularly for literary scholars working in earlier periods, a concern with whatever we define as "real worlds" should not be limited to excavating cultural and historical contexts. Yet how do we negotiate the tricky passages between literary and literal? For me, answering this question requires a consideration of the aesthetic,[1] which bridges the two. I agree with Terry Eagleton's assertion that "aesthetics was born as a discourse of the body."[2] Yet whereas Eagleton emphasizes the connection between aesthetics and class as a socialist corrective to what he claims are the "topical," though nevertheless important, concerns of race and gender, my argument here rests on the assertion that, in a very basic sense, the aesthetic allows us to think about gender and sexuality. Eagleton's argument grounds itself in a Marxist analysis of the connection between bodies and politics, where aesthetics is a "mediating category" that foregrounds bodies as producers of "artefacts," or works of art (where "art" also encompasses craft). While I am interested in this line of argument (particularly when it comes to Coriolanus), Eagleton's opening claim resonates throughout this book more in conjunction with the Foucauldian inheritance from which he occasionally distances himself, a line of thinking that argues the aesthetic is always more or less eroticized, and the erotic more or less aestheticized. Gender stands as the common term for this admittedly simplified equation, if only because bodies motivate and facilitate desires, whether erotic or aesthetic. Examining this dynamic as a subset of the category "exceptional life," with its concomitant focus on violence, means thinking about the connections between the figurative violence depicted in a work of art and the literal violence inflicted on bodies.

The question *What is violence?* stands at the core of the problem of exceptional life, and for me its genesis lies in the possibly unholy conjunction between political theology, gender theory, and deconstruction. Some might cavil at this triad, either because it's too old-fashioned or because it's too trendy. What is violence? poses an old question, to be sure, and I want to insist that this inquiry remains rooted in bodies both corporeal and textual. And there's the rub: while certain feminist and queer theorists would argue that patriarchy begins with our introjection of the symbolic system of language, others would argue that the much-misread Derridean claim that "*il n'y a pas de hors-texte*" entails a dangerously callous denial of physical and psychic trauma. I don't think we can separate the violence of language from the violence inflicted by and on bodies. I do think we need to tread delicately when tracing links between literary texts and what happens in the world, yet that forging such conceptual connections between real and imagined worlds should remain one primary task of literary scholarship.

To a certain extent, what the philosophers term "bare life" is always feminized; hence the necessity of bridging the gap between political theological and feminist methodologies. Political theology is only one of the more recent "turns to theory" in Renaissance studies,[3] and though Renaissance studies remains interested in theoretical questioning and investigation, it is not always critical of the theories it invokes. Readings of early modern literature shaped by feminist and queer theorists have taught us to consider the personal as political and never to ignore the corporeal in our consideration of politics, economics, and aesthetics.[4] I am interested in parsing both modern and early modern scenes of biopolitical strife, and emergences of new forms of life and government. One of my aims here is to recall that bodies remain at the center of theoretical discussions of power even when (as is the case for Schmitt) they seem most removed from the scene, and to resituate the sometimes occluded "private sphere" of domestic pain, labor, and action accordingly. This is why I choose to examine drama. In her reading of Aristotle's *Poetics*, Arendt remarks, "The [Athenian] theater is the political art par excellence; only there is the political sphere of human life transposed into art. By the same token, it is the only art whose sole subject is man in his relationship to others" (*HC* 188).[5] "Man in his relationship to others" here means not just the acting *inter homines esse* that, for Arendt as for Arisotle, characterizes political life. It is also the various relationships between writers and actors, between actors on a stage, between actors and audiences. Microcosmically refracted in the space of the stage, political action receives its aesthetic apotheosis, in Arendt's account of theatre—an account in which the early modern dramatists I discuss here might have recognized what became the commonplace notion that "all the world's a stage."

What Is Grace?

"Grace" carries a series of resonances in the early modern period—aesthetic, political, and theological—and its singular ambivalence is what interests me. On the one hand, in its aesthetic (and, concomitantly, social) register, grace denotes seemliness or proportion, to which we might also affix the rhetorical terms decorum or measure. On the other hand, the juridical and theological uses of grace indicate what goes *beyond* measure, outside the limits of the law (as in the sovereign's pardon or mercy) or, indeed, any sense of mortal comprehension (the grace of God). In this second, political-theological sense, grace already implies a state of exception, a movement outside juridical norms or human terms of reciprocity. Yet it never entirely loses its own other, the sense of a *striving toward* measure.

What I am calling grace's movement toward measure can most easily be seen via a brief excursus on various usages of the word itself. For Weber, grace appears primarily in the ancient guise of *charisma*, rooted in the Greek term *charis*, which retains its theological charge even in Weber's analysis of the secularized apparatuses of modern statecraft. In Weil's late mystic writings, *grâce* counterpoints gravity, a "force" whose transcendendent drive opposes the "descendent," fleshly pull of gravity (*pesanteur*). While these usages focus on the word as a noun, it's worth recalling that it is also a verb: if you *grace* my party with your presence, you bring aesthetic and affective pleasure to me and the other guests. If the king graces a gathering with his presence, though, we're again in the realm of the political theological, for now the verb carries the reminder of divine regency. In the latter example, especially, the king's gracing presence might seem to exemplify what Aristotle called *kreitton*, that which exceeds political life. Yet both of these verbal examples turn on the trope of hospitality, community, care for guests and strangers. As both noun and verb, then, grace is what we might call *transitive*—it entails an object, even if it might exceed its object. Here we recollect that the term "transitive," which grammatically refers to a verb requiring a direct object, most simply means "that which goes across." In this etymological reading, transitivity means that grace becomes a bridge, a path between subject and object, host and guest, giver and recipient—even, perhaps, sacrificer and sacrificed. So this transitivity implies a certain mutuality, though not an equivalence.

Such a transitivity might seem to stand against violence, yet as the example of sacrificer and sacrificed implies, the two cannot always be separated. In the latter third of my argument, Paul's conversion becomes one example of the symbiosis between violence and grace. But we might also go back to the example of hospitality. Derrida reminds us that hospitality contains the trace of hostility, the *hostis* or "enemy" we might be entertaining, possibly unaware. Derrida's notion of "hostipitality" turns us toward Carl Schmitt's definition of the state of exception or emergency, as, for Schmitt, political relationships must be forged according to a fundamental distinction between friend and enemy.[6] Yet Schmitt is not interested in grace, per se, despite his claim that the sovereign decision constitutes the secular equivalent of a miracle (*PT* 36).[7] Miracles might be understood as evidence of grace, so it's possible to argue that grace shadows Schmitt's formula for exception—yet, for Schmitt, both violence and grace remain abstract, as I demonstrate in chapter 2.

If the aesthetic valences of grace in relation to gender and sexuality seem fairly clear, the theological valence appears less so—unless we think of divine grace as simultaneously feminizing and utterly outside any consideration of gender. I use *feminizing* here in an admittedly contested sense, as an emptying out of subjectivity, a radical openness that both constitutes and denies its own eventuality. By using the term this way I am casting back to medieval mystics, such as Julian of Norwich or Teresa of Ávila, who characterize religious ecstasy in erotic terms. In this line of thinking, what appears as subjective annihilation sparks generation—a dynamic Agamben, once again following Aristotle, terms "the abyss of impotentiality."[8] According to such a formulation, Coriolanus's spectacular undoing echoes Saul's epiphany on the road to Damascus, or perhaps even Weil's insistent call for a "decreation" or "uprooting" of the self as a necessary prelude to receptivity to the divine. I sketch these connections loosely here, noting that in each instance we might discern the radical *potential* of grace only in the presence of an initiatory moment of oblivion that, perhaps, becomes also a moment of oblation. Schmitt's characterization of the sovereign exception, in which any concept of the miraculous remains under erasure, does not do justice to this turn. My task begins by recuperating the gendered bodies that perform and become acts of both violence and grace.

Exceptional Life between Aristotle and Schmitt

Any enquiry into what constitutes exceptional life must take into account Aristotle's famous definition of the "natural" condition of man as that of a "political animal."[9] Aristotle exemplifies possible exceptions to this rule as follows: "He who by nature and not by mere accident is without a state, is either a bad man or above humanity; he is like the 'tribeless, lawless, hearthless one,' whom Homer denounces—the natural outcast is forthwith a lover of war" (I.1253a.5–10). In Aristotle's schema, exceptions to political life occur either in accordance with nature (*phusis*) or by accident. But what "accident" (*tukhê*, generally "chance" or "fortune") can render one "tribeless, lawless, hearthless"? Is it ever an "accident"? Who or what might be able to cast one from humanity to inhumanity, the state not of the political animal (*politikon zôon*) but of mere life, *zôon*? And what is the condition of *zôon*? Aristotle tells us, using the words of Nestor, that most politic of counselors, that it is a condition where one is *like* the *aphrêtôr*, *athemistos*, *anestios*—one "without *phratrai*, law, or hearth." Thus he removes us to a literary scene that turns on Nestor's counsel against a hasty war—and not just a war against external enemies but civil war (*polemou epidêmiou*), for Nestor's full line is *aphrêtôr athemistos anestios estin ekeinos / hos polemou eratai epidêmiou okruoentos*, "a clanless, lawless, hearthless man is he who loves the horror of war among his own people." Turning back to Aristotle, then, it seems that *zôon* is not just "without *phratrai*" but specifically *against phratrai*, an enemy to his own brothers.[10] Thus the condition of *zôon* is never "mere accident" but a decision, perhaps the gods' (considering Aristotle's turn to Homer, this seems logical); but, perhaps, the man's: ironically, the man can decide to cast himself beyond decision. If rational choice, *proairesis*, gives rise to political life, then, paradoxically, the decision to declare oneself outlawed or to move beyond the place of rational choice becomes the final marker of political life. *Themistos*, like *nomos*, specifically designates *human* law, the law of custom and precedent—thus to be rendered *athemistos* is to be cast beyond civil bonds. If we perceive the first two terms as belonging to the public sphere, the third term, *anestios*, "hearthless," goes even further, declaring that *zôon* is not only an apolitical animal but an *undomestic* animal—if the first terms depict what we might call absolute civil war, the third term does not allow us to think in terms of civility at all.

The condition of *zôon* is thus a state of absolute exception, but Aristotle gives two possible readings for the exception: he is either less (*phaulos*) or more (*kreitton*) than human. If one is stripped of citizenship and its rights, then one might be considered "less" than human; the sovereign, also outside or above citizenship, is generally taken to be "mightier" than human. Aristotle reformulates this apparent dichotomy later in Book I: "He who is unable to live in society, or who has no need because he is sufficient for himself, must be either a beast [*thêrion*] or a god [*theos*]; he is no part of a state" (*Politics* 1253a.29). In both instances, the first terms would seem to indicate the life of the citizen stripped of civility (if we identify "civility" here as consisting of economic and social interdependence), the second term the condition of the sovereign: the citizen who is no longer a citizen becomes something less than human, bestial, whereas the sovereign attains the status of the transcendent, apotheothized ideal. Jacques Derrida, however, has argued that the apparent dualism collapses on further investigation, merging the two terms: the sovereign is always bestial, the beast always sovereign. Derrida has also argued that the beast/

sovereign distinction is always predicated on hierarchies of sexual difference, coding the bestial as feminine, the sovereign as masculine.[11] Each of the plays I consider in the following pages supplies a different face for this dialectic, arcing between sovereignty and what Aristotle calls "life that endures much suffering,"[12] or what Walter Benjamin terms "bare life."

This same question—what might constitute exceptions from political life?—preoccupies the early- and mid-twentieth-century political thinkers assembled in the following pages. While Aristotle offers one starting point for this intellectual genealogy, Carl Schmitt provides another opening—one that still, perhaps perversely, might be linked back to Aristotelian ethics and politics. In the now well-known opening formula of Schmitt's *Political Theology*, "Sovereign is he who decides on the exception."[13] Even this seemingly most decisive statement turns on a certain amount of equivocation, an equivocation that begins with two central terms, "decides" (*entscheidet*) and "exception" (*Ausnahmezustand*, translated elsewhere as "state of emergency").[14] In the fourth paragraph of his work, Schmitt claims that "the exception, which is not codified in the existing legal order, can at best be characterized as a case of extreme peril, a danger to the existence of the state, or the like" (*PT* 6).[15] In this sentence one of the primary problems of "deciding the exception" emerges, and it is a problem of definition. Like that oldest of legal terms, "equity," exception "is not codified in the existing legal order." But with the next clause we enter a zone of radical indeterminacy: the exception "can at best be characterized as a case of extreme peril, a danger to the existence of the state, or the like." The problem of decision appears here partially as a *grammatical* problem: the sentence is in the passive voice, a most undecisive mode, and the sliding chain of "characteristics" that Schmitt employs rapidly devolves into uncertainty: "extreme peril" morphs into the more indeterminate "danger to the existence of the state," and thence into the completely ambiguous "or the like."

Of course, all of these terms ("peril," "extreme," "emergency") are subjective, and this is where the difficulty arises: the Schmittian sovereign is the only subject who can decide on the very criteria for the decision—in Schmitt's formulation, the horizon of the decision blurs in the very act of its articulation. Thus the absolute dictum "Sovereign is he who decides on the exception" unfurls itself as infinitively recessive, endlessly non-decisive in its very decisionism. Schmitt's non-definition of the state of emergency or exception, obscure though it is, perhaps takes its origin in Aristotle's discussion of equity in Book Five of the *Nicomachean Ethics*.[16] Aristotle argues that justice is "complete virtue, not without qualification, but in relation to another person," and also that "justice is a kind of a mean—not in the same way as the other virtues, but because it is concerned with a mean [*tò méson*], while injustice is concerned with extremes [*hê d'adikía tôn ákrôn*]" (*NE* V.1129b, 1133b). But this notion of the "mean," equality, entails a nuanced reformulation of the claim that justice is the supreme virtue, for justice must take into account the fact that law itself might be the source of inequalities. Thus Aristotle turns to the notion of equity (*epieíkeia*):

> Equity, though just, is not legal justice, but a rectification of legal justice. The reason for this is that law is always a general statement, yet there are cases which it is not possible to cover in a general statement. In matters therefore where, while it is necessary to speak in general terms, it is not possible to do so correctly, the law takes into consideration the majority of cases, although it is not unaware of the error this involves. . . . When therefore the law lays down a general rule, and thereafter a case arises which is an exception to the rule, it is then right, where the lawgiver's pronouncement because of its absoluteness is defective and erroneous, to rectify the defect by deciding as the lawgiver would himself decide if he were present on the occasion, and would have enacted if he had been cognizant of the case in question. . . . This is the essential nature of the equitable: it is a rectification of law where law is defective because of its generality. (V.x.1137b–1138a)

Equity, then, addresses the problem of the juridical exception and itself constitutes something of an exception. The realm of equity might be defined as both inside and outside statutory law proper ("universal" or "unqualified justice"), and Aristotle specifically locates the prerogative for equitable decision in the person of the judge or the sovereign (*nomothétês*, "the lawgiver").

So far, Schmitt would seem to follow Aristotle, though he is concerned with "national security" and not with individual justice—though distinguishing a split between the two gives rise to profoundly troubling consequences, as we continue to witness today. In a broader sense, the very concept of equity as a legal corrective becomes distorted when the juridical decision to move outside the circumscribed realm of statutory law inscribes itself as normative—or when, we might say, the exception becomes the norm. It is precisely this difficulty that one encounters with Schmitt's notion of the sovereign decision governing the state of exception, for Schmitt's decisionism is both indebted to and utterly divorced from Aristotle. On the one hand, one term that remains somewhat fixed in Schmitt's sliding designation of the state of emergency is "extreme" (*äußerster*). So, for example, he writes in the passage already discussed of "extreme peril," which in the next paragraph becomes "extreme emergency": "The precise details of an emergency cannot be anticipated, nor can one spell out what may take place in such a case, especially when it is truly a matter of an extreme emergency and how it is to be eliminated" (6–7). Right away, then, the notion of "peril" has been subsumed by "emergency," that which had been the occasion for *declaring* or *deciding* what constitutes the state of emergency almost instantly effaced. In this slippery transition we might detect a trace of Aristotle's notion of justice warped in the absolutism of its declaration, justice distorted to produce injustice. Exception is not equity: it considers not the unintended cruelties that the law might inflict in its extremity but how existing laws do not precisely address a specific extremity. Yet once the sovereign decision to suspend the law in the name of the law takes effect, it distorts the foundations of the "rule" (to use Schmitt's term) it replaces.

Schmitt's phrase "state of exception," as Giorgio Agamben reminds us, designates "not a special kind of law (like the law of war); rather, insofar as it is a suspension of the juridical order itself, it defines law's threshold or limit concept" (*SE* 4).[17] Agamben's work takes up the double paradox that emerges with Schmitt's construction of "the legal form and the decision," for the "legal form" of the state of exception is itself anti-constitutional: though defined as the suspension of law, the "state of exception" or emergency can be determined only by the sovereign, who is himself both outside and inside the word of law in any case. He is "outside the law" inasmuch as he is not subject to its enforcement, "inside the law" inasmuch as he instantiates it in pronouncing it (*HS* 15). Agamben renders this paradox in two ways: "'the law is outside itself,' or 'I, the sovereign, who am outside the law, declare that there is nothing outside the law.'" (*HS* 15) This rhetorical doubling itself offers an example of the doubled formulation it expresses: the initial, simpler statement embodies "law" even as it depersonalizes the sovereign, rendering him a juridical abstraction. Agamben's second, more complex formulation of the paradox re-bodies both sovereign and law: the sovereign himself is the "subject" of the sentence, both grammatically and literally. He is the auto-interpellator, the "I" who can first say "I" and define himself as subject. However, that very interpellation turns about and is assimilated into "nothing." "Nothing" marks the site of the sovereign decree; law defines itself by its absence. Agamben's illusory "nothing," the evacuation of law, metaphorically demonstrates the way the sovereign decision, the decree that actualizes the state of emergency, creates an extra-legal space.[18]

Political Theological Conversations

While the oeuvres of Weber, Benjamin, Schmitt, Kantorowicz, Arendt, and Weil proceed from very different moments and locations, each of these thinkers addresses the strain of the theological in its sometimes overt and sometimes residual appearance in a variety of modern guises, branching from the legal and political to the philosophical, literary, and historical. Max Weber, a teacher of both Schmitt and Kantorowicz, provides both a chronological beginning and end point for the intellectual genealogy the book traces, for though his work belongs to an earlier generation of scholars, his insistence on the political-theological double valence of "calling" significantly shapes the thought of his intellectual inheritors. Of the remaining political thinkers whose works I address here, Walter Benjamin appears as the first of Schmitt's obvious interlocutors, citing Schmitt's *Political Theology* (published in 1922) in his *The Origin of German Tragic Drama* (written 1924–1925, published in Berlin in 1928) and revisiting the notion of the "state of exception" or emergency in his last published work, the "Theses on the Philosophy of History" (written 1939–1940, published in 1950).

In her introduction to *Illuminations*, one of the collections of Benjamin's late, short essays posthumously published in English, Hannah Arendt characterizes Benjamin as a "collector," a "man of letters" of a peculiarly nineteenth-century German-Jewish bourgeois type. Arendt refers to his methodology as "pearl diving": assembling mosaics of quotations, *layering* works, concerned with the passages that glance across the different citational surfaces placed in conjunction with one another like arcs of light. For Arendt the glittering surfaces of Benjamin's thought-mosaics allusively recall Ariel's song from Shakespeare's *Tempest*, from which she draws the epigraph for the final section of her introduction. Despite the materialist preoccupations that she attributes to the bourgeois collector, though, it is perhaps Prospero's, not Ariel's, ghost who haunts her portrait of Benjamin, whom she characterizes as a philosopher/mystic in some ways unequipped to deal with the realities of the world he inhabits and the immensity of his own "bad luck." Quoting, naming, assembling: like the hieratic figure of the philosopher-king who closes Eliot's "The Waste Land," that seminal document of modernism, Benjamin shores his fragments against the ruins of time. Arendt writes,

> Benjamin later gave up [his] theological background but not the theory and not his method of drilling to obtain the essential in the form of quotations. . . . This method is like the modern equivalent

> of ritual invocations, and the spirits that now arise invariably are those spiritual essences from a past that have suffered the Shakespearean "sea-change" from living eyes to pearls, from living bones to coral. For Benjamin to quote is to name, and naming rather than speaking, the word rather than the sentence, brings truth to light.[19]

Benjamin himself, in the essay on "The Storyteller" contained in this volume, distinguishes between story and novel, story and history: stories derive from epic and lyric, oral forms, linked with the repetitive functions of labor, concerned with the evocation and transmission of experience and not with explication.[20] The story is a pearl, singular, many layered; its nacreous impenetrability and self-enclosure resist psychological explanation. Yet at its heart lies the grain of sand or fragment of shell—an irritant, something irreducible, something dead or inanimate that spins itself out at the core of a living creature, gathers to itself the iridescent layers of truth that harden into regular form. Storytelling, as opposed to novel reading, is communal, intimate, performative: repetition works as incantation, binding teller, tale, audience. In this it resembles drama, though Benjamin does not mention theatre here. What he does mention is history, both "natural" and narrative: "Death is the sanction of everything that the storyteller can tell. He has borrowed his authority from death. In other words, it is natural history to which his stories refer back" (94).[21] The sedimented traces of generations of storytellers revivify with each new telling; each telling both invokes and wards off death, the end of every tale as it is the end of every human experience. Linked to the spiraling rhythms of this "natural history" are the histories of the chroniclers, whose genealogy Benjamin sketches from Herodotus to the medieval monastics to their modern, secularized avatars, storytellers.[22] Yet despite his secular moment, for Benjamin the modern storyteller, exemplified by Nikolai Leskov, remains an initiate: plumbing the illimitable depths of experience, dredging up truths wrapped in the cryptic folds of the human psyche.

The tension between mysticism and materiality that animates Benjamin's essay on storytelling finds its dramatic corollary in *Trauerspielen*, the German baroque mourning plays that form the subject of his most sustained work of literary criticism. In the melancholic, creatural figure of the tyrant, history phenomenalizes itself in dramatic form; in the formal codes of allegory, natural history reaches its apotheosis in its own dissolution. The baroque artist, like the storyteller, retains the key to something hidden, but in the fallen world that characterizes the baroque work of art, the hidden always remains inaccessible, even at its seemingly most transparent (such as the emblem, with its gloss). In his last published work, the fragmentary "Theses on the Philosophy of History," Benjamin reconsiders Schmitt's notion of the state of emergency or exception that he had earlier argued it was "the primary function of the sovereign" in *Trauerspiel* to avert.[23] In the Eighth Thesis, Benjamin writes,

> The tradition of the oppressed teaches us that the "state of emergency" in which we live is not the exception but the rule. We must attain to a conception of history that is in keeping with this insight. Then we shall clearly realize that it is our task to bring about a real state of emergency, and this will improve our position in the struggle against Fascism. One reason why Fascism has a chance is that in the name of progress its opponents treat it as a historical norm. The current amazement that the things we are experiencing are "still" possible in the twentieth century is *not* philosophical. This amazement is not the beginning of knowledge—unless it is the knowledge that the view of history which gives rise to it is untenable.[24]

What Benjamin calls for here is not only a philosophical treatment of Fascism but also a political *response* to the normative state of emergency imposed by its deadening grip. Hannah Arendt, in *The Origins of Totalitarianism* (1951), begins to answer both calls, but it is in her later reflections in "The Concept of History" (1954) and *The Human Condition* (1956) that she most fully takes up Benjamin's challenge for a conceptual historiography shaped in response to political crisis.[25]

If *The Origins of Totalitarianism* diagnoses the bureaucratic state of emergency that has become the norm, both *The Human Condition* and "The Concept of History" seek to resuscitate the ancient political and historiographic modalities eradicated by modern technocracy. Like Benjamin, Arendt begins the genealogy of history with Herodotus—but also with Aristotle, in whose work she locates the thread of the ultra-mortal "natural history" that so drew Benjamin. The classical idea of history, Arendt argues, was linear: bright swathes of mortal human time cutting across the immortal, curvilinear cycles of the natural world:

> What is difficult for us to realize is that the great deeds and works of which mortals are capable, and which become the topic of historical narrative, are not seen as parts of either an encompassing whole or a process; on the contrary, the stress is always on single instances and single gestures. These single instances, deeds or events, interrupt the circular movement of daily life in the same sense that the rectilinear *bios* of the mortals interrupts the circular movements of

> biological life. The subject matter of history is these interruptions—the extraordinary, in other words. (*CH* 43)

In Arendt's account, classical historiography becomes a narrative of exceptions: "interruptions—the extraordinary, in other words." Arendt's words here uncannily echo Schmitt, to whom she acknowledges a debt in her own work—though she of course distances herself from his politics.[26]

In *The Origins of Totalitarianism* Arendt lays bare both the political and philosophical genesis of what she calls "total domination," the utter subjection of human life in the "holes of oblivion" bureaucratically manufactured in modernity. Part of "total domination," according to Arendt, concerns *narrative*, the human capacity to tell stories: in her analysis, one of the most horrifying and insidious effects of the concentration camps is their capacity to silence not only the living but also the dead—not just to eradicate juridical personhood but also to utterly obliterate memory and history (*OT* 452). The "organized oblivion" of the camps mass-produces anonymous corpses, rendering even mourning impossible. Arendt writes,

> The Western world has hitherto, even in its darkest periods, granted the slain enemy the right to be remembered as a self-evident acknowledgment of the fact that we are all men (and *only* men). It is only because even Achilles set out for Hector's funeral, only because the Romans allowed the Christians to write their martyrologies, only because the Church kept its heretics alive in the memory of men, that all was not lost and never could be lost. The concentration camps, by making death itself anonymous (making it impossible to find out whether a prisoner is dead or alive) robbed death of its meaning as the end of a fulfilled life. In a sense they took away an individual's own death, proving that henceforth nothing belonged to him and he belonged to no one. His death merely set a seal on the fact that he had never really existed. (*OT* 452)

This obliteration of individual death as the end point of the annihilation of individual life, and the correspondent impossibility of mourning, the ceremonial recognition of both life and death, also means that narrative itself becomes impossible—even survivors cannot adequately voice their sufferings. For Arendt, the true task and test of human life is political action, and history, the narrative of "interruptions" and "extraordinary moments" that characterize even the most "ordinary" lives, becomes one strand of political action.[27] But it is in the theatre, not just in narrative, that action takes both political and aesthetic shape.

Ernst Kantorowicz's *The King's Two Bodies* appeared in 1957, a year after Schmitt's *Hamlet oder Hekuba* (itself a belated response to Benjamin's *Trauerspiel* book) and Arendt's *Human Condition.* Though chronologically the last of the modern works I engage in the following pages, *The King's Two Bodies* is also perhaps the first to allusively assemble the conversation between Benjamin and Schmitt. Schmitt appears only indirectly—not least in the subtitle of the book—in Kantorowicz's monumental work of modern historiography, yet his notion of exception haunts Kantorowicz's account. Like Benjamin, Kantorowicz is a "collector," a pearl fisher, amassing different types of texts and citations under the heading "political theology." His constellation begins with a Tudor "legal fiction" but quickly moves from jurisprudence to the pages of Shakespeare's *Richard II.* Unlike Weber, Benjamin, Schmitt, and Arendt, however, Kantorowicz explicitly disavows engagement with the recent past, even as his glancing references to the ongoing, international state of emergency set in motion during the war belie this intent.

While Simone Weil's philosophical training and early political writings already mark her as a radical among radicals, it is her late religious or mystical writings that I address here. Like Arendt, Weil has been castigated by some feminists, who deplore her peculiar form of self-abnegating religious consciousness. To Weil, in the end, both political and religious action mean embracing suffering in its purest form. In 1942, the year before her death, she wrote,

> Love is a divine thing. If it enters a human heart it breaks it. The human heart was created to be broken in this way. It is the saddest waste if it is broken by anything rather than the divine love. Because the divine love breaks only those hearts which consent to be broken; and this consent is difficult to give.[28]

Simultaneously hailed as a saint by some critics and reviled for repudiating her Jewish roots by others, Weil stands alongside the other political theological thinkers gathered here for the first time. I bring her into the conversation precisely *because* I think it's worth reevaluating her contributions to the canons of both feminist and political theological thought. This is more difficult for the former than the latter—yet if feminism is still, at its core, about making sure women are seen and heard, even if we don't agree with them, then it's crucial. Weil is hardly an invisible figure, yet statements such as the one quoted above mean that liberal feminist scholars might not accept her brand of radicalism. It's a version of what Cynthia Marshall called "the shattering of the self"[29]—one that also calls for the subject's "consent," and this seems to me the most difficult to accommodate aspect of Weil's thought. Yet perhaps more than any other thinker I discuss in the following pages, it is Weil who most clearly articulates the inseparability of violence and grace.

The five chapters of *Violence and Grace* fall into two parts, "States of Affliction" and "States of Grace," which nevertheless remain attentive to both the contradictions and the overlaps inherent in these formulations. I take the term "affliction" from English translations of Weil's late writings (her word is *malheur*). Weil distinguishes between purely physical suffering and *malheur*, which seizes and corrupts the very foundations of sensible life. Weil's translators seemingly choose "affliction" for its roots in the medieval and early modern periods, when it denotes self-inflicted religious suffering. Part 1, "States of Affliction," considers various cases of life marked outside the law, simultaneously formed and abjected by sovereign decree. Pairing *The Taming of the Shrew* with Hannah Arendt's *The Human Condition* and *The Origins of Totalitarianism*, a brief prologue claims that Shakespeare's troubled and troubling comedy provides a literary example of the ways those reduced to a condition of extremity are simultaneously deprived of autonomous expressions of sexuality and forced to enact grotesque parodies of gendered norms. Accordingly, I argue that the audience's complicity in Petruchio's "politic rule," contrived through the expectations generated by the comic framework, provides a chilling analogue to the annihilation of normative civic responsibility in the shadow of totalitarian regimes. Just as Arendt's diagnosis of the "wordlessness" of love and pain indexes Kate's predicament, so Kate's taming illuminates the gendered implications of Arendt's account of the bureaucratic "rule by nobody" that characterizes the modern human condition.

Chapter 1 analyzes Marlowe's *Edward II* and Ernst Kantorwicz's seminal 1957 study, *The King's Two Bodies*, tracing the connection between the originary "history play" and medieval saint plays. While Marlowe's modern critics generally read his works as testaments of either atheism or radical Protestantism, I argue that his elegiac portrait of a martyred homosexual king covertly recalls the recently executed Mary, Queen of Scots, both in its dramatic focus on letters and in its allegoric reprisal of Catholic Eucharistic and reliquary rituals. Marlowe's metadramatic poetics, in turn, sheds light on the political intervention performed by Kantorowicz's peculiarly literary brand of historiography, which critiques the recent events of World War II and the lingering remnants of sacral sovereignty that enable extraordinary forms of violence in modern absolutist states.

Chapter 2 places Thomas Middleton's *The Revenger's Tragedy* against a series of writings by Weimar (later Nazi) jurist Carl Schmitt. I begin by considering Montaigne's musings about cruelty and acts that exceed "simple death," arguing that a political conception of the limits of death must necessarily complement the juridical construction of bare life, and that Montaigne's eroticized descriptions of cruelty and torture usefully gloss both revenge drama and Schmitt's early political writings. Schmitt and Middleton both perform readings of Shakespeare's *Hamlet*, and this chapter argues that the farcical logic of exception that governs ultimately sterile modes of extra-legal retribution in Jacobean revenge drama helps us to reconsider Schmitt's grounds for equating sovereign authority with the emergency suspension of law. Montaigne's and Middleton's hyper-erotic spectacles counterbalance Schmitt's account of the miraculously disembodied sovereign decision and its effects and point up the occluded erotic underpinnings of Schmitt's own arguments in his 1956 monograph on *Hamlet* and a triad of his Weimar-era political works (*Political Theology*; *The Concept of the Political*; *Roman Catholicism and Political Form*).

Reframing juridical exception in terms of the aesthetically, politically, and theologically ambivalent pull of grace, part 2 interrogates various facets of this dynamic. Chapter 3 contends that Shakespeare's account of the life of the virile citizen-soldier, Coriolanus, stages a meditation on the political economy of the gift and the human pain and suffering at its core. Drawing on Shakespeare's main source, Plutarch's *Lives*, Machiavelli's and Cicero's accounts of the Roman Republic, and Walter Benjamin's conception of the equivocal yet inalienable sacrality that distinguishes human life from what he calls the "mere" or "bare" life of the creature, I argue that the imperfect evacuation of sacrificial ritual, the ultimate and impossible gift, continues to unsettle the nascent Republic in Shakespeare's play. Coriolanus has seemed to some recent critics to exemplify bare life. Yet, ultimately, both Benjamin's and Shakespeare's insistence on the peculiar grace that attends the exile, even in extremity, begs for a reconsideration of the limits of political life.

My last two chapters address the theoretical "return to Paul" over the past fifteen years as a way to examine the relationship between aesthetics, temporality, and gender. Judith Butler argues that "the way in which debates within sexual politics are framed is already imbued with the problem of time, and of progress in particular, and with certain notions of what it means to unfold a future of freedom in time."[30] In chapter 4, I consider Shakespeare's *King Lear* in conjunction with the temporally fraught aesthetics conjured in the letters of Saint Paul and Simone Weil's elliptical writings, as well as Jacques Rancière's recent work. Weil posits Shakespeare's play as a meditation on gravity, the "base" or descendent force that opposes the transcendent drive of grace. Yet the textual and performative seams that emerge in *Lear* can help us to think through Weil's apparent dichotomy. If *Lear* offers not a dichotomy but a dialectic of gravity and grace, "grace" emerges as a moment not of transcendence but of suspension. Posing a series of interlocked questions about *Lear*'s distended ends and problems of representation, I argue that the play's misogyny cannot be separated from its treatment of a skeptical messianism.

Reapproaching Paul via Max Weber's proto–political theological conception of *charisma*, chapter 5 examines Shakespeare's play in conjunction with 2 Corinthians' meta-epistolarity. Drawing on the double sense of "calling" (vocation and profession) teased out by Max Weber and picked up by Giorgio Agamben in his reading of messianic time in Paul's writings, I argue that the play's "calling" fuses eros, politics, and poiesis. In *Cymbeline* reading and writing, like perspective and retrospective acts of viewing, twine together to form a meditation on being and living both now and to come. This untimely hermeneutic, in turn, intersects with the play's obsession with sleeping and dead bodies. Such a preoccupation represents, on the one hand, a figure yoking Paul's seeming condemnation of letter and flesh. On the other hand, the ways people *misread* bodies alert us to the dangers of misreading Paul. *Cymbeline* thus reforges Pauline notions of flesh, letters (both epistles and *gramma*), temporality, and community. I conclude with a brief epilogue, which examines *Timon of Athens*'s multiplied and refracted "last words" in order to reiterate the stakes of reading and writing when it comes to defining exceptional life.

In her first book on Hannah Arendt, Margaret Canovan differentiates between modern "political thought" as such and Arendt's praxis as follows:

> What Hannah Arendt means by [political] thought . . . consists [of] the endless effort of human beings to make sense of what they experience, to get their minds round the things that confront them, the activities they engage in, and above all the events that happen among them. Her work is political thought, not in the sense of being the application of a pre-existing method, whether scientific or philosophical, to political material, but in the sense of representing the free play of an individual mind round politics, making sense of political events and placing them within an unfolding understanding of all that comes within that mind's range.[31]

My own project is motivated by a desire to think about the politics of pain, torture, and particularly sexualized violence as they appear in the world today. While it proceeds from a specific ethical and political impetus, my argument remains primarily literary in nature. In what follows, I make a case for the dilemma of life that is not yet precisely political but potentially or becoming-political in six early modern plays. I also seek to engage in "political thinking" in the characteristically Arendtian sense outlined by Canovan, that of allowing for a "free play of the mind" over two very disparate texts and the socio-political contexts of their inceptions in order to approach "the events that happen" here and now.

Part One

States of Affliction

Prologue

The Sexual Politics of Pain

Hannah Arendt Meets Shakespeare's Shrew

> *Peri de hēdonēs kai lupēs theōrēsai tou tēn politikēn philosophountos: houtos gar tou telous arkhitektōn, pros ho blepontes hekaston to men kakon to d' agathon haplōs legomen.*
>
> It is part of the job of the political philosopher to study pleasure and pain, since he is the master-craftsman, and lays down the end which is the standard whereby we pronounce things good or bad in the absolute sense.
>
> —Aristotle, *Nicomachean Ethics*, VII.xi.1152b.1–2

Aristotle, in the *Poetics*, decrees that "comedy is mimesis of baser but not wholly vicious characters: rather, the laughable is one category of the shameful [*aiskhron*]. For the laughable comprises any fault or mark of shame which involves no pain or *destruction* [*anôdunon kai ou phthartikon*]: most obviously, the laughable mask is something ugly and twisted, but not painfully [so]."[1] Both *odunê* and *lupê* (the former in this passage from the *Poetics*, the latter in the passage from the *Nicomachean Ethics* included as the epigraph) can indicate both bodily and emotional pain, like the Latin *dolor*. Half unworked by its framing in the mesh of Sly's dream, Shakespeare's troubled and troubling vision of domestic taming depends upon the conceit of bodily and emotional pain and destruction as "laughable." Thus I begin with an old question: what do we recognize as violence?

Like *The Merchant of Venice*, *The Taming of the Shrew* is a play profoundly concerned with what Hegel would call "civil society," the space of commerce, traffic, and exchange necessary in the passage to the political order of the state that remains, itself, only partially or becoming-political.[2] For Hegel, marriage (along with the Corporation) functions as one of the two "fixed points round which the unorganized atoms of civil society revolve," but like the Corporation, marriage is, for Hegel, paradoxically unfixed, disrupting the translation of individual interests to the State even as it enables that movement.[3] What, then, can Petruchio and Katherina's delayed marriage, a most *un*fixed point in the insular, propertied Paduan civil society that Shakespeare depicts, have to do with the question of the political?[4] Kate and Petruchio's satirically interrupted wedding ceremony might be read as the flip side of Claudius and Gertrude's "o'erhasty marriage," and though the link to *Hamlet* is admittedly a tenuous one, it can be instructive. Like *Hamlet*, *Shrew* presents an interrupted hierarchy—that is, a *domestic* state of exception, one that Katherine's final speech supposedly reinstates and valorizes.

The irony of Kate's final oration—the longest speech in the play, it promotes wifely submission and silence—prompts many critics to argue that the "taming" itself is in some sense undone. If Kate's final speech marks her as, finally, "conformable," fit for civic reintegration after her banishment to the country only because she will now uphold normative order, this process is analogous, in a strange way, to what happens in the bureaucratic "rule by nobody" that characterizes Hannah Arendt's social realm, which itself owes something to Hegel's civil society. Thus, in these opening pages, I sketch a preliminary reading of what we might term *potentially political* or *becoming-political* life as it appears in Shakespeare's play in order to gesture toward the larger predicament engendered by the heteronormative model of citizenship assumed in certain modern works of political philosophy. I have divided the argument into three moments: (1) a brief exegesis on an aporia in Giorgio Agamben's work, which might be traced in part to his reading of Hannah Arendt; (2) an attempt to recuperate Arendt from Agamben's critique; and (3) a literary exemplum of the Arendtian dilemma in Shakespeare's play.

Reading Agamben, Reading Arendt: Gendering Bare Life

In the passage from the *Nicomachean Ethics* I have taken as my epigraph, Aristotle writes, "It is part of the job of the political philosopher to study pleasure and pain, since he is the master-craftsman, and lays down the end which is the standard whereby we pronounce things good or bad in the absolute sense" (*NE* 1152b.1–2). It's a curiously Socratic statement, for Aristotle: surely the "architect of the end" (*telous architektôn*) ought to designate the political *actor*—whether citizen or sovereign—not "the political philosopher" (*politikên philosophountos*)? While Hannah

Arendt does not refer specifically to this passage in her writings on Aristotle,[5] it might almost be an epigraph for *The Origins of Totalitarianism* (1951), the first book she published in English, in which she carefully traces the ideological underpinnings of Russian labor camps and Nazi death camps. It might also serve as an epigraph for Giorgio Agamben's *Homo Sacer*, the first volume of his investigation of the phenomenon of "the camp as *nomos* of the modern."[6] In this book, Agamben begins to trace the metaphysical history of the contemporary state of exception through its early-twentieth-century origins in the theories of, primarily, Walter Benjamin and Carl Schmitt in order to fill in the gaps he perceives between Arendt's conceptualization of the rise of totalitarian states and Foucauldian biopolitics. Following Aristotle, Agamben argues that "bare life" is life stripped of civic value—life abandoned by the polis. But he does not always take into account the fact that women, who are rarely considered full citizens in any sense, already constitute an exception from the masculinist juridical paradigm. Gendered acts of violence form a dimension of the state of exception that remains largely uninterrogated in Agamben's work. Though Agamben recognizes sexuality and sexual difference as "the pure political element" in the works of the Marquis de Sade, and he also notes the "particularly grotesque" nature of one form of sexual torture, in the end he reproduces, to a certain extent, the omissions with which he charges Foucault and Arendt (*HS* 134, 155).

This aporia becomes clear in Agamben's reading of Marie de France's *Bisclavret*, which he cites in a long footnote to chapter 6, "The Ban and the Wolf" (*HS* 107–8/120). Agamben draws on the twelfth-century Breton *lai* in order to demonstrate the inextricable link between the beast, he who has been "banished," and the sovereign, who pronounces the decision that institutes the "ban." But Agamben can explicate the connection only by suppressing half the story, the relation between the half-bestial nobleman that becomes the *bisclavret* and his wife, who by the end of the *lai* has herself become the beast, monstrous and abandoned.[7] Agamben's reading focuses on the sovereign's recognition of Bisclavret's essential humanity, his "rational mind," displayed in the act of begging for mercy, for life.[8] Agamben reads this scene as the first touching incidence of the "special proximity between werewolf and sovereign" ("*Anche la particolare prossimità fra lupo mannaro e sovrano si ritrova ulteriormente nella storia*," *HS* 108/120) but does not account for the ways this "proximity" is, in Eve Kosofsky Sedgwick's term, homosocial, or, in Carol Pateman's, a fraternal social contract.[9]

For Agamben, the wife serves as a mere footnote to the footnote itself, a dismissable plot device. He treats the violent episode of the wolf's revenge with a certain cavalier humor: "The inevitable encounter with the ex-wife and the punishment of the woman follow" (*Segue l'immancabile incontro con l'ex moglie e la punizione della donna*), he states, before going on to argue that the important thing about the tale is the wolf's transformation "on the very bed of the sovereign" ("*Ma importante è che, alla fine, il ridiventar uomo di Bisclavret ha luogo sul letto stresso del sovrano*," *HS* 108/120).[10] This is a crucial point and nicely illustrates Agamben's argument about the formerly temporary character of the state of exception that has now become permanent. However, there's more going on here than just the "special proximity" of sovereign and beast. In Marie's *lai*, "bare life" comes into being with the woman's betrayal,[11] not the sovereign decree; in fact, the sovereign decree here *reverses* the state of exception, reincluding Bisclavret in the social order as a privileged member of the king's household.[12] Bisclavret's reinstitution into the civil sphere occurs only with the disfigurement, torture, and banishment of the sexually unruly female, who literally can't deal with the "animal" side of her marriage. As demonstrated by her daughters' "noselessness," women continue to bear the marks of their banishment in ways that men, perhaps, do not.[13]

I retell the *lai* at such length here both to set up certain preliminary parallels between the "bare life" of the *bisclavret*'s wife and the situation of Shakespeare's Katherina (which I will outline in the third section of this argument) and to illustrate the need for a much more thorough accounting of the ways sexual difference and sexuality are both produced and effaced by the ideology of the camp. Midway through *Homo Sacer*, Agamben himself articulates a clear call for what must come next in any theorizing of, or resistance to, the political paradigm of the camp: "In the notion of bare life the interlacing of politics and life has become so tight that it cannot easily be analyzed. Until we become aware of the political nature of bare life and its modern avatars (biological life, sexuality, etc.), we will not succeed in clarifying the opacity at their center" (*HS* 120). This call proceeds from Agamben's critique of Hannah Arendt: why, he asks, did one of the greatest theorists of totalitarianism never address how "the radical transformation of politics into the realm of bare life (i.e., into a camp) legitimated and necessitated total domination" (120)? But I will argue that Arendt does, in fact, address some of the very biopolitical processes that Agamben claims she elides. By paying close attention to Arendt's reading of Aristotle's *Politics* in *The Human Condition* and extending it to *The Origins of Totalitarianism*, we can uncover her more implicit argument about what Agamben parenthetically designates as "biological life, sexuality, etc."

Reading Arendt, Reading Aristotle: Political Life and the Place of Pain

Love and pain, according to Arendt (who follows Heidegger in this, to a certain extent),[14] constitute the two experiences that remain absolutely outside the public realm of political action. Whereas for Aristotle love in the form of the "union between man and woman" is the originary moment in the passage to man's "natural" political state, according to Arendt, "Love, in distinction from friendship, is killed, or rather extinguished, the moment it is displayed in public" (*HC* 51).[15] Arendt's distinction between "killed" and "extinguished" here is telling, for while "killed" suggests a violently active cut, a decisive blow delivered from without, the connotations of "extinguished" (though surely neither precisely passive nor lacking violence) imply an almost involuntary suffocation, a slower, more insidious demise that is, almost, from within—love exposed to the public gaze collapses in upon itself, withers away. If the quintessential role of the former private sphere was "the shelter of intimacy," she claims, since the post-Enlightenment rise of the social realm, "the intimacy of the heart . . . has no objective tangible place in the world, nor can the society against which it protests and asserts itself be located with the same certainty as the public sphere" (*HC* 38–39).[16] While this prologue cannot delve extensively into the shifting territory of Arendt's disquisitions on love, what it means, the forms it might take, and it is surely a gross oversimplification to refer to marriage in general as a relationship grounded in "love" (rather than necessity, as it is for Aristotle), I would suggest that the *proximity* of Arendt's points about love and pain compel a certain interpretive coupling, that what Arendt calls the "worldlessness" of the former can provide a useful, if somewhat paradoxical, gloss on the utterly effacing power of pain. Such a coupling also suggests that a literary example of the particular "worldlessness" Arendt describes might usefully be traced not, as one might expect, through tragedy, but through comedy or romance.

Like love, Arendt says, pain cannot be "transform[ed] into a shape fit for public appearance"; it is "truly a borderline experience between life as 'being among men' (*inter homines esse*) and death, so subjective and removed from the world of things and men that it cannot assume an appearance at all" (*HC* 50–51). For Arendt, as for Aristotle, of course, the capacity for rational choice (*proairesis*) as expressed in speech distinguishes man as a *political* animal (*politikon zôon*) from other "gregarious animals," who may only express pleasure and pain.[17] Arendt claims that pain is "at the same time the most private and least communicable of all [experiences]," locking the sufferer away from self as well as world, as it "actually deprives us of our feeling for reality to such an extent that we can forget it more quickly and easily than anything else" (*HC* 50–51).[18] Extreme pain translates the political animal to mere life, traps intellect and soul within the suffering body to the extent that it can render us what Arendt calls "a bundle of reactions" (this is particularly true of prolonged and systematic pain inflicted from without) (*OT* 438). It is, paradoxically, both the most and the least individualized of experiences, since it can be experienced only by the individual, yet its incommunicability and (for those who survive it) rapid effacement from memory obliterate the individual's agency. It casts one outside the realm of the human, outside the realm of judgment (a crucial act, for Arendt); it can never truly assume a rational discursive "shape" and can be spoken of only in retrospect, usually by analogy with a wound or a physical weapon (such as stabbing, shooting, pounding, and so forth).[19] Arendt's account in *The Human Condition* of the incommunicability of pain bears some resemblance to what she says of the paradox of memory and communication in *The Origins of Totalitarianism*. It is impossible to comprehend the camps without having been there, but equally impossible for anyone who has survived the camps to convey much of the experience. Noting the "peculiar unreality and lack of credibility" that she claims attaches to survivors' accounts of death camps, Arendt argues that

> The more authentic [the reports] are, the less they attempt to communicate things that evade human understanding and human experience—sufferings, that is, that transform men into "uncomplaining animals." None of these reports inspires those passions of outrage and sympathy through which men have always been mobilized for justice. On the contrary, anyone speaking or writing about concentration camps is still regarded as suspect; and if the speaker has resolutely returned to the world of the living, he himself is often assailed by doubts with regard to his own truthfulness, as though he had mistaken a nightmare for reality. (*OT* 439)

Here Arendt is more specific than she will later be in *The Human Condition*: pain disables not just voice but *narrative*—it inhabits the phantasmagorically liminal space of "nightmare," what she calls "a phantom world" (*OT* 445).[20] The inability to communicate the experience means that even survivors remain, in some ways, inside the camp. Somewhat like Milton's Satan, for whom "which way I fly is hell; myself am hell," in Arendt's account such an internalization of the ideology and regimes of the camp is what truly constitutes "total domination." It becomes something approaching what Foucault terms biopolitics, which means that the steps implemented to "kill the person" cannot be simply erased or negated.

But what about what we might term "the place of pain" *outside* the camps? I began my reading of Arendt by suggesting that her statements regarding love can tell us something about her points about pain. In *The Human Condition*, written in the late 1950s (i.e., more than five years after the publication of *The Origins of Totalitarianism*), Arendt situates pain not in the "phantom world" of the camps but in the domestic or private realm that she claims the rise of the social has eclipsed:[21]

> It has always been the bodily part of human existence that needed to be hidden in privacy, all things connected with the necessity of the life process itself, which prior to the modern age comprehended all activities serving the subsistence of the individual and the survival of the species. Hidden away were the laborers who "with their bodies minister to the [bodily] needs of life" [Arendt's citation: *Politics* 1254b25] and the women who with their bodies guarantee the physical survival of the species. *Women and slaves belonged to the same category and were hidden away not only because they were somebody else's property but because their life was "laborious," devoted to bodily functions.* (*HC* 72; emphasis added)

Pain does not even belong to the *oikos*, properly speaking, though the *oikos* "shelters" it even as it obscures it. The rise of the social means that the experience of pain loses all meaning, both for the private individual (in the loss of intelligibility) and for the public that the individual anonymously serves. Here we might think of the paradox of remembering and describing the experience of the death camps in *Origins*, and also of Aristotle's, and Homer's, *aphrêtôr, athemistos, anestios*—the "tribeless, lawless, hearthless one" (*Politics* I.1.1253a5–10)—but we must also recall Aristotle's claim that even "life that endures much suffering" (*enousês*) contains "something of well-being and sweetness" (*tinos eumerias kai gluktêtos*) (*Politics* III.3.1287b23–31). Arendt's conceptualization of pain, then, seems to move beyond the Aristotelian model to which she is indebted, at least at this moment. Pain is one defining characteristic of the *animal laborans*, which stands explicitly opposed to active, political life, but pain (like labor, though Arendt distances herself from the notion of the gendered division of labor, *HC* 47–48n38) is also gendered, as we see here.[22] The social sphere "hides away" pain more effectively than the supposed separation of public and private, for it covertly replaces labor with work, which retains public value but can never be recognized publicly. Here we must note that though Arendt's essential point about the non-political, obscured labor of both women and slaves is true, the first part of her formulation, strictly speaking, is not, at least for Aristotle in the *Politics*. Aristotle distinguishes between women and slaves, arguing that identifying the two is the mark of barbarian societies (I.1.1252b1–9). Arendt argues that "while we have become excellent in the laboring we perform in public, our capacity for action and speech has lost much of its former quality since the rise of the social realm banished these into the sphere of the intimate and the private" (*HC* 49)—public recognition and honor, which for Arendt as for Aristotle motivate citizens in their pursuit of the good life, are no longer possible, for work has become anonymous, corporate, mechanized. Since the rise of the social realm has transformed individuals into "cogs" in a bureaucratic machine, this extreme removal reveals, finally, the social's truly world-destroying capacity: as it allows no recognition of pain in its members it becomes able to inflict pain on others. The most negative face of such anonymity and decorporealization is the totalitarian regime of the Nazi concentration camp. The superlogical, accretive methodology of "total domination" that Arendt had outlined six years previously retains little of Aristotle's sense of *tukhê*, the "fortune," "chance," or "accident" that Aristotle initially argues might render the "naturally" political animal "tribeless, lawless, hearthless"—for Arendt, as indeed for Aristotle, in the end there's no "accident" to such processes.

Reading Shakespeare: The Camp as *Nomos* of the Marriage

Though it might seem counterintuitive to examine practices of subjugation and taming in a comedy rather than in a tragedy, *Shrew* provides an instructive *mise-en-scène* for a literary framing of the claims I'm making about Arendt precisely *because* of the generic conventions of comedy—but most comic conventions are rather harrowed by this play in particular.[23] Like most comedies, Shakespeare's comic romances focus not on the married *state* but on its potential, stopping short at the threshold (or at the curtains of the marriage bed). *The Taming of the Shrew* (ca. 1592), however, presents several anomalies, beginning with Katherina and Petruchio's wedding, which takes place in act 3.[24] Many critics have noted the particular ways delayed or disrupted rituals (most obviously the wedding) in *Shrew* function in terms of dramatic tension and plot structure, and I would suggest that the peculiar anxieties in this play must also be thought of as carrying an implicit political valence.[25] In

Shakespeare's plays, comic violence does not generally serve as a major plot device but as a more or less lighthearted diversion from the mainly marriage-bound trajectory, often relegated to subplots—perhaps a Dogberry or a Lucio or a Malvolio threatens or endures comic blows (outside a duel), but a Benedick or a Claudio or even an Angelo does not stoop to such low slapstick. Part of the strangeness of *The Taming of the Shrew* is that it is, of course, all about comic violence, the domestication of the unruly Katherina—a process, Petruchio tells her, by which he will bring her "From a wild Kate to a tame Kate / Conformable as other household Kates" (II.i.266–67).

The play is set in Padua, part of the Venetian Republic: the action occurs in locations that symbolize the bastions of Paduan mercantilism—the marketplace itself, the church, the home of Baptista Minola, Kate and Bianca's merchant father, and Petruchio's country house. *Shrew* thus bears certain similarities with that other play centering on the exigencies of civil society in mercantile Venice.[26] The framing narrative (the dream of the tinker Sly) and certain other metatheatrical moments in the play (such as Petruchio's "Prithee, Kate, let's stand aside and see the end of this controversy," V.i.48) set up a dramatic context that continually calls into question the very nature of what constitutes performance or "show." The courtly "show" continually staged by and around Elizabeth I, another unmarried shrew, provided what was arguably the biggest theatrical draw in town; conversely, much political comment and criticism happened on Elizabethan stages. Kate's final speech (whether read ironically, as some critics have, or not) valorizes patriarchy in a way that could not but be supremely topical in the England of the 1590s. Petruchio's soliloquy at IV.i activates the common analogy between husband/wife and sovereign/subjects that Kate's final speech addresses in much more detail:

> Thus have I politicly begun my reign,
> And 'tis my hope to end successfully.
> My falcon now is sharp and passing empty,
> And till she stoop she must not be full-gorged,
> For then she never looks upon her lure.
> Another way I have to man my haggard,
> To make her come and know her keeper's call,
> That is, to watch her, as we watch these kites
> That bate and beat and will not be obedient.
> She ate no meat today, nor none shall eat;
> Last night she slept not, nor tonight she shall not.
> As with the meat, some undeservèd fault

I'll find about the making of the bed,
And here I'll fling the pillow, there the bolster,
This way the coverlet, another way the sheets.
Ay, and amid this hurly I intend
That all is done in reverend care of her.
And, in conclusion, she shall watch all night,
And if she chance to nod I'll rail and brawl
And with the clamour keep her still awake.
This is a way to kill a wife with kindness,
And thus I'll curb her mad and headstrong humour.
He that knows better how to tame a shrew,
Now let him speak—'tis charity to show. (IV.ii.159–82)

Petruchio founds his "politic" reign, then, on practices of surveillance ("to watch her, as we watch these kites") and deprivation—practices that, as Emily Detmer suggests, must be considered more than "mere" domestic violence.[27] As we witnessed some years ago during the U.S. Senate Judiciary Committee wiretap hearings, the question of whether or not "surveillance" may be accounted "force" continues to be a problem that blurs whatever lines may arbitrarily be drawn between personal rights and communal good. And the outrages at Guantánamo, Abu Ghraib, and Bagram might be cited as recent (and ongoing) examples of the ways depriving prisoners of sleep and food do amount to torture. As we continue to witness, torture often takes explicitly sexualized forms. Much has been said of Petruchio's characterization of Kate as animal, monster, demon, and whore in this play, and we might recall the nameless, monstrous, banished wife of Marie de France's *lai* in this context. Here, Petruchio's analogy of the "sharp and passing empty" falcon who must "stoop" before she is to be "full-gorged" suggests that his taming strategy involves more than depriving Kate of food. In conjunction with his intention to "man my haggard" and all the talk of disturbed nights and violently tossed-about bedclothes that follows, the specter of sexual violence here cannot be ignored.[28]

Petruchio concludes his soliloquy with a couplet: "He that knows better how to tame a shrew, / Now let him speak—'tis charity to show" (ll.180–82). His quasi-legalistic call here enjoins a certain movement beyond the dramatic framework of the play, and his language recalls (with a twist) the rites of marriage itself. That is, he melds and perverts theatrical and politico-religious topoi, comically exhorting the audience to "show" (i.e., do the actor one better) and alluding to the legal publication of banns, the purpose of which was to give anyone who wished to present a pre-contract a chance to do so. The soliloquy thus both begins and ends with a focus on marriage as a legal and political (rather than a primarily domestic) institution, a public binding that models the relationship between sovereigns and subjects. Obviously, the situation of characters in a Shakespearean comedy cannot be compared with the all-too-real events I cite, but Shakespeare's play can provide a literary and theoretical framework for thinking about some of the ideologies that underlay such events. I propose a more or less allegorical reading of Katherina's situation, which we might, tweaking Giorgio Agamben's formulation slightly, term "the camp as *nomos* of the marriage."

I began this argument with the assertion that the next step to thinking about "the camp as *nomos* of the modern" is to, as Agamben himself suggests, focus on the "modern avatars of bare life," in the form of the production and control of sexualized bodies and identities. What would this mean, and what can a four-century-old play have to say about such things? Precisely this: Arendt argues that in order to "kill the spontaneity" in individuals, in order to render them truly stateless, anonymous "bundles of reactions," it is first necessary to obliterate all traces of "the differentiation of the individual, his [*sic*] unique identity" (*OT* 453). Sexual difference and sexuality are one locus of individualized identity, and the process of total domination simultaneously effaces them utterly and enforces grotesque parodies of gendered norms in the form of certain types of torture (genocidal rape is one of the most extreme examples). Shakespeare's Kate is obviously not subjected to torture in this way, but the play does illustrate the transformation to a social sphere that denies the "protection" afforded by the private realm even as it also annihilates any potential for political action and public recognition of that action. And the generic conventions of comedy mean that as an audience, we don't know quite how to respond to this play: with the exception of the happy ending (the "ending" that is nevertheless called somewhat into question by the unclosed framing narrative), a bare sketch of the main plotline sounds rather like the beginning of something written by Webster thirty years later—it's a tragedy wrenched somewhat unconvincingly into comedy by Kate's kiss in V.i.122 and, of course, by her final speech.[29] That is to say, in order for the audience to buy the comic resolution, the entire "taming" process we've just seen needs to dissipate like Sly's dream—and for that to happen we need to become, to an extent, complicitous in the taming, accomplices after the fact. In order for Petruchio's "politic reign" to "end successfully," I submit, it is necessary for the audience to participate by proxy in the "show" of marital taming he stages, and it is necessary that the "show" of Katherina's defiance be covered over or "hidden away"—de-politicized, devalued, and eventually erased. "Submitting" to the comedy here requires not just acceptance but also internalization of what Petruchio calls his "awful rule and right supremacy" (V.ii.109)—the audience's "taming" occurs along with Kate's, and mimics it, to a certain extent.

If the audience is drawn into the web of Petruchio's "taming," what then? In "Collective Responsibility," a 1968 lecture delivered at the annual meeting of the American Philosophical Society, Arendt distinguishes between "guilt" and "responsibility" as follows: "Where all are guilty, nobody is. Guilt, unlike responsibility, always singles out; it is strictly personal. It refers to an act, not to intentions or potentialities. It is only in a metaphorical sense that we can say we *feel* guilty for the sins of our fathers or our deeds or mankind, in short, for deeds we have not done."[30] What I am suggesting is not that we as spectators are "guilty" in the literal sense that we are implicated in the taming; rather, that recognizing the ways in which we are "responsible" for our "responses" (two words with the same root) to the comedy can serve as a corrective for this detachment—and that the first step in moving *away* from "the camp as *nomos* of the modern" is to translate this lesson in spectatorship to a lesson in more engaged citizenship.

CHAPTER ONE

Undead Letters

Reading the Relic between Marlowe and Kantorowicz

> History is the scene of a most intensive life, which ends time and again in ruins.
>
> —Karl Löwith, *The Biblical View of History*

I begin by borrowing Eric Santner's conception of the "undead," from his reading of Walter Benjamin's natural history:

> Because human beings have not only natures but also *second natures*, when an artifact loses its place in a historical form of life—when that form of life decays, becomes exhausted, or dies—we experience it as something that has been *denaturalized, **transformed into a mere relic of natural being***. . . . Natural history is born out of the dual possibilities that life can persist beyond the death of the symbolic forms that give it meaning and that symbolic forms can persist beyond the death of the form of life that gave them human vitality. Natural history transpires against the background of this space between real and symbolic death, this space of the "undead."[1]

Taking up Santner taking up Benjamin, we might ask: what is a relic? Most simplistically, of course, it is that which is left back or left behind (*re + linquo*), a thing (*res*) once connected to (or part of) a body that continues—or, perhaps, begins—to exert its power though corporeally severed. Locus of a mystery: the relic's potency also lies in its partial occlusion, its protected secretion *away from* the community that gathers in its name.[2] Letters, like relics, exert their power prosthetically. Tangible themselves, they recall the bodies that penned them only in the scribes' absence—whether that absence is temporary (the correspondent writes from far away) or permanent (the posthumous letter).[3] A letter from the deceased, like a relic, exerts a terrible and seductive pull all its own in its dual ability to conjure the dead and to remind the reader of that final absence.

Over fifty years ago, Irving Ribner asserted that "distinctions between history and tragedy as dramatic genres are meaningless and unnecessary," yet much modern criticism of Elizabethan chronicle dramas remains divided, reading them as either "history plays" or "tragedies," assuming that the genres remain separable and serve different ends.[4] This disjunction, in turn, rests in part on the ancient notion of "history" and "poesy" as distinct modes of expression. According to this model, history constructs a teleological narrative of facts that takes as its impetus either legitimation or critique of nationalist identities.[5] Tragedy, on the other hand (to paraphrase Sidney paraphrasing Aristotle), makes no such claims to be bound by historical truth, though it may certainly draw on historical sources and serve a similar purpose.[6] To turn to Ernst Kantorowicz's formulation of the king's two bodies and extend it to genre as well as political theology, we might say that history tells the story of the office of kingship, of succession and preservation, while tragedy presents that of the body of the king, mortal and declining, spectacularly dislocated from history.[7] If history synthesizes, tragedy rends: most strikingly, of course, it rends the body of the king, whose staged death typically provides its climax. Tragedy paradoxically dismembers the sense of unity and progress instantiated by history in its offering of hermetically closed-off, aestheticized tableaux of death; it deconstructs the teleological narrative of history even in the act of drawing on it. Yet though the death of the sovereign in tragedy is always the death of the Kantorowiczian body of the king, tragedy goes beyond the death of the sovereign to stage the moment of succession, gesturing back toward the office of kingship and the progress of history.

A critical reforging of the notional distinction between history and tragedy thus becomes necessary, and a reading of Christopher Marlowe's *Edward II* that takes into account both its play with chronicle sources and its implicit commentary on the very present dangers of the political-theological rifts in Elizabethan England enables such a move. Marlowe's play, according to Ribner, constitutes a starting point for a generic genealogy of the history play, as it is both "our first important tragedy based on the chronicles" and "a mature tragedy of character in which a potentially good man comes to destruction because of inherent weaknesses which make him incapable of coping with a crisis which he himself has helped to create."[8] But it is only with Kantorowicz's seminal *The King's Two Bodies: A Study in Mediaeval Political Theology* that the "crisis" can be diagnosed: *Edward II* depicts the collapse of the king's two bodies, the subordination of political body to personal exigency. As Kantorowicz notes in the chapter he devotes to Shakespeare's *Richard II*, the very idea of "the king's two bodies" is almost inherently tragic in nature: each body threatens to engulf or otherwise destroy the other, yet neither can exist separately. Kantorowicz defines a dialectical relationship between the "political" (corporate and metaphysical) office of kingship and the frail, vulnerable body natural that inhabits the office. The ambivalent bond between the king's two bodies thus mimics the dialectical relationship between historiography and tragedy, yet these tensions drop out of some recent readings of both history plays and the submerged political play of Kantorowicz's monumental "study in mediaeval political theology." Kantorowicz was hardly the first to point out the theological scaffolding of kingship in Shakespeare's play, which derives from Marlowe's but tends to supersede it, in the modern critical landscape. Yet it is in tracing Marlowe's often obscured or vexed theological contours that the nature of Kantorowicz's critical engagement with the political action entailed by historiographic practice emerges most clearly.[9]

If the king's two bodies can be considered what Kantorowicz calls a "mystic fiction" (3), this "mystic fiction" itself may also be considered a trope—a figure of speech, a *turn* from the literal or corporeal (the body of Tudor law) to the metaphorical and metaphysical, and also a turn between its pre-modern subject matter and its modern points of articulation. Consider *facere*, "to make" or "to do": the Latin root of "fiction" recalls a usefully neutral sense, one that avoids the potential of false binaries (such as fact/fiction—two terms born of the same root—or truth/fiction). At this basic etymological level, the coupling of *making* and *doing* is suggestive, recalling the political impetus to action that seemingly underlies Kantorowicz's account. Though his preface names his study as an excavation of myths of state, as formulated in the exiled philosopher Ernst Cassirer's final work (xix),[10] Kantorowicz quickly turns away from further citation of Cassirer, and though acknowledging his "debt" to the legal scholarship of Frederic Maitland, he never names the controversial jurist whose work stands in his own subtitle.[11] These scholarly passages, not quite ellipses, suggest both Kantorowicz's ties to "myths" or "fictions" of state and also his suspicions of the same.[12] Ultimately, Marlowe's generic fluidity finds a somewhat uncanny double in Kantorowicz's peculiarly literary historiographic practice, which cloaks its own critique of the reemergence of absolutist doctrines in modern totalitarian states in the deliberately mystified guise of the history of a fiction.[13]

Kantorowicz's undead letter emerges surreptitiously, via a circuitous passage between a series of Weimar-era writings by the conservative

Catholic jurist Carl Schmitt and the German-Jewish thinker Walter Benjamin that excavate not just the mystic but also the martyrological aspects of early modern sovereignty.[14] *Edward II* might be considered Marlowe's undead letter, an undigested remainder that inhabits both Shakespeare's later play and Kantorowicz's reading of it. And, too, biographical speculation about "Marlowe the man" continues to shadow critical readings of the play. The infamous "Baines Note"—"information" written by a former spy and Cambridge contemporary of Marlowe's, to whom Baines attributes various remarks concerning the sodometrical trio of atheism, treason, and, of course, homosexuality—was hastily copied and anonymously delivered to the authorities while Marlowe was held for questioning after Kyd's similar accusations. This decidedly undead letter continues to shape Marlowe's reception, as Jonathan Goldberg and Stephen Orgel have argued.[15] Given this proto-secular, bad boy "Poet/Spy" persona[16] (initially derided, now critically prevalent), it seems that the most truly perverse thing of which one could accuse Marlowe would be that he employs a Catholic theological scaffolding upon which to erect his radically Protestant, skeptical, or atheist plays—which is exactly what I propose here.

In linking the development of chronicle drama mainly to the "Tudor myth" arguably promulgated by historians such as Holinshed and Hall, E. M. W. Tillyard and his intellectual inheritors tend to de-emphasize the connection between the rise of history plays and the decline of miracle or saint plays.[17] Tillyard, who opines that *Edward II* "shows no prevailing political interest: no sense of the sweep or pattern of history," claims that "[Marlowe] never confuses the legitimate cutting off of princely parasites with the illegitimate lifting of the hand against the Lord's Anointed."[18] Ribner counters this:

> The truth is that the political milieu of *Edward II* is the same as that of *Tamburlaine*, in which *the unquestioned absolutism of the king is based not upon divine ordination, but upon human power, and in which the king is not controlled by any responsibility to a God who will destroy him if he neglects his duties to his people, but only by the limits of the king's own ability to maintain his power in spite of any opposition.*[19]

Ribner's claim that "the king . . . [is controlled] only by the limits of [his] own ability to maintain his power in spite of any opposition" acquires an illuminating gloss when we turn to Benjamin's notion of the sovereign's role in what he calls "the state of emergency" in *Trauerspielen*.[20] Benjamin differentiates between tragedy and *Trauerspiel* by locating both the subject matter and the "true object" of the latter in "historical life as it was conceived at that time," whereas tragedy focuses on "myth . . . the past age of heroes."[21] Remarking that, for baroque dramatists, "the sovereign, the principal exponent of history, almost serves as its incarnation," Benjamin reminds us that "like the term 'tragic' in present-day usage—and with greater justification—the word *Trauerspiel* was applied in the seventeenth century to dramas and historical events alike," resisting the tragedy/history split so prevalent in readings of English plays of the period.[22]

In Benjamin's account, the monarch in mourning plays thus functions as the "bearer of history," the tyrannical, melancholic, and indecisive *Kreatur*, while *Trauerspiel* itself yokes the terrible burden of sovereignty to the ongoing condition of political crisis that inevitably occurs in these dramas.[23] Benjamin links the two as follows:

> Whereas the modern concept of sovereignty amounts to a supreme executive power on the part of the prince, *the baroque concept emerges from a discussion of the state of emergency, and makes it the most important function of the prince to avert this.*[24] The ruler is designated from the outset as the holder of dictatorial power if war, revolt, or other catastrophes should lead to a state of emergency. This is typical of the Counter-Reformation. . . . The theological-juridical mode of thought, which is so characteristic of the century, is an expression of the retarding effect of the over-strained transcendental impulse, which underlies all the provocatively worldly accents of the baroque. *For as an antithesis to the historical ideal of restoration it is haunted by the idea of a catastrophe. And it is in response to this antithesis that the theory of the state of emergency is devised.*[25]

Here Benjamin references Schmitt's *Political Theology: Four Chapters on the Concept of Sovereignty* (first published in March 1922), whence he derives both the designation and the definition he employs—and whence Kantorowicz will later take his own subtitle. Opening with the magisterial declaration, "Sovereign is he who decides on the exception" (*Souverän ist, wer über den Ausnahmezustand entscheidet*)—the "decision" being when to suspend normative law and declare a juridical state of emergency—Schmitt's work traces the secularized afterlives of theological concepts in modern statecraft. For Schmitt, "the exception in jurisprudence is analogous to the miracle in theology."[26] Recalling James I's conceit of the king as *lex loquans*, Schmitt's analogy abstracts the sovereign decider utterly from the scene of law even in the act of his pronouncing it.[27] In 1930,

Benjamin wrote to Schmitt—another undead letter that to some taints Benjamin's intellectual legacy—and sent him a copy of his book, but his debt to Schmitt already appears in the preceding passage.[28]

Schmitt's political-theological excavation is later taken up by Kantorowicz, in the work that adopts Schmitt's title as its subtitle and moves from "Christ-Centered Kingship" to "Man-Centered Kingship." Kantorowicz's analysis, however, proceeds from a position arguably closer to that of Schmitt's interlocutor, Walter Benjamin, in terms of both methodology and content, than to Schmitt himself.[29] Like Benjamin, Kantorowicz provides a heterodox reformulation of the Schmittian doctrine of sovereign exception. While he cites Schmitt in the preceding passage, Benjamin's careful unfolding of the state of emergency or exception [*Ausnahmezustand*] eventually refutes Schmitt's elegiac portrait of decisionist sovereignty. If Schmitt's sovereign embodies the "state of exception" inasmuch as he is, himself, always already the juridical exception,[30] Benjamin's emphasis on the tyrant's melancholy and indecisive embodiment hollows out Schmitt's apotheotic concept. Benjamin argues that "in the *Trauerspiel* monarch and martyr do not shake off their immanence," and his linkage of the two figures regrounds the Schmittian sovereign, insisting on a kingship that remains precariously corporeal. For Benjamin, the king (even, and perhaps especially, the tyrant of *Trauerspiel*) is not excepted from the world and its laws; he is in fact *more* subject to contingency, "haunted by the idea of catastrophe." In this way, the sovereign in *Trauerspiel* more closely approximates the ambiguously hallowed figure of the martyr than either the Nietzschean superman or the Schmittian decisionist.[31] This series of partially submerged links between Kantorowicz, Schmitt, and Benjamin allows for a rethinking of the bifurcated construction of history and tragedy, one that reanimates the decidedly *non*-secular scripture—what Karl Löwith called "the [reiterated] story of action and suffering"—that ultimately underpins both.[32]

Possibly the last play Marlowe wrote, *Edward II* has no recorded performance before his death in 1593.[33] In 1594 an octavo edition appeared, entitled "The troublesome raigne and lamentable death of Edward the second, King of England: with the tragicall fall of proud Mortimer." This first printing announces its generic ambivalence, grafting the overtly literary topos of Mortimer's "tragicall fall" onto its quasi-historic description of Edward's "troublesome raigne and lamentable death."[34] Marlowe's play both demonstrates Kantorowicz's sovereign dialectic and calls attention to some cracks in the facade of the notionally "Reformed" Elizabethan polity. In the argument that follows, I propose that the imprisonment and execution (and, to some at the time of the play's composition, martyrdom) of Mary, Queen of Scots, in 1587 forms a potent though covert dramatic nexus for Marlowe. Critics have long pointed out parallels between the homosexual Edward II and both Henri III of France and James VI of Scotland, each of whom presented a certain threat to the English succession.[35] While these topical referents certainly remain valid, yet another ghost sits at the table in *Edward II*, that of James's mother, Mary Stuart: the queen in exile, the French, Catholic threat whom Elizabeth had finally and so unwillingly cut down a mere five years before Marlowe wrote his play. *Edward II* draws together tropes of Catholic martyrdom (which codes the pierced, mutilated body of the saint as feminine) and a complex discourse of sovereignty that foregrounds the political theological relationship between inscription and spectacle. Thus Marlowe's play presents a disassembled and prismatic Mary Stuart, an at times nearly hagiographic triptych portrait of the queen's fate dispersed among its portrayal of Edward II himself, Gaveston, and the "miserable and distresséd Queen," Isabella (4.170). This fraught conjunction points up the tensions that tend to undermine the notion of the "office" of kingship as the stable part of the sovereign dialectic limned by Kantorowicz.

"Enter reading on a letter that was brought him from the king"

"Enter Gaveston reading on a letter that was brought him from the king": the opening stage direction of Marlowe's play activates a focus on the sovereign's written word that Mortimer's "unpointed letter" will repeat with variations.[36] It is just this concentration on *writing*, or inscription, and its peculiar conjunction with theatrical artifice that I want to focus on here, recalling the prominent part played by letters (the so-called casket letters and, later, the Babington letters) at both trials of Mary Stuart.[37] Taken together, the first two lines of the play (the stage direction and Gaveston's letter) convey a great deal about both the political and the philosophical problems the play will address. While the opening stage direction establishes a context that blurs distinctions between spoken and written words, it also foregrounds two senses of acting: as dramatic performance, and as "doing," the opposite or extension of thinking, speaking, writing. In the ancient model of the *vita activa*, acting or doing is always now, always present—it may later become the stuff of history, but its tangibility and immediacy must be juxtaposed with the abstraction and removal of the *vita contemplativa*.[38] But an actor, pacing the stage, "reading on a letter," quite literally melds the two modes—and when the actor is "reading on a letter . . . from the king," we might say that the figure of history abruptly enters the scene—or is it the figure of tragedy? We can only say that it is the figure of the sovereign—the sovereign absent, ventriloquized, perhaps disfigured in the recitation, as Mary argued she had been in the presentation of the casket letters.[39]

Gaveston's letter invokes not one but two absent kings—the "deceased" Edward I and the non-present Edward II. The words of the living but invisible, offstage Edward II convey the image of the dead Edward I: "My father is deceased; come, Gaveston, / And share the kingdom with thy dearest friend" (1.1–2). In this first line, the caesura marks a severance in sovereign perpetuity even as it announces the succession—the semicolon stands in for both sempiternal kingship and the inevitable decay and fall of the individual body of the sovereign. The letter Gaveston reads thus figures a literal interregnum, the breath or pause between the two speech acts of the cry "The king is dead . . . long live the king!"[40] Here the first part of Edward II's statement, "My father is deceased," constatively echoes the first part of the traditional formulation "le roi est mort." Though Edward elides the second part of the formulation, the announcement of the perpetuity of kingship in the cry "Vive le roi!" that same almost magical adjuration hovers behind and above his order to "come, Gaveston / and share the kingdom with thy dearest friend." Rescinding Edward I's order for Gaveston's banishment, Edward II figuratively crowns himself in the written command. "Come, Gaveston" thus performs an act of sovereign superscription, the living body of the king blotting out the shrouded shadow of the dead king.

For an Elizabethan audience, Edward's invitation to "share the kingdom with thy dearest friend" would provoke a certain pause. By 1592, nearing sixty, Elizabeth had not yet declared an heir, and the specter of a headless, internally divided state haunted the popular imagination and the stage. The king's address to his "friend" evokes the inevitable dark double of the flatterer, while the adjuration "share the kingdom" conjures the image of an England divided within itself. If friendship in the broadest sense constitutes the sometimes unspoken *civil* contract that establishes horizontal links between equals rather than vertical or hierarchical bonds, friendship is also a *civic* contract between citizen equals or citizen subjects.[41] But the nominal "contract" of friendship must necessarily be complicated when one friend *is* the sovereign; the prince ("first citizen") cannot have equals, as is the case for Edward. In the tradition of the *speculum princeps*, the office of the sovereign's friend must be that of the counselor, mirroring the monarch's best qualities and pointing out fallibilities, or the friend becomes the flatterer. In a very real way, then, the friend mediates the hierarchical link between the physical body of the king and the metaphorical body of office.

Just as Marlowe's compressed history telescopes the twenty-three years of Edward's reign, it also condenses three external threats: France, Scotland, Ireland. Critics have long noted the ways "channel water" figures both symbolically and structurally in *Edward II*. In both scene 1 and scene 22, though, while the "channel" is a ditch or gutter, that other Channel must also be imaginatively present, as, indeed, it is throughout the play. Gaveston's opening soliloquy conjures it: "Sweet prince, I come. These, thy amorous lines / Might have enforced me to have swum from France, and, like Leander, gasped upon the sand, / So thou wouldst smile and take me in thy arms" (1.6–9). Like Isabella, the "sister of the French king," Gaveston is aligned not so much with France as a *land* but with the Channel that separates yet binds France and England: fluid, shifting, ever potentially treacherous; this, in turn, associates him with the feminine in terms of humoral theory. In all of these ways, too, both Gaveston and Isabella covertly recall the threat posed by Mary, Queen of Scots, whose continual insistence that she be considered "absolute queen" of a sovereign nation, thus unsubject to England's laws, echoes the influential writings of the French legal historian Jean Bodin.[42]

In his 1576 *Six livres de la République*, which Marlowe apparently read either in the original French or in the author's 1586 Latin translation, Bodin provides a striking visual allegory of the dangers attendant upon any division of rule, and particularly upon any elevation of a subject:

> For just as a crown no longer has that name if it is breached, or if its rosettes are torn away, so sovereign majesty loses its greatness if someone makes a breach in it and encroaches on a part of its domain. . . . By the same reasoning all [the jurists] agree that the rights of the crown (*droits Royaux*) cannot be relinquished or alienated, and cannot be prescribed by any period of time. *And if it should happen that a sovereign prince does share them with a subject, he would make a companion of his servant and, in so doing, would cease to be sovereign. For the notion of a sovereign (that is to say, of someone who is above all subjects) cannot apply to someone who has made a subject his companion.* Just as God, the great sovereign, cannot make a God equal to Himself because He is infinite and by logical necessity (*par demonstration necessaire)* two infinites cannot exist, so we can say that the prince, whom we have taken as the image of God, cannot make a subject equal to himself without annihilation of his power.[43]

Here it is Bodin's concept of the inalienability of sovereign authority as represented by the Crown that must draw our attention, for it provides a useful gloss on the threat posed by Edward's invitation to "share the kingdom." As the audience learns during a later exchange between the two Mortimers, the barons' problem with Gaveston is not so much his sexual relationship with the king, for "the mightiest of kings have their minions," but "that one so basely born / Should by his sovereign's favour grow so pert, / And riot it with the treasure of the realm / While soldiers mutiny for want of pay" (4.393, 404–7). While Edward would divide the kingdom by "shar[ing] it with [his] dearest friend" (as he would later share the throne, divide the kingdom among the peers, relinquish the royal seal, and empty the treasury), he would never divide himself from Gaveston, as we see in his greeting: "Why shouldst thou kneel; knowest thou not who I am? / Thy friend, thy self, another Gaveston!" (1.139–42). Edward admits neither ceremony nor separation between them, for he is "another Gaveston"; when Gaveston is exiled the second time, Edward is "banished from [him]self." Employing the characteristic language of the friend as double, Edward subsumes the office of kingship, subordinating it to the body of the king. To return to Bodin's conceit of the broken crown, he in effect "make[s] a servant his companion." Accordingly, the barons reprimand Edward in much the same terms Mary, and even Elizabeth herself, were criticized for presuming to elevate their own favorites.

Mary's letters to Elizabeth turn upon the conceit of the monarch as, quite literally, peerless—or, we might say, friendless. Drawing out the ties of blood and gender that she shares with Elizabeth, Mary rhetorically constructs sovereignty as a link that binds the two of them while separating them from their respective subjects, as she does in a letter after the exposure of the Ridolfi conspiracy:

> From Sheffield, the 29th October, 1571
>
> Madam,—The extreme severity which by your orders I am used, so convinces me, to my great regret, of the misfortune which I have, with many others, not only of being in your disfavour, but, which is worse, *esteemed by you as an enemy instead of a friend, as a stranger instead of a relative,—even the more detested as it does not permit the exercise of Christian charity between parties so nearly related by blood and propinquity*,—that for some time past I have felt so perplexed as to hesitate whether I should write to you or not. . . .[44]

Here, uncharacteristically, Mary's form of address to Elizabeth does *not* inscribe their "blood and propinquity" so insistently as her customary address, "Madam, my Good Sister" (Elizabeth, on the other hand, generally addresses her cousin as "Madam"). Mary deployed this rhetorical line in a different way at her treason trial in 1587. Maintaining that she could not be tried by Elizabeth's court, for that to subject herself to the laws of England would "prejudice her own royal majesty, the King of Scots her son, her successors, or other absolute princes," Mary declared that she would speak only if the court acknowledged her near claim to Elizabeth's throne, declaring her "next to the succession . . . next of kin to the queen."[45] As Jayne Lewis notes, reiteration of her own sovereignty served as Mary's main defensive strategy during her trial.[46] Yet Mary's continual assertions of "absolute" queenship marked her as dangerously French, relying on a Bodinian theory of absolute monarchy.[47] Such perilous affiliations sound a sympathetic node that chimes with Marlowe's play.

The very current threat of a schismatic body politic only nominally headed by a monarch who places erotic desire above political control finds its corollary in the play's formal disruptions. Much has been made of Gaveston's metatheatrical soliloquy later in the opening scene, in which he outlines his plans to "draw the pliant King which way I please" via "Italian masques" and "pleasing shows" (1.49–70). The barons later castigate both Gaveston and Edward for their effeminate and un-English theatricality—decrying Gaveston's "proud fantastic liveries" and Edward's player-king appearances on the battlefield—and the play demonstrates the sort of consciousness of itself as theatrical production that will become more common later in the period (4.408–16; 6.154–57, 179–84).[48] But such metadramatic tropes must be thought of in conjunction with a certain broader *metageneric* consciousness, simultaneously sketching and dissolving its generic borders and classifications. Scene 6, one of the longest and most episodically packed in the play, contains two important moments, each of which figures generic interludes (emblematic and historic) that also serve as metatheatrical commentary (6.11–28). In the first episode, the action of the busy scene freezes, translating stage business into an emblematic tableau that the barons antiphonically gloss. While the barons' *imprese* function as the true mirror for the prince Gaveston is not, they borrow his own techniques to do so, turning the theatricality of the "triumph" Edward plans for Gaveston against them both. After Mortimer Senior's capture and Edward's refusal to ransom him, the barons' condemnation becomes prophetic, almost choric (6.154–66). A few lines later, Mortimer laments that "Libels are cast against thee in the street, / Ballads and rhymes made of thy overthrow" (6.174–75), cloaking his own potentially treasonous accusations in the safety of rumor—and, too, drawing popular history in the form of "ballads and rhymes" into a scene already virtually overburdened by intergeneric citation. Marlowe's turn from Holinshed to Fabyan as a source for the "fleering Scots jig" included here underscores the metageneric momentum of the moment, echoing the ways Fabyan's own work comprises something of a generic patchwork.[49] The scene, then, exemplifies Marlowe's methodology, soldering together a varied range of dramatic, literary, and iconographic tropes and seemingly calling attention to each of these moves.

Relic/Passage I: Marlowe's Golgotha

For both Marlowe and Kantorowicz, the king's funeral always already precedes his deposition. This proleptic fall is perhaps most clearly figured by Kantorowicz in a fascinating "digression" (417) into the study of funeral rituals and burial practices (411–36), which substantiates the idea of the simultaneous identification and gap between King (office) and king (body). If the funeral effigy or the tomb likeness of the office of kingship supersedes the frail, mortal body natural, perception of the effigy as immortal, self-perpetuating, depends on both its proximity to and its distance from the decaying body natural. That is, the effigy must not be entirely inseparable from the body natural; although it may present a highly idealized likeness, it must still be a *likeness*. Kantorowicz notes that Edward II himself was likely the first English king for whom an effigy was made (perhaps due to the body's mutilation, or simply its decay, as—contrary to Marlowe's suggestion—it was three months before the body was interred), and that "with the funeral of Edward II there begins, to our knowledge, the custom of placing atop the coffin the 'roiall representation' or 'personage,' a figure *ad similitudinem regis*" (419–21). The immortality of the King thus assumes the qualities of an elaborate masquerade, a pantomime perpetuity, and the effigy acquires meaning only through its proximity to, yet apparent separation from, the dead or dying body of the king. That said, it is also the careful preservation of the space *between* the undying King and the dying king that enables the fiction. This gap may be seen in the open space between the glorious effigy on top of the tomb and the skeletal representation enclosed beneath. The unchanging representation of the office must never be allowed to collapse *entirely* into the remains of the mortal placeholder below, but neither is it to be autonomous or entirely disincarnate.

A linguistic corollary to this open space appears in Marlowe's characteristic play with "over" compounds (e.g., in this play, overbear, overpeer, overrule, overdaring, overthrow, overstretched, overwatch), which perhaps most clearly demonstrate the collapse of the king's two bodies, the ever-present risk of the Bodinian crown metaphorically ruptured. In conjunction with the hyperbolic and punning "over," we must also consider the covert "under" terms (decline, subscribe, underwrit) reiterated throughout the play. While Marlowe's "overs" generally play on the doubling of ruling and seeing, as sovereignty accords with visibility, his "unders" play on tropes of writing—the monarch's word is law, and the "decline" of the king corresponds with the emptying of intelligibility from the office itself. This repeated correlation between sovereignty, inscription, and spectacle becomes most evident—and is most closely linked with the property of the crown—in the deposition scene.

Inasmuch as the crown iconographically echoes the halos of the saints,[50] it assumes a dual status something like that of a relic: both tangible object and metaphysical symbol, it memorializes the sovereign/martyr's terrible vulnerability even as it announces his transcendence. Like the martyr's halo, like the host, the crown encompasses a ghostly community, circumscribing the ever-renewing body politic even as it circles the dying brow of the king. It is thus a *relic* of sovereignty in the truest sense, both sempiternal remainder and mortal casing, its "hollow round" metaphorically striated and strained between fleshliness and transcendence, individual and communal, much as the cruciform scoring of the Eucharistic wafer inscribes a compact both spiritual and temporal.[51]

Reading the relic alongside Lacan's *Seminar XXIII*, Julia Lupton argues that "the presence of the saint in the relic resembles the presence of Christ in the Eucharist."[52] The briskness of Reformation debates about Eucharistic presence points up the fraught nature of this "resemblance," which I would also call a *subtext*, yet another undead letter: like the flayed and broken body of the martyr when it has finally been parceled into relics, the Eucharist remains a palimpsestic text.[53] Reformation debates about Eucharistic presence center on both the semantic and the ontological status of "is" in the ritual repetition "This is my body, to be given up for you."[54] According to the Catholic doctrine of transubstantiation, codified at the Council of Trent between 1551 and 1552, the host *becomes* the body of Christ at the moment of elevation that occurs immediately after the sacring (the repetition of the words "Hoc est enim Corpus Meum"). Miri Rubin notes that between the twelfth and fourteenth centuries, "The elevation was a token both of sacramental meaning and of the exclusive priestly power of its mediation and it becomes common in the decoration of the text of the mass in missal."[55] Indeed, this "priestly power" became a particular point of contention for English reformers, as the twenty-fifth and twenty-eighth Articles of Religion demonstrate.[56] In this case we might consider the priest's utterance, an echo of Christ's words at the Last Supper, a performative speech act of a peculiarly doubled nature: at the moment of elevation the priest both performs *as an actor*, imitating Christ, and also performatively translates bread into body, word into flesh.

The notion of Christ's presence in the Eucharist, in its turn, always recalls Golgotha and the scene of crucifixion—particularly John's and Luke's accounts, which emphasize the mocking inscription of sovereignty Pilate orders the soldiers to nail to the cross.[57] Pilate's "I have written what I have written" (John 19:22) recasts Yahweh's "I am what I am," but here the word does not become but surmounts the flesh—a naming before death that becomes a naming *into* or *unto* death, in the martyrological superscription "King of the Jews." This linkage between the spectacle of the mortified Christ and the ironic exscription of his sovereignty raises again the ambiguous status of the decidedly *un*dead letter and its peculiar conjunction with the sovereign/martyr dyad.[58] Keeping the debates encircling Eucharistic presence and crucifixion as the Eucharistic subtext in mind, let us turn back to Marlowe's play, for these stratified exegetical allusions surface in scene 19, with the capture of Edward I—the king surprised in the garden, surrounded by his few followers—a scene that, in Marlowe as in Holinshed, seemingly recalls the evening of the Last Supper, Christ's last vigil at Gethsemane.[59] At the end of scene 18, Mortimer's lines eerily foreshadow Edward's capture; he refers to Edward and the followers who have "shipped . . . for Ireland with the King" as "rebellious runagates" (18.66, 85; 85n).[60] Edward, Baldock, and Spencer, it transpires, have taken refuge in an Irish monastery, where Edward delivers a set speech contrasting "rule and empery" with "this life contemplative" (19.14, 21). Far from the Edward who flouts the church and has the Archbishop of Canterbury "christen'd anew" in the gutter in the opening scenes, this Edward seeks solace as well as shelter with the monks:

> Good father, on thy lap
> Lay I this head, laden with mickle care.
> O might I never open these eyes again,
> Never again lift up this drooping head,
> O never more lift up this dying heart! (19.39–44)

Kneeling to place his head in the monk's lap, the king enacts a tableau of sovereignty in abeyance, fragmented into "eyes," "head," "heart"—a dismembered emblem of martyrdom. In this setting, the repetitive crossings of "never again" and "lift up" and the consonantal echoes of "this drooping head," "this dying heart" suggest a sort of inverse consecration ceremony that simultaneously invokes the Eucharistic elevation and prefigures the deposition scene. Abasing himself before the monk, Edward figures himself as both the celebrant and the Eucharist itself, perpetually consumed, eternally renewed to be consumed again—yet renewed only partially, as a body endlessly suffering. A few lines later he offers himself as a sacrifice, in an image that recalls both the hunted hart motif of Gaveston's final moments and the "sacred heart" emblem so popular in medieval martyrologies: "Comes Leicester, then, in Isabella's name / To take my life, my company, from me? / Here, man, rip up this panting breast of mine / And take my heart in rescue of my friends" (19.64–67).

Relic/Passage II: Kantorowicz's Acts and Monuments

Selectively occluding and revealing its politically potent interiors, Kantorowicz's history of a Tudor "legal fiction" itself becomes a reliquary of the *present*, or at least the more recent past: studded with footnotes, bracketed with parentheses, an ornamented carapace protecting its only superficially "mystic" content. Just as Kantorowicz's historical argument provides a useful theoretical gloss on Marlowe's rather perverse political theology, so Marlowe's poetics offers a methodological mirror for Kantorowicz's peculiarly literary brand of historiography. Consider the following characterization of Kantorowicz, drawn from the opening paragraph of Alain Boureau's book on the historian's life and work:

> Ernst Kantorowicz transformed himself into a monument or shrine when he died in 1963. In his will he had asked that all private papers be destroyed. During his lifetime, an exaggerated penchant for secrecy made him keep silent about all but the scantiest biographical details. Fortunately, only a few years before his death, he had completed a magnificent cenotaph, *The King's Two Bodies*. In the way some books have of identifying with their authors, and vice versa, this book would henceforth be conflated with Kantorowicz himself.[61]

As his subtitle (*Stories of a Historian*) intimates, Boureau argues that before his death Kantorowicz consciously crafted a *fiction* of his own scholarly development and political agendas. What does it mean, to consider Kantorowicz himself as "a monument or shrine," his last work a "magnificent cenotaph"? I would suggest that we consider all of these terms in conjunction with the generic argument I have been trying to trace in this chapter. Kantorowicz's "self-fashioning" (to redeploy Stephen Greenblatt's famous phrase in this new context) results in what Boureau suggests is a sort of iconic reconstruction, a monolithic Self-Portrait of The Historian that always reveals the cracks in the monument. So, too, does Kantorowicz continually draw attention to the *fictiveness* of history in the very act of historiographic production:

> The tenet of the King's Two Bodies and its history served in this case as a unifying principle easing the assemblage and selection of facts as well as their synthesis. The origin of this study will explain how it happened that the author swerved again (as in his study on the *Laudes*) from the normal tracks of the mediaeval historian and broke through the fences, this time of mediaeval Law, for which he was not prepared for his training. For this trespass he owes apologies to the professional jurist who, undoubtedly, will find many a flaw in this presentation, although the author himself is aware of some of the more likely shortcomings: overlaboring of texts on the one hand, missing of salient points on the other. But those are the hazards to which the outsider will usually expose himself; he will have to pay the fine for intruding into the enclosures of a sister discipline. (xix)

It's an odd passage—in both senses of the word "passage"—for in this excerpt or passage Kantorowicz's metaphors describe the authorial passage outside the "enclosures" of medieval history. In some ways it is a very conventional passage for a medievalist, for it employs that oldest of tropes, the humility topos—yet that topos turns against its own effacement by positing the historian as a sort of dashing adventurer, a pirate raiding the sanctuaries of his "sister disciplines." And what emerges from these authorial introjections, these "intrusions," or, perhaps more properly, *excursions*, beyond the "fences" of the traditional territory of the medieval historiographer? Kantorowicz's apology here casts the work of the historiographer as a sort of archaeology (in the Foucauldian sense), a practice of not just unearthing but "assembling" and "synthesizing" a narrative product. And it is precisely the "swerves" that Kantorowicz here apologizes for, his turns *away from* "the normal tracks of the mediaeval historian," that tell us something interesting about history as narrative production.

Kantorowicz's apology requires us to ask three questions: First, and most obviously, if this monolithic monograph is *not* to be considered a "normal" history, what is? Second, and slightly less obviously, who is the "professional jurist" to whom Kantorowicz apologizes? And, third: why *only* apologize to scholars of law for "trespassing," when surely the chapters on Shakespeare and Dante might be considered an incursion into the territory of literary scholars? In the opening pages I suggested that the shadowy "professional jurist" to whom Kantorowicz apologizes and, more tentatively, acknowledges a debt, is likely not just Frederic Maitland but also Carl Schmitt. Thus I turn now to the third query, and so, eventually, back to Marlowe. Like Marlowe's play, Kantorowicz's history comprises a generic and methodological patchwork—something to which he calls attention with a certain rueful humor in his preface and introduction. In these two brief sections Kantorowicz outlines his intention, claiming that his work will engage with "What has been called 'The Myth of the State' (Ernest Cassirer) . . . although it is restricted to one leading idea, the fiction of the King's Two Bodies, its transformations, implications, and radiations" (xix). Kantorowicz's passing reference to Cassirer here must be considered more than mere citation, for by drawing a connection between his own work and Cassirer's sober yet impassioned critique of modern "techniques" of nationalist myth making,[62] Kantorowicz certainly invokes the shadow of the modern totalitarian state and the ways that the "transformations, implications, and radiations" of political theology continued to impact post-war nation-states. Kantorowicz has already alluded to some of these contemporary "implications and radiations":

> Such as it now stands, this study may be taken among other things as an attempt to understand and, if possible, demonstrate how, by what means and methods, certain axioms of a political theology which *mutatis mutandis* was to remain valid until the twentieth century, began to be developed during the later Middle Ages. It would go much too far, however, to assume that the author felt tempted to investigate the emergence of some of the idols of modern political religions merely on account of some of the horrifying experience of our own time in which whole nations, the largest and the smallest, fell prey to the weirdest dogmas and in which political theologisms became genuine obsessions defying in many cases the rudiments of human and political reason. Admittedly, the author was not unaware of the later aberrations; in fact, he became the more conscious of certain ideological gossamers the more he expanded and deepened his knowledge of the earlier development. (xviii)

Though he does not cite Cassirer in this passage, Kantorowicz's assessment of the "political theologisms [which] became genuine obsessions, defying in many cases the rudiments of human and political reason" in "our own time" bears a marked resemblance to Cassirer's own opening remarks. Kantorowicz's rhetorical focus on the subordination of "the rudiments of human and political reason" echoes Cassirer's, whose analysis commences with a call to understand the underlying structure of the myths whose pervasive power has so recently, and so destructively, been deployed as a new kind of political tool, one that eclipses "rational thought."[63]

If Kantorowicz's monumental study of "medieval political theology" can be seen as a critique of modern totalitarian regimes, and a concomitant appraisal of the sovereign state's monopoly on violence—and I think it must—this critique bears out Kantorowicz's affiliations with Benjamin's reformulation of Schmittian sovereignty. In the fragmentary "Theses on the Philosophy of History," written just before his tragic suicide, Benjamin notes that "'the state of emergency' in which we live has become not the exception, but the rule."[64] Similarly, Kantorowicz's brief but dense outline of the fiction of *perpetua necessitas* traces the evolution of the temporary "emergency of the realm" (284) to a state of permanent emergency:

> The state had become permanent, and permanent were its emergencies and needs, its *necessitas*. . . . Around 1300, the notion of *necessitas* began to be focused also upon the ordinary and (so to speak) budgetary needs of administration, and to meet these administrative needs the governments arrived at the new fiction of a *perpetua necessitas*, implying (not unlike the modern tenets of "perpetual revolution") the perpetuation of something that, by definition, indicated an exception, some singular condition or some momentary deviation from the rule. (286)

It would, perhaps, stretch a point to interpret this passage as an allusive critique of the modern totalitarian state, but certainly Kantorowicz's parenthetical comparison with "modern tenets of 'perpetual revolution'" emphasizes his corrective to Schmitt's formulation of the state of exception. Though less overtly, Kantorowicz draws a Benjaminian parallel between the medieval concept of *perpetua necessitas* and the all-too-recent creation of an ongoing, international state of emergency. Similarly, the line Kantorowicz traces between taxation and military service (*cavalcata* or *chevauchée*, 289) may be linked with Benjamin's analysis of military law and military violence, and the state's monopoly on violence in the name of the law.[65] In these two parenthetical passages, Kantorowicz ultimately, though more elliptically, ends where Benjamin does, redrawing Schmitt's absolutist thesis by regrounding sovereignty in corporeality. In so doing, Kantorowicz invokes the political action implicit in historiographic production, much as Marlowe allusively suggests the intimate ties between chronicle play and Passion play.

The Relic, Returned

Marlowe's last scenes fill the evacuated space of sovereignty with a litter of relics: Edward II's handkerchief and crown; Mortimer's "unpointed letter"; Isabella's jewel; the "puddle water" in which Edward is shaved, symbolically "unanointed" as he has been uncrowned; the table, featherbed, and spit employed in his murder; the royal seal; finally, and most spectacularly, the severed head of Mortimer placed atop Edward II's hearse. Scene 20, the deposition, begins with Edward musing on the "strange exchange" of sovereign immunity for imprisonment (20.35), a "strange exchange" phenomenalized in the crown, the blood-stained handkerchief, and the letter that Edward rends "as though [he] may rend [Mortimer's] name that rends [his] heart" (20.139–44). It is this curious crossing of properties—each, in its way, now a razed reliquary—that recalls to us the spectral, fragmented figure of Mary, Queen of Scots, that has haunted the entire play. Stage properties proliferate, yet their very significance is often obscured (Mortimer's letter) or doubled (Isabella's jewel, which becomes Edward's final gift to a favorite, Lightborne).[66] Signs and symbols lose their meaning; the crown alone reverses this trend, preserving its symbolic integrity while Edward himself devolves and declines.

Eerily echoing both the play's opening lines and the written "decree" that forces him to renounce the crown, Edward's death turns on the repetition of a letter—as did Mary's. This time it is Mortimer's "unpointed letter," which he obligingly glosses:

> This letter, written by a friend of ours,
> Contains his death, yet bids them save his life:
> [*He reads*] "*Edwardum occidere nolite timere, bonum est;*
> Fear not to kill the King, 'tis good he die."
> But read it thus, and that's another sense:
> "*Edwardum occidere nolite, timere bonum est;*
> Kill not the king; 'tis good to fear the worst."

> Unpointed as it is, thus shall it go,
> That, being dead, if it chance to be found,
> Maltravers and the rest may bear the blame,
> And we be quit that caused it to be done. (23.6–16)

As in Gaveston's letter at the beginning of the play, the punctuation (or lack thereof) signifies a great deal: like that first semicolon, the caesura, the ghostly comma literally marks the place of the breath or pause between life and death—an interpretive pause, the momentary suspension of decision. Both Mortimer's letter and Gaveston's elicit what can only be called a sovereign decision, in the Schmittian sense, but whereas Gaveston's letter inserts the figure of the friend beside and between the king's two bodies, Mortimer's letter ironically overturns this fleshly conjunction ("this letter, written by a friend of ours"). "Being dead," the dangling modifier in line 14, already models Edward's assassination in its grim refusal of both agency and referent; Mortimer's letter grammatically effaces Edward's "kingly body" even before the murder. In this way the letter perfectly exemplifies Mortimer's regency itself, which has always been ambivalent, attenuated, prosthetic, "underwrit" by the authority of the nominal king, Edward III. Yet, ironically, the dangling modifier also models the sempiternity of the king's *other* body: "*being* dead," not just "dead"—Edward's kingly "being" spins itself out, gathers itself up in the endlessly progressive -ing. As Edward II himself notes just prior to passing on the crown, "Edward's name survives, though Edward dies" (20.48). Edward III's coronation and condemnation of the usurping Mortimer in the final scene emblematically superscribe the passage of sovereign authority, rearticulating the sundered political body:

> Thou shalt die; and on his mournful hearse
> Thy hateful and accursèd head shall lie
> To witness to the world that by thy means
> His kingly body was too soon interred. (25.29–32)

In characteristically perverse fashion, Marlowe returns us to Golgotha, for Mortimer's head, like Pilate's "title," assumes the status of a dead letter that won't stop speaking. Mortimer's severed head becomes one more relic of the sovereign dialectic in the play, the spectacle of his decapitation standing in for that which Marlowe had earlier denied, the depiction of Holinshed's infamously graphic account of the brutal murder of Edward I's "kingly body." Much as the headless, mutilated Mary assumed a certain phantasmatic tenacity in Elizabeth's imagination,[67] Holinshed's iconic description of Edward's assassination haunts Marlowe's play even, and perhaps especially, as it seeks to turn away from a clear depiction of this most definitive rupture of the king's two bodies.

Yet finally, perhaps, Marlowe's fictional queen, who herself becomes a sort of relic, most clearly melds the anxieties represented by both the childless Elizabeth and the foreign mother of the probable heir, Mary Stuart. In the last scene Isabella emerges as the survivor (*relict*), the remainder, the reminder of all that has gone before: the aging dowager, the "unnatural queen" now also an unnatural mother, an unnatural woman. Condemned to the tower by her own son upon his accession at the end of the play, Marlowe's Isabella simultaneously represents the triumph of the fragile balance of Edward III's new order and undermines its fledgling stability. Unlike Mortimer's, unlike Mary's, Isabella's head stays on at the end of the play—but what of that? At the beginning of the final scene, her words ironically underscore the metadramatic momentum of the entire play: "Now, Mortimer, begins our tragedy" (25.23). But her fate cannot, precisely, be accounted tragic in the same way that Gaveston's or Edward's or even Mortimer's "fall" might be. Isabella is not another Marlovian Dido. Throughout the play Isabella serves as its most consciously (and self-consciously) literary voice, her formalized rhetoric of complaint in the first half of the play shading almost imperceptibly into the political power-playing of her speeches of the second half. But in these final moments that very literariness undercuts itself, and Isabella is cast back into history even as her ambiguous fate casts the Elizabethan audience back into their own uneasy present.

I end my remarks about Marlowe's loosely allusive triptych by way of a brief excursus on two actual paintings of Mary Stuart, which function as something of an iconic corollary for my argument.[68] The first of these, an unattributed portrait of Mary in captivity, dressed in nunlike (though fashionable) black and white, wearing two crucifixes, casts her as a pious Catholic.[69] This image, in turn, served as the model for the memorial portrait commissioned by Elizabeth Curle, Mary's former lady-in-waiting, which reimagines the queen as a Catholic martyr (see plates 1–3). The latter portrait functions as something of an iconic narrative, blending historic events with hagiographic tropes. The portrait fuses several iconographic and narrative discourses: state portrait (the central image and the royal seal); saint's *vita* (the execution scene and the Latin glosses); popular or broadside images (the execution and mourning scenes). Schematically, the painting recalls a compressed triptych, in which the miniature scenes of Mary's execution at Fotheringay and her weeping ladies-in-waiting flanking the iconic central image of Mary herself serve as narrative supplements to the hieratic simulacrum of the martyred queen. The three scenes represent the sovereign martyr's progress from living flesh to decaying, disarticulated body, and thence into the space of mourning, memory, and narration: in other words, into historiography and hagiography.[70] Much like the hand of Jane Kennedy (Latinized as "Joanna Kennethie"), reaching beyond her own representational space of mourning to touch the gown of the as-yet-undead Mary (whose own gesture, as she raises her crucifix, echoes or perhaps prefigures that of her lady-in-waiting), the memorial portrait forces together past and present. Like the act of mourning, the actual moment of martyrdom itself is visually represented as both a singular occurrence, an exceptional rupture that lifts both mourners and mourned out of time, and as a fall *into* temporality, in which the martyrdom is continually reenacted in the flowing tears of Elizabeth Curle and Jane Kennedy and the flowing blood of Mary herself, whose horribly botched, interrupted decollation appears in the two bleeding incisions (see plates 2, 3). Interpellating these scenes, the royal seal and the Latin tags that identify Mary as a dutiful daughter of both Church and state, wife, and mother both gloss and interrupt the visual narrative production of Mary as historic and hagiographic subject.

In this fluid economy, the memorial painting becomes an alembic, transmuting martyr's blood and mourners' tears into a narrative artifact that discursively melds all of these tropes, a visual allegory of the ways that the nominally differentiated genres of history, hagiography, and tragedy continually slide into one another. And, too, Curle's commission of a memorial painting of such a contentious personage must be considered not just a memorial act but also a *political* act, a carefully negotiated announcement of political theological affiliations that remained perilous even after the queen had lost her head. Marlowe, Benjamin, and Kantorowicz each remind us that history itself partakes of this same fiction: it is always, in some sense, both monument and ruin, composed of fragments and citations, interpellated scenes and wandering glosses—a work of mourning that continually strives to move beyond the "scenes of action and suffering" that give it rise.

Plate 1. Memorial portrait of Mary Stuart. By kind permission of the Blairs Museum Trust, Aberdeenshire, Scotland.

Plate 2. Detail of the Blairs memorial portrait, showing the execution of Mary Stuart.

Plate 3. Detail of the Blairs memorial portrait: Jane Kennedy and Elizabeth Curle mourning.

Chapter Two

The Revenger's Decision

Exceptional Law between Middleton and Schmitt

In *Shakespeare among the Moderns*, Richard Halpern demonstrates how modernist constructions of Shakespeare continue to inflect both performance and literary criticism today.[1] Turning not to Shakespeare but to his young contemporary and sometime collaborator Thomas Middleton in this chapter, I take up Halpern's line from a different angle. Much as our arguably "post-modern" Shakespeare relies on what Halpern terms "historical allegory," the nostalgic modes that impel the influential readings of, primarily, T. S. Eliot and Walter Benjamin, so the revised canon of "early modern drama" depends upon our memorial reconfiguration of the years between 1914 and 1950. This is much the same as the impetus that, according to Halpern, characterizes Eliot, who "has constructed an image of Elizabethan drama largely in response to what he sees as a crisis in contemporary theater. His discussion of the historical past is thus largely governed by his grasp of the immediate cultural situation."[2] Eliot is also, of course, responding to a larger crisis: the killing fields of the Great War and the assemblage of totalitarian states in Europe loom within his dramatic criticism of the 1920s and '30s as much as within his earliest poems. "Webster was much possessed by death / and saw the skull beneath the skin," he wrote in 1920: the "skull beneath the skin" gapes grinningly in Eliot's own works, and the political imaginary sketched in and around his revalorization of these "minor" dramatists must necessarily be taken into account in any discussion of his critical methodology.[3] While not a dedicated fascist supporter like his sometime collaborator and editor, Ezra Pound, in the early 1930s, some of Eliot's remarks, expressing antisemitism and a desire for a "homogenous," non-liberal state, draw him frighteningly and perhaps unexpectedly close to Carl Schmitt.[4] But in his scholarly methodology, and in his reasons for revisiting his own early works on the "minor" dramatists in the mid-1950s, Eliot comes closer to Walter Benjamin. All three of these figures, then, will reappear in the pages that follow.

Thus while I agree with Halpern's brilliant thesis, I want to push it further, looking beyond the "Shakespeare horizon."[5] In a way, then, the subtitle of this chapter might as well be "*NOT JUST* Shakespeare among the Moderns," for while I take up some of the same twentieth-century critics (notably Eliot and Benjamin), my "proof text" here is *not Hamlet*, as it is for Halpern—despite the fact that Hamlet's ghost is always present in *The Revenger's Tragedy*, in verbal echoes as well as visual citations.[6] As many have noted, the now-preferred period designation "early modern" (as opposed to Renaissance, or Tudor, Stuart, Elizabethan, Jacobean) rejects certain lineages only to create another—an *avant le lettre* teleology that posits "our" historical and socio-political moment as the end point. Similarly, the descriptor "early modern drama" (rather than "minor Elizabethan" or "minor Jacobean" drama—the "minor" meaning "anyone who wasn't Shakespeare") attempts to escape the Shakespeare vortex but does not quite manage to do so. Thus it is that an anonymous play *perhaps* written by one of the period's most prolific and flexible collaborators provides such a unique occasion for thinking about the problem of "early modern drama" as such, as well as its fabrication by "modern" or "post-modern" literary critics.

The Revenger's Tragedy presents a number of critical conundrums. There is the initial question of authorship: anonymously entered in the Stationers' Register on 7 October 1607, it was first credited to Cyril Tourneur (the author of *The Atheist's Tragedy*) in a 1656 play list by Edward Archer.[7] While the attribution to Tourneur was largely invalidated by the mid-1950s, textual scholars have not been able to definitively assign it to Middleton, who nevertheless seems the most likely candidate.[8] Second, there is the question of genre, and the self-consciousness of intergeneric movement within the play. A metatheatrical mélange that incorporates elements of Senecan blood tragedy with medieval allegory and morality plays, *The Revenger's Tragedy* gleefully undoes the conventions of all three. The reemergence of critical interest in this and other plays by so-called minor Elizabethan dramatists in the early part of the twentieth century also marks a shift in the scholarly terrain. Around 1900, A. H. Thorndike coined the phrase "revenge tragedy" to refer to certain plays by Shakespeare and some of his contemporaries, which Aristotle would perhaps have recognized only as inferior derivatives of the "tragedy of suffering."[9] With J. W. Cunliffe's *The Influence of Seneca on Elizabethan Tragedy* (1893), F. L. Lucas's *Seneca and Elizabethan Tragedy* (1922), and T. S. Eliot's "Seneca in Elizabethan Translation" (1927) and "Shakespeare and the Stoicism of Seneca" (1934), each of which traced a lineage from the Stoic dramatist to the plays now commonly referred to as revenge tragedy (usually taken to begin with Thomas Kyd's *Spanish Tragedy*, ca. 1587), revenge tragedy acquired a new critical prominence.[10] In "Seneca in Elizabethan Translation," commissioned as an introduction to Thomas Newton's 1581 rendering of Seneca's *Tenne Tragedies* in the Tudor Translation Series, Eliot elevates Seneca to the same status as Montaigne and Machiavelli, arguing that this triumvirate definitively shaped the Elizabethan poetic imagination. Some years later, Fredson Bowers's *Elizabethan Revenge Tragedy 1587–1642* (1940) expanded and refined the definition of revenge tragedy, also framing the analysis in terms of the Senecan trajectory but providing a historical, religious, legal, and literary context for the Elizabethan construction of revenge.

All of these critics share a basic definition of the revenger as a malcontent who distrusts both religious and social morality and who (perhaps illegitimately, or too precipitously) assumes the "burden of proof" (to employ Stanley Cavell's phrase) for the original crime and, with it, the roles of judge as well as executioner.[11] Many of them also read the plays as symptoms of a generic instability (exemplified most in tragicomic double plots, such as that of Middleton's *The Changeling*,[12] and in the emphasis on violent spectacle) that is itself a symptom of a decaying society. Writing in the early 1930s, Eliot claims that "the general attitude toward life of the Elizabethans is one of anarchism, of dissolution, of decay"; by 1940, Fredson Bowers speaks of the pervasive mood of revenge drama as "a curious moral atrophy."[13] For Halpern, these expressions exemplify a displaced anxiety about Western imperialism. It is this "historically displaced and geographically internalized image of the effects of contemporary imperialist penetration into indigenous third-world societies" that Halpern terms "a kind of historical allegory at work," in which modern critics project their own fears of dissolution backward upon the screen of "the English Renaissance."[14] Whereas most early twentieth-century criticism followed this trend, emphasizing the ethical degeneracy of these spectacularly violent and eroticized plays, more recent critics (such as Jonathan Dollimore, Katharine Eisaman Maus, John Kerrigan, and Cavell, in his essay on *Hamlet*) tend to read the violent, hypersexualized, and misogynist elements of the plays as signs of political instability rather than as indications of the moral depravity of either the period in or the audience for which they were composed.[15]

My own argument draws from both the earlier and the later strands of criticism but attempts to ask slightly different questions. Rather than "what can this play tell us about the early Jacobean temperament/system of justice/social hierarchies/gender roles?" (although each of these queries colors the analysis that follows), by drawing the play into conversation with both early and late works by Carl Schmitt (paying particular attention to Schmitt's belated response to Benjamin's *Trauerspiel* book), I am asking both what these thinkers can tell us about the play's baroque politics and aesthetics and what the play's farcical, episodic structure and its deeply skeptical metatheatricality can tell us about Schmitt's thesis. While both *Edward II* and *Coriolanus* occasionally suggest the sadomasochistic subtexts of their sexual politics, Middleton's play foregrounds an inextricable link between violence and eroticism, in which "mere life" assumes overtly sexualized contours. Fredson Bowers declared that *The Revenger's Tragedy* "stands practically at the crossroads of Elizabethan tragedy," both the last of the "Kydian" or Senecan revenge dramas and "the distinct forerunner of the new school of the true horror tragedies."[16] Bowers is also among the first to remark positively on the play's structure, usually derided as melodrama or farce, by noting that "the scene was the [principle dramatic] unit and the plot is composed of a series of strong, brilliant situations, each occupying a single scene, somewhat loosely strung together."[17] Some years earlier Eliot also had high praise for Tourneur (to whom the play was then attributed), though he singles out not the play's episodic structure but its language and staging.[18] Eliot, though himself far from a psychoanalytic critic, offers perhaps one of the earliest Freudian-inflected readings of the play. In a passage that recalls the idea of the "objective correlative" from his well-known essay on *Hamlet*, Eliot writes,

> The cynicism, the loathing and disgust of humanity, expressed consummately in *The Revenger's Tragedy*, are immature in the respect that they exceed their object. Their objective equivalents are characters practising the grossest vices; characters which seem merely to be specters projected from the poet's inner world of nightmare, some horror beyond words. So the play is a document on humanity chiefly because it is a document on one human being, Tourneur; its motive is truly the death motive, for it is the loathing and horror of life itself. To have realized this motive so well is a triumph; for the hatred of life is an important phase—even, if you like, a mystical experience—in life itself.[19]

Reading these lines, one is tempted to apply the idea of the objective correlative to Eliot's interpretation as well as to its object—for the play itself, peopled by the hollowed figures of allegory, hardly provides the deeply psychologized "death motive" Eliot detects here. Yet the play's continual movement beyond the pleasure principle to discover the death drive—after all, it opens with "the skull beneath the skin" literally center stage—as well as its interweaving and undoing of satire, morality play, and blood tragedy, sparked a renewed critical interest just at the time Freud's works were first translated in England and published by Virginia and Leonard Woolf's Hogarth Press, which also published some of Eliot's own works.[20]

Set in a decayed Italian court, with all the Catholic baggage such a backdrop entailed for its uneasily Reformed audience, the play yokes together political, sexual, theatrical, and theological topoi. As in medieval morality plays, the characters' allegorical names index their characters—yet the allegory and its attendant morality are continually undone by Vindice, the titular "revenger." In a recent book that charts a lineage of revenge tragedy from the *Oresteia* to the rhetoric of Vietnam and the Cold War, John Kerrigan notes that retribution begins with the "transference" of the burden to act from the dead to the living.[21] Vindice's pell-mell plot against the corrupt Duke hinges on two such transferences, two violations: that of his "poisoned love," Gloriana, who kills herself rather than submit to the Duke's "palsey-lust," and that of his father, whose "dejection" from the court prompts his death by "discontent, the nobleman's consumption" (I.i.14, 34; I.ii.123–25). Vindice thus emerges as the typical Jacobean malcontent, whose initial distance from the court allows his satirical commentary on its corruption. Assisted in his plot against the Duke by his brother, Hippolito, Vindice takes a place at court as a pander to the Duke's eldest son, Lussorioso—only to discover that the lady "not far from court" that Lussorioso has his lecherous eye on is his own sister, Castiza. Now disguised as Piato, Vindice woos his sister on Lussorioso's behalf. When his suit to the "virtuous maid" fails, he tries instead to tempt his money-hungry mother, Gratiana, to seduce her daughter for Lussorioso—for "women with women can work best alone" (II.i.246; II.ii.63). Seduction, consumption, revenge: all entwine in the vocabulary of labor and commodity saturating the opening scenes of the play. "Work[ing] best alone" ironically describes not only the doubly-displaced seduction of Castiza (handed, as it were, from Lussorioso to Vindice to Gratiana) but also the supplemental transferences of revenge—even when it seems Vindice "works alone," the robotically widening gyre of retaliatory violence always implicates more than the maverick avenger, always engulfs more than the solitary victim.

Meanwhile, another plot creaks into motion with the rape of the wife of a prominent citizen, Lord Antonio. Neither the lady herself nor her rapist, the Duchess's youngest son by a previous husband, are named in the play text.[22] When, much like Gloriana, the unnamed lady kills herself rather than "live dishonored," Lord Antonio incites his followers (including Hippolito) to avenge her. Imprisoned for the rape, Junior Brother provides the motivation for yet another subplot involving the inept machinations of his two elder brothers, the Duchess's sons Ambitioso and Supervacuo. Spurio, a bastard son of the Duke's, completes the family group, and in the course of the action becomes something of a foil for Vindice. Like Vindice, who recognizes the inevitability of his role, Spurio claims that "adultery is [his] nature"; thus adultery (with his stepmother the Duchess) will be his means of retribution: "there's the vengeance that my birth was wrapped in, / I'll be revenged for all: now hate begin, / I'll call foul incest but a venial sin" (I.ii.177; 167–69). Piato/Vindice, told of the "incestuous" liaison by Hippolito, prompts Lussorioso to surprise the two in bed and kill Spurio. Lussorioso, with dagger drawn, "discovers" instead the Duke and Duchess and is promptly charged with treason for the apparent attempt on his father's life.

All is now in place for Vindice's *coup de théâtre*, the murder of the Duke, which takes place in the middle of the play (III.v). Yet any sense of pathos at the Duke's parodically overdetermined death is immediately undercut by the scenes that bookend it. Determined to free Junior Brother and, at the same time, to move themselves up in the succession, Ambitioso and Supervacuo concoct a false death warrant for "their brother," intending Lussorioso to lose his head. But their plans go awry when the Officer instead executes Junior Brother, freeing Lussorioso—now, unwittingly, the Duke. Incensed at Piato's mistake in urging him on against Spurio and the Duchess, Lussorioso decides to have Piato killed; the ever-trusty Hippolito recommends his brother, Vindice, for the "preferment." Hired to kill himself, Vindice garbs the Duke's corpse in his Piato rig and informs Lussorioso that the deed is done—pausing to engineer the "conversion" of Gratiana to "natural" motherhood and the reconciliation of Castiza and Gratiana. The play's final set piece occurs during the festivities Lussorioso has planned to celebrate his ascension to the Dukedom, during which two groups of masked revengers take advantage of the revels to murder Lussorioso and his favorites. Supervacuo declares himself the Duke; Ambitioso, jealous of the succession, stabs his brother, who returns the favor. Supervacuo's servant, mistakenly thinking Spurio has killed his master, turns his dagger on Spurio. The bloodbath is interrupted by Lord Antonio wondering "how the old duke came to be murdered," and Vindice proudly declares that it was "All for your Grace's good. . . . 'Twas we two murdered him!" (V.iii.94,

98, 100). Now installed as sovereign, Lord Antonio orders the brothers executed for treason. The play closes with his couplet: "Bear up / Those tragic bodies; 'tis a heavy season. / Pray heaven their blood may wash away all treason" (V.iii.129–31)—lines we shall have occasion to revisit.

Simple Death and the Erotics of Violence: Montaigne on "Mere Cruelty"

I turn now to a divagation on Montaigne in order to highlight two things: one, the strange rhetorical passages that reason might take, by way of proving itself; two, the always-potential imbrication of eros and violence. In speaking of the spectacular violence that attended corporal punishment, Montaigne writes that "even in matters of justice, *Whatsoever is beyond a simple death, I deeme it to be meere crueltie*."[23] Thus far I have focused on the idea of mere or bare life, variously defined: for Arendt, we might liken the condition of the prisoner subjected to "total domination" to something approaching mere life; for Benjamin, mere life can only be conceived of as creaturely existence, and man's innate sacrality means that the human condition never really approaches this final threshold, whereas for Agamben, mere life *does* approximate something like the apoliticized life of the creature (as we shall see in chapter 3). In each of these cases, the distinction between "mere life" and political life hinges on its proximity to death, and to the sovereign decision that might pronounce death, whether legitimately or illegitimately. Yet a new problem with the definition of "mere life" arises with the entrance of this phrase of Montaigne's, *la mort simple*, which Florio renders as "simple death" but which we might also think of as "mere death." In this chapter, then, I want to consider this new constellation of terms. What relation does "mere life" bear to "simple" or "mere death"? Or, to put it another way, how does the progression beyond "simple death" illuminate what might constitute "mere life"?

The extravagant violence and violations that characterize *The Revenger's Tragedy* provide an occasion for considering these questions. The problem of revenge tragedy might be said to be the problem of the decision, in the Schmittian sense. Carl Schmitt's 1922 *Political Theology: Four Chapters on the Concept of Sovereignty* opens with the magisterial declaration, "Sovereign is he who decides on the exception" (*Soverän ist, wer über den Ausnahmezustand entscheidet*) (5/8). Usurping the sovereign or divine right to punish or to pardon, the Jacobean revenger takes upon himself the burden of "deciding the exception." In "Of Revenge," Francis Bacon writes,

> Revenge is a kind of wild justice; which the more man's nature runs to, the more ought law to weed it out. For as for the first wrong, it doth but offend the law; but the revenge of that law putteth the law out of office. Certainly, in taking revenge, a man is but even with his enemy; but in passing it over, he is superior; for it is a prince's part to pardon.[24]

Bacon's characterization of revenge as "put[ting] the law out of office" might also be thought of as the usurpation of the sovereign decision, the right to choose between the sentences of life and death.[25] In the explosive, ultimately counterproductive actions of revenge tragedy, the ultimate spectacle of what Montaigne called "a succession of fresh cruelties, each intended to smother each other," we might read a corrective for Schmitt's decisionist politics.

In Montaigne's analysis, what Kerrigan has called the "economy of vengeance" shows its infinitely expanding nature. Similarly, Bacon, in the brief lists that constitute his *Antitheses of Things* (1623), begins the columns on Revenge as follows:

For	Against
Revenge is a kind of wild justice.	He that did the first wrong made a beginning of mischief; he that returned it made no end.[26]

Revenge thus emerges as a kind of feedback loop of infinite regress—yet it is infinite regress with a supplemental difference. Its movement is profoundly ironic, because it is inimical to decision, even as the revenger seizes the power of deciding—for of course what the revenger "decides" is to punish violence with violence. Revenge strives for symmetry, for *isonomia*, but though the avenger desires to re-create the original crime and requite suffering with suffering, vengeance typically reaches outside its initial object. This might mean that the avenger's violence engulfs more than the intended victim, or it might also be seen in the revenger's excessive acts of cruelty, in the desire not just to kill but to utterly obliterate, to prolong the agony of dying or mutilate the corpse (as with the Duke's spectacularly extended death). To the revenger this sort of overkill functions as a period, the decision inscribed and reinscribed on the criminal's body, as in Kafka's penal colony, brutally reducing the human subject of law (the "person," in juridical terms) to a dehumanized object. Yet, as we shall see, in his inability to recognize "simple death" as a threshold, the revenger exemplifies the monstrous potentiality of decisionist sovereignty.

Schmitt's conception of sovereignty rests on the notion that the sovereign decree that allows for the emergency suspension of the law cuts through the liberal democratic "delays" of discussion and negotiation. We take our primary meaning of "decision" from the second sense of the Latin *decido*, *decidere*, *de* + *caedo*, literally, "to cut down, cut off; to cut short, to settle, to arrange." But the primary sense of *decido*, *de* + *cado*, is lost in contemporary usage: *decido* is also "to fall down; to fall dead, die."[27] For Schmitt's purposes, the sovereign is he who *always* decides in the second sense, that of "cutting off" or through parliamentary negotiations and judicial processes. He is both above and behind this sense of decision: "above" inasmuch as he is not accountable to the law, and "behind" inasmuch as his is the decree that phenomenalizes (and nominalizes) law. But in the first sense, "to die," the sovereign *never* decides or is subjected to the decision—and in this way he *becomes* the absolute exception, the exception par excellence. Yet an unacknowledged problem at the core of Schmitt's decisionist thesis emerges when we turn to revenge drama, in which the escalation of cruelties the revenger's decision sets in motion creates further delays rather than slicing through them. Schmitt himself, in a short monograph on Shakespeare's *Hamlet* that he published in 1956 as a belated response to Benjamin's *Trauerspiel* book, aligns the famously *in*decisive prince with James I—though not because of his indecision. In his reading of the play, Schmitt argues that James's anxieties about his mother's reputation constitutes a historic "intrusion" within the aesthetically delimited confines of the play within a play. In a section that appropriates the language of the Freudian family romance (despite his preliminary distancing of his own reading from the "excess of psychological interpretation," which he describes as "an inescapable labyrinth"),[28] Schmitt claims that the "tabooed" figure of the dead Mary, Queen of Scots, haunts the play, prohibiting any true consideration of Gertrude's complicity in the murder of Old Hamlet. This taboo against portraying the potential "guilt of the mother," Schmitt reasons, symbolically extends the rift between Catholics and Protestants, since the former typically defended Mary against any accusation, while the latter assumed her guilt. In its double removal from reality, Schmitt argues, the play within a play becomes the only space in which the queen's potential guilt can be staged. So, Schmitt argues, Shakespeare handily addresses a cause célèbre that would have attracted his audience yet avoids offending his company's patron, the new king. The buried erotics of Schmitt's reading of *Hamlet* will become the ghost in the machine (or under the floorboards, the "old mole" itself) in my own reading, for *The Revenger's Tragedy* makes explicit what *Hamlet* seeks to repress, gleefully violating what Schmitt called "the taboo of the queen." Thus it is in its ironic citations of *Hamlet* as much as in its parodic excesses that Middleton's play can help us to arrive at a critique of the psychotheological substrata of Schmitt's argument.[29]

Montaigne's clearest examples of the cruelty that exceeds mere death include the torture of prisoners and the prolonged terror of hunted animals—though, as he says, he himself "enjoys the hunt enormously" (481). Both his examples, in this sense, are perhaps already concerned with the designation "mere life," since both the condemned prisoner (or even the prisoner of war, which he addresses more fully in "On Cowardice") and the beast would already be, in the eyes of many, less than, or other than, human. In his essay "On Cruelty," Montaigne brings the idea of what exceeds mere death closer to home, as it were, by likening the effects of torture and orgasm. Thus, he argues, both the infliction of pain and injury and the experience of sexual pleasure obliterate the human capacity for rational action. Or, at least, he tells us, this is what others might have us think, namely, "those who have to write against sensual pleasure." These unidentified and ill-advised (and, he implies, sexually frustrated) writers, Montaigne claims,

> like to use the following argument to show that it is entirely vicious and irrational: when its force is at its climax it overmasters us to such an extent that reason has no way to come into it; they go on to cite what we know of that from our experience of lying with women—
>
> > *cum jam proesagit gaudia corpus,*
> > *Atque in eo est venus ut muliebria conserat arva*
> > [as when the body already anticipates its joy, and Venus is about to scatter seeds broadcast in the woman's furrows]
>
> —in which it seems that the delight so transports us outside ourselves that our reason could not possibly perform its duty then, being entirely transfixed and enraptured by the pleasure (481).[30]

Montaigne's argument here enacts a sort of striptease, moving in and out among a series of screens: the unidentified "those" slide behind the quotation from Lucretius, which itself depicts the moment of orgasm indirectly, almost impersonally, the "body" of the (presumably male) lover disappearing behind "Venus," who scatters his seed. The threat of failure to "perform its duty" is deflected from "the body" to "reason," and in all of these ways the ultimate corporeal event becomes, in the retelling, utterly decorporealized, prosthetic.

Montaigne rhetorically recuperates the poor spent lover even before he takes the stand, as it were, to defend him. In the next paragraph, ever at pains to reconcile sensual experience with rational capacity,[31] Montaigne refutes the decoupling of eros and logos on the basis of his own erotic practice:

> If we have the will, we can sometimes manage, at that very instant, to bring our soul back to other thoughts. But we must vigilantly ensure that our soul is taut and erect. I know it is possible to master the force of that pleasure; and I am quite knowledgeable about the subject; I have never found Venus to be as imperious a goddess as several people, chaster than I am, attest her to be. (481)[32]

Montaigne's language here asserts his own rational superiority over the vicissitudes of "the body's joy," reinscribing eros within the realm of reason by attributing a phallic tumescence to the soul itself—spiritual readiness, here, assumes a corporeal immediacy. Like his unnamed interlocutors in the previous paragraph, who approach their points only obliquely, Montaigne approaches reason in a curiously circuitous way, via the "soul"—that which (like desire) must also be considered uncircumscribed by the limits of reason alone.

I mention Montaigne's intriguing circumlocutions here by way of introduction to his essay—for the passage in question is, in its entirety, something of a byway to Montaigne's main argument, which concerns cruelty. The two paragraphs occur immediately after Montaigne has stated his theme: "Among the vices, both by nature and judgment, I have a cruel hatred of cruelty, as the ultimate vice of them all," he writes (480–81).[33] Here again Montaigne ironically doubles back upon his own claim; his "hatred" of cruelty must necessarily partake in cruelty, if only rhetorically. Just as, in the following paragraphs, he seeks to rebind reason with pleasure, even if only by way of an ironic passage *around* reason, so here "cruelty" necessarily appears in his disavowal of cruelty. The extremity of his "cruel hatred" then gives way to the analogy to "sensual pleasure," with the results that we have seen. The consideration of cruelties that exceed the limits of "mere death" and the connection between mere death and revenge tragedy emerge more fully in another of Montaigne's essays, "On Cowardice, the Mother of Cruelty." Here Montaigne defines vengeance as follows: "The first acts of cruelty are done for their own sake;

from them there is born fear of a just revenge; that produces a succession of fresh cruelties, each intended to smother each other" (793).[34] In this essay Montaigne links both vengeance and cruelty with tyranny, arguing that the illegitimate ruler's fear of overthrow breeds an unjust "lust for blood" (792). The logical outcome of this terror, Montaigne argues, is that "their cowardly minds can furnish them with no other means of security save exterminating all those who simply have the means of hurting them, women included" (792).[35]

Singling out violence against women (as he had earlier separated the cruelty of the hunt from the torture of prisoners) as a special case, Montaigne nevertheless does not say much more on the topic here—except for including almost verbatim an account from Book XV of Livy's *History*, the story of the "courageous mother" Theoxena, who vows to kill her own children rather than handing them over to Philip of Macedon, one of Montaigne's types of the bloodthirsty tyrant. Understandably alarmed by Theoxena's plan, her husband, Poris, instead convinces Theoxena that all of them will be better off sheltering with "some of his faithful vassals" in Athens, and they escape by sea. Pursued by Philip's soldiers, Theoxena decides that death is the only escape:

> When they were overhauled, while Poris was busy urging the sailors to flee faster Theoxena, raving mad with love for the children and for vengeance, returned to her original plan; she got weapons and poison ready; she then showed them to them saying, "Come now, my children; from henceforth death is your sole means of defence and remaining free; and it will provide the gods with something to work their hallowed justice upon. These drawn swords and these goblets open the way to it for you. Be brave. And you, my oldest son, grasp this blade and die the bolder death." The children, with this staunch counsellor on one side and the enemy at their throats on the other, frantically ran to whatever goblet was nearest to hand and were thrown still half-dead into the sea. Theoxena, proud of so gloriously having saved all her children, threw her arms passionately around her husband and said, "Let us follow these boys, my love, and let us enjoy the same grave with them." Clasped thus in each other's embrace, they plunged headlong into the sea. (793–94)

Theoxena's story thus illustrates not violence executed against women by a tyrant, per se, but the extremity of a situation in which the actions of the tyrant have so perverted the course of justice that what might be considered one of the most fundamental of human bonds must itself be twisted out of shape to thwart the sovereign's malfeasance. Thus Theoxena, "raving mad with love for the children and for vengeance," may escape the tyrant's decision only by pronouncing the death sentence herself. The children, in turn, "frantically run" to embrace what turns out to be only a partial death. Both poison and the sword prove insufficient, for "[the children] were thrown still half-dead into the sea." Half-dead, not half-alive: a linguistic quibble, perhaps, but a telling one. Delayed in its ultimate execution, the children's suspended sentence propels them across a terrible threshold, where "mere death" ceases to even be an option.

However unintentionally, the loving mother seemingly inflicts the cruelest of punishments and prolongs the suffering of dying; yet Theoxena's act does not, for Montaigne, exemplify the cruelty that exceeds "simple death." Theoxena is no Medea. On the contrary, this haunted and haunting exemplum serves as an aesthetic counterpoint to the already disjointed account of the horrors endured by criminals and prisoners of war. Montaigne commences his retelling of Theoxena's tale with the remark, "Beautiful topics can always hold their own, no matter where you strew them. I who am more concerned with the weight and usefulness of my writings than with their order and logical succession must not be afraid to place here, a little off the track, an account of great beauty" (793). Yet the "beautiful account" of the "beautiful topic" centers on a love that takes the form of "vengeance," a "raving love" that finds its ultimate consummation when Theoxena and Poris plunge beneath the waves to their watery marriage bed, forever locked in their now sterile embrace.

Theoxena's story ends here in two senses—it is both the end of this exemplum incongruously "strewn" "a little off the track" of cowardice and cruelty and a more profound death, one that resonates politically as well as narratively. Theoxena herself, like Gertrude, is something of an "imperial jointress of a warlike state," a princess of Thessaly though never named as such. Her first husband having been killed by Philip and "feeling the urge to mother her nephews," she then weds her sister Archo's widower, "the leading man among the Aenians," Poris. Figuring both motherhood and wifehood as simultaneously protective and devouring, in her spectacular denouement Theoxena metonymically reenacts the entire tale, providing an exemplum nested within the larger exemplum much as the tale itself rests within the *essai*. This aesthetic jewel that Montaigne "strews" along the path of his *essai* both interrupts its rambling "progress" (as much as an essay might be said to "progress") and impels the reader in its own narrative wake. Doubly framed by Montaigne's opening apostrophe on "beautiful topics" and by the putative (and decidedly non-beautiful) topic of "cowardice and cruelty," Theoxena's tale is, itself, an apostrophe of sorts: a *turning away* from the extravagant horrors of cruelty that nevertheless enfolds spectacular violence in its narrative embrace. For like Montaigne's "cruel hatred of cruelty," his rendering of Theoxena and her doomed kindred curls back upon itself, ironically foregrounding what it notionally seeks to suppress.

Something like Montaigne's doubled motion and doubled impulse emerges in Middleton's play, which continually holds up the intricately contrived propulsions of its own plot with semi–self-enclosed vignettes that foreground precisely what the play's already parodic sententiousness would seem to decry.[36] *The Revenger's Tragedy* presents multiple revengers and motives for revenge, all of which center on the desire for political or erotic control and which cause the play itself to assume such farcical crossings and recrossings. The endless complications and reduplications of the revenge plot find their analogue in metaphors of coinage and exchange, the predominant "counters" in the self-consumptive appetites for power and sex.[37] The Duke is condemned all around: by Vindice, for Gloriana's death and his father's "dejection" (the anti–Old Hamlet); by Spurio, for effectively consigning him to live under the unnatural "sign" of the bastard; by the Duchess, for not exercising his already corrupt authority to acquit Junior Brother, and of course for being bad in bed; even Lussorioso, who does not enter into these conspiracies, would not mind being "made himself" a little early. Lady Antonio's rape and suicide, emblematically framed by Lord Antonio in I.iv, provide a second plot device, and Lussorioso's play for Castiza presents Vindice with yet another reason to purge Italy of the "nest of dukes."

Each of the main revenge plots thus takes its impetus from the desire to avenge a sexually compromised woman who becomes safely "close" or chaste only in death, yet the headlong rush to "quit" suffering with suffering keeps getting entangled by its own metatheatrical momentum.[38] As a revenger, Vindice is also like Hamlet an "instrumentalizer" or artificer, and specifically a playwright, as the Duke's eventual death and, finally, the revengers' masque attest.[39] At crucial moments the action freezes while the characters turn aside to contemplate macabre spectacles that eroticize corruption even as Vindice, the decisionist/artificer par excellence, decries it. Perhaps these paradoxical disjunctions within the farcically overwrought crisscrossings of the plots ought not surprise us, given the play's opening, Vindice's soliloquizing to the "shell of death" of his former love, Gloriana. Set against this citational figure soliloquizing to the skull, the court characters pass mutely across the stage, a dumb show that is also a royal progress (for the sake of convenience, since I will be referring to this passage again, I include the entire opening speech):

Enter VINDICE [*then*] *the* DUKE, DUCHESS, LUSSORIOSO *her son*, SPURIO *the bastard, with a train, pass over the stage with torchlight*

VINDICE
Duke: royal lecher: go, grey haired Adultery,
And thou his son, as impious steeped as he:
And thou his bastard true-begot in evil:
And thou his duchess that will do with the devil:
Four ex'lent characters!—Oh that marrowless age
Would stuff the hollow bones with damned desires,
And 'stead of heat kindle infernal fires
Within the spendthrift veins of a dry duke,
A parched and juiceless luxor. Oh God! one
That has scarce blood enough to live upon,
And he to riot it like a son and heir?
Oh the thought of that
Turns my abusèd heart strings into fret.
Thou sallow picture of my poisoned love,
My study's ornament, thou shell of Death,
Once the bright face of my betrothed lady,
When life and beauty naturally filled out
These ragged imperfections;
When two heaven-pointed diamonds were set
In those unsightly rings—then 'twas a face
So far beyond the artificial shine
Of any woman's bought complexion
That the uprightest man—if such there be,
That sin but seven times a day—broke custom
And made up eight with looking after her.
Oh she was able to ha'made a usurer's son
Melt all his patrimony in a kiss,
And what his father fifty years told
To have consumed, and yet his suit been cold:
But oh accursed palace!
Thee when thou wert apparelled in thy flesh,
The old duke poisoned,
Because thy purer part would not consent
Unto his palsey-lust; for old men lustful
Do show like young men angry-eager, violent,
Out-bid like their limited performances—

Oh 'ware an old man hot and vicious:
'Age as in gold, in lust is covetous'.
Vengeance, though Murder's quit-rent, and whereby
Thou show'st thyself tenant to Tragedy,
Oh keep thy day, hour, minute, I beseech,
For those thou hath determined. Hum, who e'er knew
Murder unpaid? Faith, give Revenge her due,
She's kept touch hitherto—be merry, merry,
Advance thee, oh thou terror to fat folks,
To have their costly three-piled flesh worn off
As bare as this—for banquets, ease and laughter
Can make great men, as greatness goes by clay,
But wise men, little, are more great than they. (I.i.1–49)

Vindice careens from addressee to addressee, image to image, apostrophe to apostrophe—his syntax mimics the broken and perversely reforged chain of meaning that becomes the revenge plot itself. The initial scene layers theatrical and political citations, allusions to Shakespeare's Hamlet and the dead Elizabeth I ("Gloriana" herself) flickering in and out of Vindice's remarks.[40] Yet though the metatheatrical echo of Hamlet discoursing on the ways of worms and men to Yorick's bony pate must certainly be present here, Gloriana's skull serves a different purpose than Yorick's. Both memento mori and murder weapon,[41] Gloriana's skull becomes a strangely doubled signifier, a stage property that is also an artifact of what Walter Benjamin might term *Naturgeshichte*. As a relic or ruin that recalls its created form in the lineaments of its own dissolution, Gloriana's skull occupies the liminal realm of what Eric Santner, in his reading of Benjamin, terms "the space between real and symbolic death, [the] space of the 'undead.'"[42] Infinitely generative even though it is a hollowed-out "shell of Death," the graveyard of Vindice's hopes yet becomes the teeming birthplace of his retribution: rather than projecting himself in his progeny, he must project himself in the negative "work" of revenge, that which Lussorioso later terms "deep policy." Gloriana's skull thus recalls the womb/tomb pairing so common in Shakespeare's sonnets, or in some of Donne's poems. Compare, too, Shakespeare's Iago, who continuously speaks of thought-work, especially revenge, as labor and expenditure. In his first soliloquy, he characterizes revenge as parturition, the "monstrous birth" he has "engendered" alone.[43]

The linkage between vengeance and perverse birth appears in part in the way Gloriana and the Duke are doubled in Vindice's rhetoric, which itself constitutes a curiously admixed epideictic—the speech of both praise and blame ends up conflating praise *with* blame.[44] This conflation is perhaps most evident in lines 23 to 29, where Vindice extols Gloriana's virtue by noting how her beauty would tempt even the "uprightest man" to sin, or "a usurer's son / [to] melt all his patrimony in a kiss." In Vindice's conceit, Gloriana's chastity is forged and reforged through her capacity to lead men astray. Though *hers* is the agency here, it is a curiously passive agency, a contradiction expressed in the very grammar: "she was able to ha'made" rather than "she made." Vindice's rhetoric ultimately condemns Gloriana's complicity in the world's corrupt consumption even as he seemingly lauds her purity. This doubled rhetorical action itself mimics one of the central paradoxes of the main revenge plot, which unfolds via the negatively supplemental logic of *usure* (both "usury" and "use," in both sexual and economic senses).

Vindice's image of patrimony dissolving in a kiss, of patriarchal inheritance "used up" both before and in the act of "use," finds its analogy in the wasteful expenditure or barren "uses" of revenge.[45] Scene 2 removes to Junior Brother's trial, whose farcical judicial shenanigans open up yet another ironically metatheatrical space within the confines of the play. Many critics have noted the parallels between the theatre and the courtroom, in this play as in Webster's later revenge dramas. Spurio, the Duke's bastard son, becomes both a stand-in for the audience and a foil for Vindice himself, whose mocking commentary on the trial undoes the Duke's seeming piety much as Hamlet's asides do during the performance of "The Mousetrap." When the Duke resists the Duchess's plea to spare her son by postponing his decision "till next sitting," Spurio remarks, "Delayed, deferred, nay then if Judgement have / Cold blood, flattery and bribes will kill it" (I.ii.83, 89–90). The bastard's recognition of the problem of justice "delayed, deferred," then enacted "out of office" (Bacon's phrase), aligns him with the malcontent Vindice. Yet where Vindice insists that blood must requite blood, Spurio's vengeance (sleeping with his stepmother) takes the form of an ironic commentary on the incestuously "close" networks of the court. Vindice later likens the court to a "nest of dukes," and his image of the snaky internecine politics that pullulate within the nest suggests the popular emblematic image of the serpent eating its own tail—the sign of infinite corruption and regression, of which the Duchess and Spurio's quasi-incestuous coupling becomes only one signifier.

"Glorious acts": Metatheatre and Mourning

Lord Antonio, whose "silver hair" will eventually usher in the new "silver age" at the play's close, makes his first stage appearance in the dual character of mourning husband and theatrical impresario:

Enter the discontented lord ANTONIO (*whose wife the duchess's youngest son ravished*)*; he discovering* [*her dead body*] *to certain lords and* [*to* PIERO *and*] HIPPOLITO.

ANTONIO: Draw nearer lords and be sad witnesses
Of a fair comely building newly fallen,
Being falsely undermined. Violent rape
Has played a glorious act: behold my lords
A sight that strikes man out of me. (I.iv.1–5 and stage direction)

As in Vindice's opening speech, punctuated by his grisly apostrophes to Gloriana's skull (and Gloriana is perhaps obliquely recalled here via the "glorious act"), Lord Antonio's emblematic reframing of his wife's rape and suicide employs a woman's dead body to set in motion the machinery of a revenge plot. As a "discontented lord," Antonio recalls Vindice and Hippolito's deceased father, he of whom Vindice remarks, "Surely I think he died / Of discontent, the nobleman's consumption" (I.i.125–26). In a play much concerned with noblemen's (and women's) corrupt consumption, in which any appetite seems disease, Lord Antonio's "discontent" already marks him as a character who may be less laudable than he initially appears—as does his theatrical flair, which aligns him with Vindice. His "discovery" (drawing aside the curtain of the stage's discovery space) of Lady Antonio's body to the circle of lords acts as a play within a play, a metadramatic turn that his lines underscore: "Violent rape / Has played a glorious act: behold my lords" (I.iv.3–4). Antonio's line echoes Hippolito and Gratiana's gossipy exchange in the opening act:

GRATIANA: What news from Court son Carlo?[46]
HIPPOLITO: Faith mother,
'Tis whispered that the duchess' youngest son
Has played a rape on Lord Antonio's wife.
GRATIANA: On that religious lady! (I.i.106–10)

Whereas Hippolito's remark fixes the rape on its perpetrator, "the duchess' youngest son," Antonio's lines entirely remove the rapist from the scene: "violent rape" plays itself out, creating an auto-instrumental *theatron* that further instrumentalizes its spectators.

Antonio's retelling of the crime continues the motif of rape as a spectacularly violent "act" in the theatrical sense. Rape goes unregarded during the noise and spectacle of a courtly masque:

Last revelling night,
When torchlight made an artificial noon
About the Court, some courtiers in the masque
Putting on better faces than their own,
Being full of fraud and flattery, amongst whom
The duchess' youngest son—that moth to honour—
Filled up a room; and with long lust to eat
Into my wearing, amongst all the ladies
Singled out that dear form, who ever lived
As cold in lust as she is now in death—
Which that step-duchess' monster knew too well—
And therefore in the height of all the revels,
When music was heard loudest, courtiers busiest,
And ladies great with laughter—Oh vicious minute!
Unfit, but for relation, to be spoke of—
Then with a face more impudent than his vizard
He harried her amidst a throng of pandars
That live upon damnation of both kinds
And fed the ravenous vulture of his lust.
Oh death to think on't! She, her honour forced,
Deemed it a nobler dowry for her name
To die with poison than to live with shame. (I.iv.27–48)

License already characterizes the "reveling night," with its carnivalesque inversions of normative social and political order, and here the midnight escapades take place in an unnatural, torchlit noon that nevertheless conceals more than it reveals.[47] In Antonio's retelling, the topsy-turvy world of the festival seemingly enables the crime it covers, neatly including rape in the catalogue of the putatively unlawful "acts" it temporarily condones.

It is worth remarking, however, that it is Antonio's unnamed Lady who initially sets up a metadramatic—or perhaps a metageneric—reading. Arranging her deathbed as an emblem of wronged chastity, she stages her suicide and provides a helpful gloss in case her act should be misread:

ANTONIO: I marked not this before:
A prayer book the pillow to her cheek;
This was her rich confection, and another
Placed in her right hand with a leaf tucked up,
Pointing to these words:
Melius virtute mori, quam per dedecus vivere.
[*Better to die virtuous, than to live dishonored.*] (I.iv.13–18)

It is of course a period commonplace that the only truly chaste woman is a dead woman;[48] here "that most religious lady," like Gloriana, like Lucrece and Lavinia, forever seals her chastity in death. Lord Antonio compares his wife to "a fair comely building newly fallen, / Being falsely undermined" (I.iv.2–3). After swearing himself to revenge her death (in a passage that alludes directly to *Hamlet*), Hippolito likens the lady to a ruined monument: "'Twere pity / The ruins of so fair a monument / Should not be dipped in the defacer's blood" (I.iv.67–69). Piero, his co-conspirator, continues the analogy, planning a "wealthy funeral," for, he says "her name / Merits a tomb of pearl" (I.iv.70–71). All this talk of razed and ruined edifices strikes a curious note. Like Shakespeare's "wronged Hero," vindicated in epitaph, Lady Antonio's raptured virtue would be lithographically reinscribed by means of the "tomb of pearl,"[49] which in its unblemished luster visually suggests the moon and thus the goddess of chastity herself. Yet the play has already questioned the efficacy of an unblemished tomb if the "name" it encrypts is besmirched. Consider the exchange between the corrupt Duke and the toadying Judge that opens the second act:

> DUKE: Duchess it is your youngest son, we're sorry,
> His violent act has e'en drawn blood of honour
> And stained our honours,
> Thrown ink upon the forehead of our state
> Which envious spirits will dip their pens into
> After our death, and blot us in our tombs.
> For that which would now seem treason in our lives
> Is laughter when we're dead. Who dares now whisper
> That dares not then speak out, and e'en proclaim
> With loud words and broad pens our closest shame.
> I JUDGE: Your Grace hath spoke like to your silver years
> Full of confirmed gravity; for what is it to have
> A flattering false insculption on a tomb
> And in men's hearts reproach? The bowelled corpse
> May be cered in, but, with free tongue I speak—
> 'The faults of great men through their cere-cloths break'.
> (I.ii.1–16)

Middleton's focus on tombs and the monumental reinscription of honor is perhaps a topical concern. As king of England, James ordered Mary Stuart's remains disinterred from Peterborough and moved to Westminster Abbey, where he had costly sepulchers built for both his mother and his predecessor, Elizabeth I.[50] By placing Elizabeth's monument next to that of her half sister, Mary Tudor (emphasizing their sororal connection rather than either's claim to the throne through Henry VIII in the epitaph), and Mary Stuart's near the tomb of Henry VII, James lithically rescripted his own royal lineage. Both the locations of the monuments themselves and their inscriptions underlined his own legitimacy and right to the Tudor throne, even as he relegated Elizabeth to the role of bastard, childless spinster. Elizabeth's tomb was finished in 1606, a year before the play was recorded in the Stationers' Register. Though Mary's body was not moved until 1613, twenty-four years after her death, James seems to have begun work on the new tomb at the same time work commenced on Elizabeth's—that is, immediately after assuming the throne. The discovery space thus redoubles its visual significance, recollecting the tombs of the dead queens at the same time as it metonymically represents the theatre as a whole.

James's sepulchral rehabilitation of his mother monumentally "insculpts" what he had already written to his son, Henry, in the prefatory matter of *Basilikon Doron*.[51] Defending himself against the charge that he "should seeme to nourish in [his] minde, a vindictive resolution against England, or at the least, some principals there, for the Queene [his] mothers quarrell," James directs his son

> not to heare nor suffer any unreverent speeches or bookes against any of his parents or progenitors: wherein I do alledge my owne experience anent the Queene my mother; affirming, that I never found any that were of perfit aage the time of her reigne here, so stedfastly trew to me in all my troubles, as these that constantly kept their allegiance to her in her time. (5)

Like Mary Stuart, Antonio's lady can be recuperated only synecdochically, via her "name," a name that, ironically, neither audience nor avengers ever learn. In a play where allegorical names provide such telling indexes to character, the honorable name that remains under erasure thus signifies a complete evacuation of symbolic meaning even as first the lady herself, then her husband, then her avengers, struggle to assert it. The name that is important here is Antonio's, of which the tomb, a tangible symbol of his wealth and position, would provide a constant reminder. Ceremonial mourning, like the ceremonies of judgment, end up "deferred, delayed," staged as hollow spectacle rather than acted out as civic ritual. Yet unlike Hero, whose tale is told for her in the inscription on her tomb and ventriloquized by her accuser, Claudio, or Lavinia, mutely struggling to signify her rapists, Antonio's unnamed lady provides her own emblematic motto with her prayer books: "A prayer book the pillow to her cheek; / This was her rich confection," Antonio remarks (I.iv.14–15). "Confection" carries here its etymological sense, *con* + *ficere*, something made or compounded of disparate elements, but also the common sense of something *sweet*—it thus points back to the unwholesome appetites, themselves so curiously mixed, that characterize the corrupt court. It is linked to the "quaintness" of revenge. As Vindice has already done with Gloriana, then, Antonio rhetorically inculpates his dead lady at the very moment he exculpates her, aligning her stagy "confection" with the masqueing and machinations of the decayed court. Yet perhaps even a third sense of "confection" is at play here, that of the mass and its recollection of sacrifice[52]—a sense deepened by both the discovery space's visual parallels to the catafalque of Elizabeth I and the parodic twist on *Hamlet* I.v that the conspirators are about to enact as they vow themselves to vengeance (I.iv.56–78).

Grafted onto the usually mute figures of women whose chaste silence can be ensured only by death, political and religious tensions within the play also might be traced in the language of conversion that continually attends the question of virginity. As we have already seen with Antonio's wife, "that most religious lady," Middleton's play insistently links marital fidelity with religious fidelity yet calls into question these same marital and religious structures.[53] Vindice's fear radiates beyond the bodies of political and sexual subjects, taking in its grip the potentially treasonous *religious* subject as well. Ultimately, the play evacuates the religious field of significance.[54] This is perhaps most evident in the second half of the play, with its self-consciously theatrical momentum. Vindice's "Has heaven an ear? Is all the lightning wasted?" is answered by a delayed stage effect:

> VINDICE: Oh thou almighty patience 'tis my wonder,
> That such a fellow, impudent and wicked,
> Should not be cloven as he stood
> Or with a secret wind burst open!
> Is there no thunder left, or is't kept up
> In stock for heavier vengeance?
> [*Thunder*] There it goes! (IV.ii.193–98)

This layering of political and theological traces that metatheatrically undo themselves in the very moment of their articulation gestures toward the play's skeptical impulse.[55] Vindice's final lines, "Our mother turn'd, our sister true, / We die after a nest of dukes—Adieu!" comically reiterate the anxieties about "turning" that have proliferated throughout the play. "Turning," like the "deep policy" of revenge (and like rhetorical seduction), is figured in terms of labor, as we see in Vindice's remarks after his failed attempts to seduce his sister for Lussorioso:

> VINDICE: The word I brought
> Might well have made indifferent honest naught;
> A right good woman in these days is changed
> Into white money with less labour far—
> Many a maid has turned to Mahomet
> With easier working. I durst undertake,
> Upon the pawn and forfeit of my life
> With half these words to flat a Puritan's wife,
> But she is close and good; yet 'tis a doubt
> By this time—oh the mother, the mother! (II.ii.24–33)

Peter Stallybrass argues that though the social order dissolves with the "slobbering" kisses of the corrupt Duke, it is at least partly reforged in the "chaste" kisses of the family, "wherein lies no lust" (IV.iv.57–59, 146–48).[56] This final "turn" occurs in IV.iv, where the Gratiana/Castiza subplot disappears after Gratiana's "conversion" to "natural" motherhood. Recalling the closet scene in *Hamlet* (III.iv), the scene opens with Hippolito and Vindice castigating their mother, Vindice enquiring, "Who shall be saved when mothers have no grace?" (IV.iv.27). Gratiana doesn't earn her name until a final "testing" of her virtue, which devolves on Castiza herself, who momentarily mimics Vindice's duplicity in re-trying Gratiana. Gratiana's "turning" becomes, perhaps, the play's sole redemptive moment: "Oh mother let me twine about your neck / And kiss you till my soul melt on your lips: / I did this but to try you" (IV.iv.146–48).

Other than dying into chastity, women in the play can achieve the ideal "closeness" only by miming men—yet Vindice himself is far from displaying the "closeness" he touts. As in *Hamlet*, in Middleton's play Vindice's anxieties about the corrupt court take explicit shape in his anxieties about the "closeness" of its borders and policies, and these fears in turn are allegorically projected to include the sexual permeability of bodies, particularly women's bodies. "Closeness," for Vindice, indicates not just chastity but also secrecy: "Why are men made close / But to keep thoughts in best? I grant you this, / Tell but some woman a secret over night, / Your doctor may find it in the urinal i'th'morning" (I.iii.80–84).[57] The capacity for secret manipulation, what Lussorioso calls "deep policy," is also rhetorical skill. Like Hamlet, Vindice is the instrumentalizer par excellence; like Hamlet, his skill at both policy and "playing" is most clearly demonstrated by his ability to manipulate language, which we see particularly in the scenes where he interacts with Lussorioso (such as I.iii, IV.ii), in which he plays the decidedly "unclose" role of the sodomite. But Vindice ultimately fails to embody the masculine "closeness" he vaunts, and vaunting is his downfall, once he has ushered in a "silver," if not a golden age.

Carl Schmitt's Decisionism

In *Die Diktatur*, published shortly before *Political Theology*, Schmitt distinguishes between commissarial and sovereign dictatorship—while the former's purpose is to reinvigorate or enforce constitutional laws as they exist, the latter's function must always be to instantiate a new juridical regime.[58] In these two types of dictatorship we might trace certain parallels to the different faces of Bacon's "wild justice" as they appear in Middleton's drama. In this play, at least, the machinations of the revenge plot are always *conservative* in their impulse, and Vindice's desire to rid the state of a corrupt ruler and shore up the shaky foundations of the existing law points, to some extent, toward Schmitt's definition of a commissarial dictator. But the revenger's decision to move outside the law in order to enforce law sets in train an endless progression of supplemental violence. Lord Antonio, by the end of the play, has become the figure of the sovereign dictator, executing the law without counsel, debate, or recourse to trial. Though Vindice's "confession" obviates this somewhat, Lord Antonio's summary decree once again steps outside normative law at the very moment when he supposedly reinstates the rule of law.

Recall the opening of *Political Theology*: "Sovereign is he who decides on the exception" (5/8). The subjective ambiguity that lies at the very core of Schmitt's dictum provides a useful parallel for thinking through the tangled etiology of retribution of Middleton's play. Schmitt's work closes with an analysis of the Catholic counter-revolutionary philosopher Joseph de Maistre's formulation of what might be termed the *decisio ex nihil* (5). In order to understand Schmitt's project, we are almost required to read the last chapter first and proceed backward to arrive at that opening assertion, for it is the decision that forms and governs the exception more than the exception can be said to govern the decision. Schmitt defines "the problem of sovereignty" as "the problem of the legal form and of the decision" (chap. 2), but as his selective intellectual history of the decision makes apparent, there is always also a certain distance or remove between the concept of sovereignty and the concept of the decision. "Sovereign is he who (always and never) decides," Schmitt's opening formula might as well run, for the "exception" is of secondary importance to the concept of sovereignty in Schmitt's depiction. We might also say "every sovereign decision is a decision of the exception" if we recall the etymology of "exception": Latin *excipere*, literally, "to take out." The sovereign takes himself out of the decision at the instant of its pronunciation and is thus, in a sense, the exceptional exception, not subject to the exceptional decree even though he defines it.

Among other things, Schmitt draws from de Maistre his definition of sovereignty as infallible. For de Maistre, this incontrovertibility finds its most prominent example in the figure of the Pope, whose symbolic, religious, and political function would provide him with the topic for what is perhaps his most influential book, *Du Pape* (1850). In the opening paragraphs of this work, de Maistre states, "*Infallibility* in the spiritual order of things, and *sovereignty* in the temporal order, are two words perfectly synonymous. The one and the other denote that higher power which rules over all other powers—from which they all derive their authority—which governs, and is not governed—which judges, and is not judge."[59] The Roman Catholic Church, in de Maistre's formulation, renders itself infallible both because of its "universality" and also because of what he claims is its relative "unity," which he contrasts with the "pullulating sects" of Protestantism (particularly Anglicanism) and Eastern Orthodoxy.[60] Taking up Aristotle's definitions of good governance and grafting them onto the body of the Church, de Maistre argues that it provides an ideal political model, combining monarchy with aristocracy. In this analogy, in which it is not difficult to trace a comparison with, say, king and Parliament, the "Sovereign Pontiff" emerges as a sort of *über*-Sovereign. Somewhat like that portrayed in the frontispiece of Hobbes's *Leviathan*,[61] in the figure of the Pontiff spiritual infallibility bleeds into temporal sovereignty, vitiating the distinction between spiritual and political governance on which de Maistre so painfully insists elsewhere:

> To the Sovereign Pontiff alone belongs essentially the right of convoking general councils, which does not exclude the moderate and legitimate influence of sovereigns. He alone is judge of the circumstances which require this extreme remedy. Those who pretended to assign this power to temporal authority [i.e., monarchs], quite overlooked the strange paralogism into which they fell. They suppose an universal and (what is more) an everlasting monarchy; they go back, without reflecting, to those times when all the mitres in

> the world could be called together by one sceptre only, or by two. (I.iii.14; note added).

Just as Bodin's figures the crown as an emblem of the indivisibility of sovereignty (which, depending on its design, might itself echo a mitre as well as a halo), so de Maistre focuses on the mitre as a symbol of the binding and decisionist powers of sovereignty. Yet de Maistre departs from Bodin in locating absolute and indivisible authority *only* in the Pope, for, he argues, "Political sovereignty being essentially neither indivisible nor perpetual [a direct contradiction of Bodin], if we refuse to the Pope the right of convoking general councils, to whom shall we grant it?" (14; note added).

In *Roman Catholicism and Political Form* (1923), his most sustained consideration of the Church's political potential, Schmitt retains de Maistre's eulogizing of the Church as an idealized political form headed by an infallible supersovereign, the Pope. For Schmitt, the Church as a model of a coherent, "concrete" political form stands against the depraved and fragmented civil society exemplified in the industrial and then technocratic rise of post-Enlightenment "economic" thinking.[62] Responding in part to Max Weber's critique of Catholic "irrationality" in *The Protestant Ethic and the "Spirit" of Capitalism* (1905), Schmitt argues that the Roman Catholic mind is profoundly rational in its syncretism and plasticity. It is, he argues, the last remaining example of a "universalism" that is nevertheless "particular" in its personalism—that is, in its representative head, the Pope. In a decidedly psychoanalytic twist that belies his avowed dislike of psychoanalytic method (in *Hamlet oder Hekuba*), Schmitt writes, "The pope is called the Father; the Church is the Mother of Believers and the Bride of Christ. This is a marvelous union of the patriarchal and the matriarchal, able to direct both streams of the most elemental complexes and instincts—respect for the father and love for the mother—toward Rome" (*RCPF* 8). Thus the devout Catholic assumes the lineaments of the Oedipal subject in the family romance, but with one important difference: this faithful subject refuses to take the Oedipal path, refuses to disavow the mother. Schmitt concludes this passage by enquiring, "Has there ever been a revolt against the mother?"—YES! Freud, would answer—but Schmitt is not Freud.[63] And ultimately the family romance does take on a somewhat Freudian patriarchal form, for the matriarchal figure of the Church can assume its pattern only from the paternal figure of the Pope: "Ultimately, most important is that this limitless ambiguity combines with the most precise dogmatism and a will to decision as it culminates in the doctrine of papal infallibility" (*RCPF* 8),

Schmitt concludes—and with the phrase "papal infallibility" Schmitt surely invokes de Maistre, though he does not cite him here.

Schmitt's use of the term "representation" demonstrates the way the doctrine of papal infallibility ends up conflating temporal and religious sovereignty, as we see here:

> From the standpoint of the political idea of Catholicism, the essence of the Roman-Catholic *complexio oppositorum* lies in a specific, formal superiority over the matter of human life such as no other imperium has ever known. It has succeeded in constituting a sustaining configuration of historical and social reality that, despite its formal character, retains its concrete existence at once vital and yet rational to the nth degree. This formal character of Roman Catholicism is based on a strict realization of the principle of representation, the particularity of which is most evident in its antithesis to the economic-technical thinking dominant today. (*RCPF* 8)

"Representation," for Schmitt, carries both aesthetic and political valences: it designates both mimetic form and juridical personhood.[64] In *The Concept of the Political* (1932), Schmitt opposes politics to ethics, aesthetics, and economics; here, though still juxtaposed with "economic-technical thinking," the nostalgically inflected political form of the Church that emerges is also an aesthetic construct.[65] "Concrete existence," representation's correlative in the quoted passage, is exemplified, again, in the person of the Pope, whom Schmitt claims remains as the last avatar of medieval allegorical modalities: "The Catholic Church is the sole surviving contemporary example of the medieval capacity to create representative figures—the pope, the emperor, the monk, the knight, the merchant" (19). Given his earlier and later eagerness to point out the Church's feminine or maternal aspects, it is curious that this tarot deck of representative figures remains entirely male.

Crudely put, one might say that for Schmitt as for de Maistre, Christ is to the Pope as the Pope is to the Church as the Church is to the secular State . . . a diminishing chain of signifiers. Schmitt writes,

> The political power of Catholicism rests neither on economic nor military means but rather on the absolute realization of authority. The Church also is a "juridical person," though not in the same sense as a joint-stock company. The typical product of the age of production is a method of accounting, whereas the Church is a concrete personality. All knowledgeable witnesses have conceded that

> the Church is the consummate agency of the juridical spirit and the true heir of Roman jurisprudence. Therein—in its capacity to assume juridical form—lies one of its sociological secrets. But it has the power to assume this or any other form only because it has the power of representation. It represents the *civitas humana*. It represents in every moment the historical connection to the incarnation and crucifixion of Christ. It represents the Person of Christ himself: God become man in historical reality. Therein lies its superiority over an age of economic thinking. (19)

Curiously enough, perhaps, it is precisely Schmitt's focus on the idea of "concrete representation" that makes this a work it is useful to consider in conjunction with both *Political Theology* (published only shortly before) and his much later short monograph on Shakespeare's *Hamlet* (published in 1956). Schmitt's insistence on the Pope as the living representative of "the incarnation and crucifixion of Christ . . . God become man in historical reality" chimes interestingly with his discussion of the Catholic theologian Donoso Cortés in the closing pages of *Political Theology*. Drawing on Cortés's critique of liberalism, Schmitt demonstrates his own dissatisfaction with the unresolvable "conversation" that characterizes liberal democracy as follows: "Liberalism, with its contradictions and compromises, existed for Donoso Cortés only in that short interim period in which it was possible to answer the question 'Christ or Barabas?' with a proposal to adjourn or appoint a commission of investigation" (*PT* 62).[66] Thus "liberalism" exists in a moment of postponement or delay of the sovereign decision, which might also be characterized as the "period between the periods" of the two sentences: life and death.[67] Yet we must note that the very moment of deferral that Cortés cites subjects God (in the feminized, subjectivated figure of Christ) to *popular* decision, *not* to the sovereign decree. To realize the implications of this reversal, we must recall that Pilate *abrogates* his authority, turning the decision over to the Jews; thus, it would *seem* to be a moment that instantiates popular sovereignty—he decides *not* to decide. For Schmitt, though, as for Bodin and Hobbes (to some extent), "popular sovereignty" does not exist, for to leave the power of the decision to the populace would divide and contravene the state's authority; thus, Schmitt cannot acknowledge the real ambivalence of Pilate's turn away from the decision.

In each of these disparate works, the figure of Christ becomes an analogical flashpoint for some kind of "intrusion" or interruption. Like Montaigne's coy lover, perpetually stopping his text at the moment of revelation, in Schmitt's analysis Christ appears behind a series of veils, utterly corporealized yet always already transcendent—no doctrinal surprises there. And like the Church itself, in Schmitt's reading, the figure of Christ emerges as a *complexio oppositorum*, melding certain essentialized notions of masculinity and femininity, emerging as a sort of hermaphroditic Tiresias figure. By a strange twist of logic, the enfleshed Christ becomes the miraculous flashpoint of exception *most exemplarily* at the moment in which he decides to die—if, that is, it is a true decision, which is a point for the theologians to debate. This example of the sovereign decision as the decision to die, after bodily torment and suffering, becomes the exception within the state of exception—as it is for Coriolanus, for Theoxena, and, eventually, for Vindice.

Schmitt begins the third chapter of *Political Theology* as follows:

> *All significant concepts of the modern theory of the state are secularized theological concepts* not only because of their historical development—in which they were transferred from theology to the theory of the state, whereby, for example, the omnipotent law became the omnipotent lawgiver—but also because of their systematic structure, the recognition of which is necessary for a sociological consideration of these concepts. *The exception in jurisprudence is analogous to the miracle in theology. Only by being aware of this analogy can we appreciate the manner in which the philosophical ideas of the state developed in the last centuries.* (36; emphases added)[68]

Leaving aside, for the moment, Schmitt's definition of his critique here as an intervention in sociology, I want to work through the complex articulations that link "the miracle" with the representative figure of Christ—this despite the fact that Schmitt insists, in his belated response to Walter Benjamin, that "Shakespearean drama in general and *Hamlet* in particular is no longer religious in the medieval sense. . . . Shakespeare's drama is no longer Christian."[69] With this provocative statement, Schmitt seeks not only to refute Benjamin but also to reassert his own argument concerning the formal and political primacy of the Roman Catholic Church. Schmitt can say "Shakespeare's drama is no longer Christian" only as much as he might say "Shakespeare's drama would not necessarily have been recognized as primarily theological, and specifically Catholic, in its origins and intents"—though of course both of these are vexed claims that continue to fuel the Shakespeare industry today. Thus Schmitt sets up an antithesis between the "barbaric" world of medieval feudal states and the emergent "political" realm of the nation-state, reserving a special exception for

England, with its maritime agenda. The modern state, Schmitt argues here as in *Political Theology*, though on different grounds, constitutes a secularized or post-theological development. Claiming that Benjamin failed to address the historical and geographical particularities of Shakespeare's England, Schmitt writes,

> Shakespeare's drama falls within the first stage of the English revolution, if one dates it (as is possible and reasonable) from the destruction of the Armada in 1588 to the expulsion of the Stuarts in 1688. During these hundred years a new political order on the European continent developed from the neutralization of confessional civil war—the sovereign state, which Hobbes called an *imperium rationis* and Hegel described as a realm of objective reason beyond theology whose *ratio* put an end to the heroic age, the age of heroic law and heroic tragedy. The century of civil war between Catholics and Protestants could only be overcome by the dethroning of the theologians, because they kept the civil war alive with their doctrine of tyrannicide and the just war. In place of the medieval order of feudal castes or estates appeared a public order of peace and security created and maintained by the legitimating achievement of the new entity: the *state*. . . . Those thinkers who no longer looked to the church but to the state for deliverance from the hopelessness of the confessional civil war, among them the jurist Jean Bodin, were called politicians, *politiciens* in a very specific sense in France, the foremost country on the European continent. The sovereign state and politics were antithetical to the medieval forms and methods of a religious and feudal domination. In this situation the word *political* acquired a polemical meaning as opposed to the word *barbaric*; concretely, it acquired the meaning of a genuine antithesis. (149)

The "primitivism" Schmitt displays in this appendix recalls Eliot's essays of the 1930s, and one is also tempted to juxtapose with this passage Virginia Woolf's lyrical meditation on the "violence" of the Elizabethan age in *Orlando*—though perhaps this is the first and last time the two will ever be mentioned together.[70] Like Woolf, like Eliot, in the *Elizabethan Essays*, Schmitt characterizes the "barbarous" Tudor and Stuart England with a certain nostalgia for its lost immediacy. Mourning the passage of "the age of heroic law and heroic tragedy" even as he celebrates the ascendancy of "the legitimating achievement of the *state*," Schmitt seemingly decries the falling away of the age's urgency, or perhaps he might say of *emergency*—or at least the falling away of the theophanic notion of sovereignty of which he sees the faded remnants in the Stuarts. In this he perfectly echoes the conservative desire for a lost Golden Age that Vindice attempts to recuperate.

Allegory in Ruins: The Revenger Unmasked

I want to return, though, to the question of representation, and to the exchanges between Schmitt and Benjamin concerning the location of sovereignty within the frame of *Trauerspiel*. As we have seen in chapter 1, Benjamin insists upon a melancholic, corporeal sovereignty bowed by the excessive weight of history—a sovereignty whose primary function is to avert the state of emergency (in this he differs from Schmitt). Part of Schmitt's divergence from Benjamin here might be said to lie in their respective constructions of history. For Benjamin, as we have seen, "history" as a narrative is in some sense always already a failed projection, a game of illusions; the "death of history" Hegel predicts and Marx ushers in assumes its apotheosis in his "Theses on the Philosophy of History." Despite its messianic drive, it is fragments shored against ruins, compulsively assembled in the face of sheer contingency.[71] Its face is the weary, grief-strained visage of the sovereign martyr, meshed in a terrible struggle with time (in the *Trauerspiel* book), or Klee's shell-shocked angel mired in the dusty wreckage of the world (in the Ninth Thesis).[72] Schmitt's figure for history emerges with the triumphant visage of Christ, perpetually resurrected in the person of the Pope, the sovereign above temporal sovereigns who (unlike the king's frangible two bodies) remains infallible *even in* his corporeality. In this way the Pope, ever providing the "concrete representation" of Christ, becomes the exception *in his very unexceptionability*—that is, in his normativeness, his perpetuity. If, in Schmitt's schema, the decision to declare a state of emergency must be founded only as a protective or apotropaic gesture—a warding off of potential "danger" or "peril," no matter how ambiguous that threat might be—his reliance upon the suffering Christ as a figure for the sovereign decision opens up a space of radical indeterminacy. For Schmitt, the Church is an essentialized, naturalized feminine body wounded by techno-economic power (hence his focus on viniculture as the Catholic form of labor par excellence, the earth as a fruitfully bleeding womb)[73]—yet even in his romantic transports it is curious that he never mentions Mary at all. Despite his insistence on the Church as a hermaphroditic edifice that incorporates and embraces both masculine and feminine essences, his analysis erases the mystic feminine, in whose place he erects an auto-generative, concrete superpatriarch, the Pope—yet in his very "concreteness," the lithic force of the Pope's "representative" function always threatens to collapse upon itself at the very moment of its realization. Like Montaigne's lover at the unrepresentable moment of orgasm, Schmitt's characterization of the Pope as the infallible "representative" of history undoes itself in its enactment—and it is this very undoing that leads us, eventually, back to Middleton's play, and the figure of the revenger (or the "intriguer," for Benjamin).

In the second half of the *Trauerspiel* book, Benjamin turns his attention to allegory as both an aesthetic and a hermeneutic, a modality that, he claims, dominates the baroque and which the post-Romantic conception of "symbols" has flattened out.[74] Allegory, unlike symbol, presents itself *self-consciously*; in this, Benjamin argues, it is like "holy writing" or "sacred scripture," a created surface that always reveals its own createdness (175), emptying itself of signification in the act of signifying. Its proper expression, Benjamin argues, is the *ruin*, for it is in the ruin that the creaturely life of humans finds itself most fully gathered up and reflected:

> When, as is the case in the *Trauerspiel*, history becomes part of the setting, it does so as a script. The word "history" stands written on the countenance of nature in the characters of transience. The allegorical physiognomy of the nature-history [*Natur-Geschichte*], which is put on stage in the *Trauerspiel*, is present in reality in the form of the ruin. In the ruin history has physically merged into the setting. And in this guise history does not assume the form of the process of an eternal life so much as that of irresistible decay. Allegory thereby declares itself to be beyond beauty. Allegories are, in the realm of thoughts, what ruins are in the realm of things. . . . That which lies here in ruins, the highly significant fragment, the remnant, is, in fact, the finest material in baroque creation. For it is common practice in the literature of the baroque to pile up fragments ceaselessly, without any strict idea of a goal, and, in the unremitting expectation of a miracle, to take the repetition of stereotypes for a process of intensification. The baroque writers must have regarded the work of art as just such a miracle. (*Origin* 177–78)[75]

Though Benjamin would not, perhaps, have placed Middleton in the same "baroque" category as Calderón and Shakespeare, this passage resonates with Middleton's play, both structurally and thematically. For it is in this work that Middleton places history (in the form of sovereign succession, as we see in the dumb-show/progress that opens the play) so definitively on the stage, in the process of its undoing—that is, in the process of transmuting itself into a ruined artifact. Hence the focus on tombs, which encase the dead in a kind of perpetuity while at the same time constituting an ineffable landscape of death. Hence the compulsively assembled "fragments" of piously sententious speech that, as R. A. Foakes argues, continually belie their speakers' true intentions. And hence, perhaps, the skeptical impulse that nevertheless continually searches for revealed meaning, Vindice's own "unremitting expectation of a miracle" that can work itself out only in crafting an anti-miracle, the negative miracle of destruction. Benjamin writes,

> It is fallen nature which bears the imprint of the progression of history. The penchant of the baroque for apotheosis is a counterpart to its own particular way of looking at things. The authorization of their allegorical designations bears the seal of the all-too-earthly. Never does their transcendence come from within. Hence their illumination by the artificial light of apotheosis. . . . Any adequate masking of content is absent from the typical work of the baroque. The extent of their claims, even in the minor forms, is breathtaking. And they lack any feeling for the intimate, the mysterious. They attempt, extravagantly and vainly, to replace it with the enigmatic and the concealed. In the true work of art pleasure can be fleeting, it can live in the moment, it can vanish, and it can be renewed. The baroque work of art wants only to endure, and clings with all its senses to the eternal. (*Origin* 180–81)

Benjamin's remarks reveal a strange irony: in this depiction, the baroque work of art is simultaneously extensive and bounded by its own extravagance; it trades "the intimate, the mysterious," for "the enigmatic and the concealed," yet only partially concealed, in the always-evident guise of allegory (exemplified above all in emblems). A few pages later, Benjamin continues, "Above all it is the offensive, the provocative quality of gesture which is baroque. . . . If it is to hold its own against the tendency to absorption, the allegorical must constantly unfold in new and surprising ways. . . . Allegories become dated, because it is part of their nature to shock" (183). In the conjunction of these passages we might see elements of Vindice, the revenger who thus also becomes a figure for Benjamin's baroque artist and, especially, for the "intriguer" (*intrigant*) whose "devilish mirth" signals the fallen ends of allegory.[76] In Benjamin's conceit, the master craftsman triumphs over time by dissolving into it—for the "apotheosis" of the baroque work of art is also its undoing, its assimilation into a creatural landscape that waits to receive it.[77] In what we might term his *willing fall* into a supranatural time-beyond-time, the baroque intriguer becomes, in the end, a figure for redemptive history even as he brings about the end of history in his fall.[78]

The correspondence between Vindice and Benjamin's intriguer/artificer is perhaps most apparent during Vindice's *coup de théâtre*, the Duke's murder via Gloriana's poisoned skull:

> VINDICE: Now to my tragic business. Look you brother,
> I have not fashioned this only for show
> And useless property, no—it shall bear a part
> E'en in its own revenge. This very skull
> Whose mistress the duke poisoned with this drug,
> The mortal curse of the earth, shall be revenged
> In the like strain and kiss his lips to death.
> As much as the dumb thing can, he shall feel;
> What fails in poison we'll supply in steel.
> HIPPOLITO: Brother I do applaud thy constant vengeance,
> The quaintness of thy malice, above thought. (III.v.98–109)

Once again, Vindice employs the language of the theatre, crossed with that of the commodity culture he seeks to undermine ("tragic business"). With "revenged / In the like strain," the supplementary law of violence that governs the logic of vengeance emerges, for "the like strain" must always incorporate an excess. Hippolito's punning response underlines its own irony: the only "constancy" possible in the play's overwrought world is the constancy of vengeance, but a constancy undone by its own "quaintness." The "quaintness" of Vindice's malice lies in its baroque overdetermination, the overdoing that becomes his undoing. For Vindice's much-vaunted "closeness" is of course not "close" at all, just as "quaint," with its pun on female genitalia, is not "close" at all.[79] Like most artists, he must have recognition for his work; hence his unmasking first to the Duke, then to Lussorioso, and, in the end, to Antonio. Vindice's compulsive repetition—"'Tis I, 'tis Vindice, 'tis I!"—mimics the overkill he enacts.[80]

Like Theoxena's children, the Duke is not to be allowed "simple death" but must suffer the graphic tortures of "millions of deaths" (III.v.177) as well as being "killed in the eyes" by witnessing the Duchess and Spurio's amorous meeting. Yet this is not Greek tragedy, Hecuba putting out her eyes with her brooch—the grotesque spectacle of the Duke's punishment turns to comedy, and any tragic potential is undercut by his own narration. Like Antonio's lady in only this way, the Duke glosses his own death, though in this case he does not direct the staging. Anatomizing his own performance, he provides a running commentary on his demise: "My teeth are eaten out"; "Oh!" "Oh!" "Oh my tongue!"; "Millions of deaths!" (III.v.158, 161, 169, 175, 179). The brothers' silencing of his still-going tongue (which proclaims its own consumption) by placing their daggers over his tongue and heart constitutes an emblematic tableau, which parodically undercuts the emblematic significance of the deathbed of Lord Antonio's lady.

In his essay on Tourneur, Eliot remarks that "the suddenness of the end of the final scene of Act V matches the sudden explosiveness of the beginning" of *The Revenger's Tragedy*.[81] After the staginess of the Duke's murder in act 3, Junior Brother's hilariously accidental offing in act 4, and Vindice's fiercely conceived "murder" of himself as Piato, Lussorioso's festivities provide the occasion for the play's final metatheatrical twist. Seizing on the opportunity the masked revels provide, both Spurio and Vindice plot to kill Lussorioso, Ambitioso and Supervacuo to kill both elder sons. The intricately intertwining figures of these two revengers' dances might be read as a stagy metaphor for the entire foregoing action—which comes to a close when Vindice and Hippolito joyfully proclaim the murdered Dukes their doing before essentially installing Lord Antonio as "the hope of Italy," whose "reverend years . . . will make the silver age again" (V.iii.86–89). Lord Antonio's first sovereign act is to haul the impenitent brothers off to be executed for treason, and the play ends with his lines, "How subtly was that murder closed! Bear up / Those tragic bodies; 'tis a heavy season. / Pray heaven their blood may wash away all treason" (V.III.129–31). This closing couplet provides a telling motto for the play as a whole, for while seemingly rounding off the "heavy season" of the tragedy, it yet lends itself to a certain ambiguity. The uncertain antecedents of the pronouns—"that murder," "their blood" (does "their" refer to the "tragic bodies" of the murdered brothers and nobles, or to the about-to-be-executed Vindice and Hippolito?)—"closes" off the mechanistic violence of retribution only by echoing the very sentiments that first gave it rise. "How subtly was that murder closed!" Antonio marvels, but the play has permanently scored both subtlety (linked to "deep policy" and "quaintness," the covert architectonics of revenge that continually bog down in spectacle) and the idea of closure. Blood begetting blood, the integral dynamic of revenge, finds a not-quite-yet-political reason in Antonio's charge of "treason" and a not-quite-yet-juridical response in his summary execution of the brothers' sentences—and the play has already demonstrated that treason, the most serious of charges, can be comically fabricated and misconstrued as much as any other. Thus Antonio's closing lines might be read as a further unclosing, the final couplet an invitation to further cruelty.

At the end of the first chapter of *Political Theology*, Schmitt writes,

> Precisely a philosophy of concrete life must not withdraw from the exception and the extreme case, but must be interested in it to the highest degree. The exception can be more important to it than the rule, not because of a romantic irony for the paradox, but because the seriousness of an insight goes deeper than the clear generalizations inferred from what ordinarily repeats itself. The exception is more interesting than the rule. The rule proves nothing; the exception proves everything: It confirms not only the rule but also its existence, which derives only from the exception. In the exception the power of real life breaks through the crust of a mechanism that has become torpid by repetition (*PT* 13).[82]

For Schmitt, the exception both precedes and illuminates juridical norms, norms that it obviates in the act of declaration. It is a strobelike flash of pure immediacy, a coruscating "eruption" that echoes the theophanic miracle to which he will compare it in later chapters, and which finds an example in the "eruption" of historical immediacy of Mary Stuart's problematic legacy as it is aesthetically reframed by Shakespeare's play. But though Schmitt disavows "the romantic irony of the paradox," he creates another irony in doing so: once the exception "breaks through [*durchbricht*] the crust of a mechanism that has become torpid by repetition," once it *declares itself as the norm* and reshapes legal structures accordingly, it too becomes mechanized, repetitious, robotic—in a word, inhuman.

Part Two

States of Grace

Chapter Three

Sacred Life and Sacrificial Economy

Coriolanus in No-Man's-Land

In this chapter I return to Aristotle's claim in Book I of the *Politics*: "It is evident that the state is a creation of nature, and that man is by nature a political animal. And he who by nature and not by mere accident is without a state, is either a bad man or above humanity; he is like the 'Tribeless, lawless, hearthless one' whom Homer denounces—the natural outcast is forthwith a lover of war" (I.1253a.5–10).[1] In these lines we might trace a precursor for Shakespeare's Coriolanus, the military hero of the early Roman Republic who turns his back on his own city to join forces with its enemies. "First Citizen" speaks the first line of *Coriolanus* (ca. 1608–9): "Before we proceed any further, hear me speak."[2] The opening lines of the play thus link the shifting status of republican citizenship to rights, and rites, of public speech and popular representation, issues again foregrounded in the election scene of act 2, scene 1. Often considered the most political of Shakespeare's plays, his last tragedy has long provided fodder for those who speculate about Shakespeare's own political affiliations, particularly his attitude toward absolute monarchy, on the one hand, or some sort of proto-democratic populism, on the other. Most recently, Andrew Hadfield takes up the issue in a series of books and articles.[3] In his latest book, Hadfield identifies his critical task as an exercise in historical "recovery" or "archaeology," commencing with the provocative query "was Shakespeare a Republican?" Unlike Hadfield, in the argument that follows I do not overtly engage this question. Rather, as A. C. Bradley said over a century ago, "I do not propose to join this dance, or even to ask whether any reasonable conjecture as to Shakespeare's political views and feelings could be formed from study of this play and of others."[4] While I certainly agree with Hadfield's assertion that understanding how republicanism was construed in the period nuances our appreciation of Shakespeare's work, I also concur with Ineke

Murakami's recent claim that, in *Coriolanus*, "rather than stage solutions, [Shakespeare] raises questions."[5] Whereas many critics feel they must answer Hadfield's inquiry one way or the other, then, it is precisely the deep *ambivalence* of Shakespeare's treatment of the emergent polity in this play that interests me.[6]

The First Folio text of the play itself invites a consideration of this doubleness. In the many "crowd" scenes of the play, the Folio stage directions distinguish between various groupings: on the one hand, there are the ignominious "rabbles" and "troupes" of Roman and Volscian "soldiers" (I.iv; I.ix) and the Roman "plebeians" (second half of II.iii; III.iii; IV.vi), as well as the Volscian "Commoners"; on the other, the highly articulate Roman "company of mutinous citizens" in I.i and in the first half of II.iii, or even the Volscian "Guard or watch" in V.ii. While it is perhaps foolish to attribute the Folio's stage directions to Shakespeare, rather than to a compositor or printer, the very fact that *someone* created a palpable distinction between an easily manipulated mob and a politically savvy "company" or "commonwealth" of nevertheless individually distinct *citizens* in this initial printing should not go unremarked.[7] It seems to me that those who favor a proto-republican reading (such as Hadfield and Patterson) focus most on the latter category, the articulate Roman citizens,[8] while those who argue for a "conservative," anti-populist Shakespeare (from Hazlitt to Huffman) emphasize the "rabble," and the vicious tribunes.[9] I will argue, however, that Shakespeare's ambivalent reception of the more idealized republic present in his main source, Plutarch's *Life of Caius Martius Coriolanus*, crystallizes around various facets of two linked but separable civic rituals: gift-giving and election, both ligatures of the embryonic political order. Yet like Coriolanus himself, his scored flesh signifying his fitness to stand for office, the very idea of election is increasingly "undone" throughout the course of the play. For Plutarch, election is tied to trial—*krisis*, in Greek. Shakespeare retains this sense of crisis attendant upon popular election yet shifts Plutarch's focus on the election of the tribunes of the people to Coriolanus's quickly rescinded election as consul, an office retaining traces of the powers accorded the banished kings.

Scarred and sacred, aphasic and abandoned: Coriolanus has seemed to some recent critics to exemplify the "bare life" typified by the archaic Roman *homo sacer* in the work of Giorgio Agamben.[10] Ineke Murakami, for example, argues that the beast language in the play corresponds to a medieval conception of natural law, a zone of intersection between theology and politics that simultaneously forms and abjects the "creaturely" or bare life that gives it rise. For Murakami, "willing divestiture stands at the heart of the play," a line of thought James Kuzner's reading takes in a different direction.[11] To Kuzner, Coriolanus exemplifies a form of "self-undoing" subjectivity that distances the play from critical accounts of "bounded selfhood" (what some might term Coriolanus's "absoluteness"). Drawing on the work of Agamben, Butler, and Jean-Luc Nancy, but aligning Coriolanus's undoing most fully with the transgressive figures of Leo Bersani's "gay outlaw" and the early modern "sodomite" in Jonathan Goldberg's work,[12] Kuzner argues that the play's political potential can be located in the "sodomitical outside" of his relationship with Aufidius—a queer un-coupling that models the radical openness needed to move beyond rigidly defined borders (either political or psychological).[13] Whereas Murakami focuses on the domains of natural law, Rebecca Lemon considers the play as a proleptic gloss on the legalism of the later Republic (the Twelve Tables) and the Empire (Justinian's Institutes), the latter especially influential in English jurisprudence via the writings of Bracton and subsequent jurists. In a closing turn to Agamben and Schmitt, Lemon argues that Coriolanus inhabits the dual space of sovereignty and exile typified by Agamben's *homo sacer*, whose "sacrificial" death fails to reconcile the tensions between an archaic military code and an incipient civil legal order.[14]

Each of these critics, in various ways, attributes to Coriolanus an "exemplary" status that is also "exceptional," a "sovereignty" attainable only via exile, comparable to Agamben's reading of the sovereign ban, which simultaneously suspends the subject from legal personhood and subjects him to the law of perpetual banishment, an extra-legal zone in which death ceases to have any sacrificial value.[15] For Agamben, this paradox forms the basis of modern biopolitics in the West, in which the "state of exception" brought about by the Schmittian decision to suspend the law inscripts itself as the new norm.[16] In this, Agamben argues, "we are all virtually *homines sacri*" (*HS* 115). To a certain extent, I would agree with this claim, yet I would have us nuance Agamben's correlation of "sacred life" with "bare life" by thinking more carefully about the peculiar economy of violence within Shakespeare's play. In the last portion of this chapter, then, I consider this claim more fully, beginning by tracing Agamben's redeployment of Benjamin's remarks concerning "mere" or "bare life" (*bloßes Leben*).[17] For Agamben's purposes, *homo sacer* comprises both "bare life" and "sacred life" precisely because of his ultimate excision from what Aristotle calls "political life," whereas for Benjamin, I will argue, "sacred [*heilig*] life" constitutes an undefinible, irreducible excess that resists the biopolitical grasp on "mere life" even at its limits.

By excavating the residues of mystic sovereignty that continue to interrupt Shakespeare's nascent Republican scene, then, this essay reconsiders the connection between what Benjamin calls "sacred life" and the operations of sacrificial economy. Like Plutarch's in this, Shakespeare's Coriolanus approaches his "world elsewhere," Antium, as a suppliant (*hiketês*). In Plutarch's account Coriolanus enters Aufidius's house in disguise, "in such clothing and attire as would make him seem, to any one who saw him, least like the man he was, like Odysseus 'He went into the city of his deadly foes' " (XXII.2.172–73), and takes his place at the hearth of his enemy—the traditional refuge of the fugitive.[18] Reimagining this scene, Shakespeare places less emphasis on Coriolanus's fugitive status, yet he does preserve a vestigial ritual of supplication by retaining the hearth as the focus of the action. By preserving this scene of supplication, Shakespeare sets the stage for a consideration of the "extremity" of what Aristotle calls "life that has endured much suffering" that nevertheless contains within itself "something of well-being and sweetness" even excepted from the bounds of the "political life" of the citizen (III.1278b.26–31). It is this sense of the *preservation* of "something of well-being and sweetness," as well as the traces of religious and civic ritual that Shakespeare likewise retains, though covertly, that exempt Coriolanus from exemplifying the commensurability of sacred life and bare life. Instead, I will argue, Coriolanus comes closer to Benjamin's notion of a *natural* life that retains its equivocal sacrality: exiled, perhaps, but maintaining even unto death the possibility of an alternative political order.

No-Man's-Land: The Citizen-Soldier and the Gift of Death

> Death can be neither taken nor given.
>
> —Jacques Derrida

Coriolanus depicts both the titular hero of the play and the Rome reemerging from the ruinous exploits of the Tarquins inhabiting an indeterminate zone, poised between (in the first instance) soldier and citizen, absolutism and negativity, sovereignty and abjection, sacred and sacrificial orders, and (in the second) between monarchy and republic. In this play, then, Shakespeare captures the state of exception coupled to the transition from monarchy (*Regnum Romanum*) to fledgling Republic (*Res Publica Romanum*), a moment of crisis never really subsumed in the reordering of civic affiliations at the play's close. To consider the paradox of the citizen-soldier, we might begin by thinking about the relationship between military and civic orders in our own time and place, which in some ways provides an instructive parallel to the situation in Shakespeare's Rome (though not, perhaps, to that in Shakespeare's England).[19] In the contemporary popular media of the United States, the soldier inhabits a strange no-man's-land, both paradigmatic citizen and negative citizen. On the one hand, the soldier is held up as an exceptional citizen, and this singularity is always figured in terms of a willingness to participate in the ultimate exchange: life for country. Yet this potential exchange in turn lends itself to endless abstraction and dilation: the willingness to give "life for country" becomes "life for democracy" or "freedom of religion." The rate of exchange is never fixed, except for the first term, "life."

I speak of the peculiar tensions inhabited by the citizen-soldier as "a strange no-man's-land," a phrase I intend not as a glib pun but as a serious analogy. The phrase originates in the fourteenth century as a reference to the place outside London's city walls where criminals were executed, but to us today it is perhaps best known as a descriptor of the area between the trenches of the Entente and those of the Central Powers during World War I, so called because anyone who ventured into the barren strip between the lines risked being shot down by both sides.[20] In the modern idiom, "no-man's-land" thus becomes a metaphor for life suspended between two deaths, life on the brink of suffering and annihilation yet precariously preserved intact, held in the balance between struggling political and ideological forces. Hinterland, border, frontier: each of these near-cognate terms fails to capture the precise sense of no-man's-land, which is perhaps the most literal representation imaginable of the space of "armed neutrality." Nullified but, perhaps, not negated, the specter of sexual difference also stands within the phrase (no-*man's*-land), which then becomes a metaphor for the contested terrain of what Giorgio Agamben and others, following Walter Benjamin, term "bare life"—something that the originary designation of the abandoned, ex-civitate zone of the executioner should already recall. "No-man's-land" thus provides a paradigm for the state of exception within Shakespeare's play, in which the hyphenated existence of the citizen-soldier exemplifies this very sense of life shivering on the edge of death.

In the latter half of this chapter, I will consider bare life in conjunction with the question of the possibility of "sacrificial economy"; for now, though, let us pause over the peculiar tensions inhabited by the modern citizen-soldier, thinking of these tensions in terms of the economy of the gift, its exploitations, impossibilities, and doublings. Since the U.S.

invasions of Afghanistan and Iraq, amendments to the Immigration and Nationality Act that place current or former active-duty personnel on a fast track to U.S. citizenship provide yet another major incentive to join the military for those who are *not* current citizens. And, too, there is the ultimate ambivalence of the gift of "posthumous citizenship" for those killed in combat, which should recall to us Derrida's "gift of death," the impossibility of sacrificing one's life to save another's.[21] The alien soldier "killed for country," dying into citizenship,[22] exemplifies this terrible dilemma outlined by Derrida, yet even the naturalized or native citizen-soldier is always, in some sense, bound by the doubleness of "death's dative," the impossibility of mortal sacrifice for the sake of a political ideal. *Coriolanus* points up the untenability of such an exchange.

In this play, Shakespeare works certain variations on his own earlier tragedy of a citizen-soldier abjected from a republican body politic, *Othello*. Indeed, as J. G. A. Pocock has demonstrated, for many Renaissance thinkers the Venetian Republic stood as the most direct political and intellectual inheritor of the ideals (if not the praxis) of the Roman Republic, for good or ill.[23] As is so often the case in Shakespeare's Venice, Shakespeare's Rome in this play occupies a stage of political transition, and the drama focuses on the birth pangs of the early Republic and in particular the so-called Conflict of the Orders, resolved in part by the creation of the plebian tribunes. While Aufidius and the Volscians provide the play's external state of emergency, Coriolanus's banishment occurs because he represents a second and potentially more deadly (because internalized) threat, that of tyranny. More specifically, Coriolanus poses the threat of the citizen turned tyrant, a fear that Brutus and Sicinius, the play's plebian tribunes, do not necessarily need to fabricate when they incite the citizens to rescind their favorable "voices" for the newly elected consul, Coriolanus. Against this specter of tyranny Shakespeare sets the all-too-corporealized image of the rotten body politic made up of "mutinous members," a patched and putrefying "many-headed monster."[24]

To examine the paradox of the citizen-soldier and the "gift of death" that remains perpetually withheld as it appears closer to Shakespeare's own time, we turn to Niccolò Machiavelli's *Arte della guerra* (1521).[25] This treatise, the only one of Machiavelli's works published during his lifetime, proved enormously influential both on the Continent and, forty years later, in Elizabethan England. Peter Whitehorne's English translation—with a dedicatory epistle to Elizabeth—was published in 1560 and reissued in 1573 and 1588, more editions than any other translation of a military work.[26] Machiavelli's preface, addressed to his patron, Lorenzo di Filippo Strozzi, opens as follows:

> Many are now of the opinion, my dear Lorenzo, that no two things are more discordant and incongruous than a civil and a military life. . . . But if we consider the institutions of the ancients, we shall find that there is a very close, intimate relation between these two conditions, and that they are not only compatible and consistent with each other, but necessarily connected and interrelated. (3–4)

Machiavelli most frequently draws upon the military order of the Roman Republic for examples of the "institutions of the ancients" that intertwined civic with military excellence. With this nostalgically idealized state he juxtaposes the "depraved" and decayed military order of modern Florence. Machiavelli's treatise takes the form of a Platonic dialogue between the papal captain, Fabrizio Colonna (here, the military Socrates), the Florentine intellectual Cosimo Rucellai, and a group of Cosimo's friends. Fabrizio argues that the military and political stability of the Roman Republic rested on the citizen militia, as professional soldiers will have no investment in maintaining a stable polity:

> Since war is not an occupation [*una arte*] by which a man can at all times make an honorable living [*vivere onestemente*], it ought not to be followed as a business [*non la può usare per arte*] by anyone but a prince or a governor of a commonwealth; and if he is a wise man, he will not allow any of his subjects or citizens to make that his only profession—indeed, no good man ever did, for surely no one can be called a good man who, in order to support himself, takes up a profession [*un esercizio*] that obliges him at all times to be rapacious, fraudulent, and cruel, as of course must all of those—no matter what their rank—who make a trade of war. War will not maintain them in a time of peace, and thus they are under a necessity either of endeavoring to prevent a peace or of taking all means to make such provisions for themselves in time of war so that they may not lack sustenance when it is over. But neither of these courses is consistent with the common good (I.15).

To a certain extent, Coriolanus exemplifies what Fabrizio identifies here as the problem of the professional soldier: like Othello when his warlike occupation's gone, once he's off the battlefield, he never truly inhabits the civil space of civilian life.[27] Machiavelli's Fabrizio seems the anti-Clausewitz, here, arguing that to the mercenary soldier, war—or at least war from the ground up—is hardly "politics by other means,"[28] a temporary expedient whose real object is always political. For the mercenary soldier whose business is fighting, war becomes an end unto itself; no political horizon bounds the military existence.[29] On the contrary, the professional soldier in times of peace constitutes a political threat par excellence, as Fabrizio demonstrates with the relatively recent examples of marauding brigands (*brigante*) formed by soldiers disbanded after the Hundred Years' War (15).[30] Fabrizio goes on to argue that the Republican citizen-soldier provided the ideal blend of civic responsibility and military prowess: "Caesar and Pompey, and almost all the Roman generals who lived after the Second Punic War, acquired their reputation as skillful men [*valenti uomini*], not as good citizens [*non come buoni*]; but those who lived before that time won glory by being both civic-minded and skillful," for "the former made war their sole occupation, and the latter did not" (I.17). During the Republic, Fabrizio claims, neither commanders nor common soldiers sought military acclaim for its own sake but only as a passing excellence:[31]

> [After war,] the commanders, contenting themselves with the honor of a triumph, returned with eagerness to their former manner of living; and the common soldiers laid down their arms with much more pleasure than they had taken them up. Each resumed the calling by which he had gotten his bread before, and none had any hopes of advancing himself by plunder and rapine. (17–18)

In Fabrizio's account, the best illustration of the temporary, bounded character of the "art of war" as practiced during the Republic exists in the triumph, the public celebration greeting the returning hero—such as the one staged in honor of Coriolanus's return.

To Fabrizio, the non-professional soldier thus combines martial *virtú* with an Aristotelian notion of good citizenship; military life serves as only one stage in a series of progressive civic occupations. The Republican *cursus honorum* essentially comprises a ladder of civic offices, beginning with the obligatory military service and progressing to that which Coriolanus eventually stands for, the consulship. In the early days of the Republic, only an aristocrat could hold this office, which constituted, in effect, the supreme elective executive power.[32] In Cicero's *De legibus*, Marcus traces a connection between the consuls and the banished kings:

> Since the monarchic form of state, although it once met with approval, was rejected not so much because of the faults of monarchy as because of the faults of the monarch [*non tam regni quam regis vitiis repudiatum est*], the title alone of king will seem to have been rejected, but the substance will remain if there is a single person

> who commands all the other magistrates [*nomen tantum videbitur regis repudiatum, res manebit, si unus omnibus reliquis magistratibus imperabit*]. That is why there was good reason for Theopompus to set up ephors at Sparta to oppose the kings, and for us to have tribunes against the consuls. For the consul has this legal authority, that all the other magistrates should obey him except for the tribune [*nam illud quidem ipsum, quod in iure positum est, habet consul, ut ei reliqui magistratus omnes pareant excepto tribuno*], who was brought into being later to avoid the state of affairs that had existed. This was the first thing that reduced the power of the consul, in that someone was created who was not subordinate to him, and also because he brought assistance not only to the other magistrates but even to private citizens who disobeyed the consul. (III.15–16.476–77)[33]

Marcus thus characterizes the power of the consuls as a vestigial or attenuated sovereignty, balanced and tempered after the creation of the tribunes. His cryptic statement about "the state of affairs that had existed" necessitating the creation of this plebian office seemingly refers to the conflicts between patricians and plebeians collectively known as the Conflict of the Orders, such as the grain riot that Shakespeare stages in the opening scene of his play.[34] Marcus does not note in this passage the primarily negative quality of the tribune's authority: his statement that of "all the other magistrates" the tribunes alone stood exempt from "obey[ing]" the consuls seems to gesture beyond the power of veto that served as the tribunes' most powerful juridical tool.[35]

Following Polybius's commendation of the Republican "mixed constitution,"[36] Machiavelli argues that the Roman Republic after the appointment of the tribunes constituted the ideal civic government because it combined the three "good" forms of government: principality, aristocracy, and democracy. In a passage from the *Discorsi sopra la prima Deca di Tito Livio* that directly corresponds to the moment dramatized in Shakespeare's play, Machiavelli writes,

> Romulus and all the other kings passed many good laws suitable to living in liberty, but because their goal was to found a kingdom and not a republic, when that city became free it lacked many public institutions which should have been organized in a manner favourable to liberty, institutions which had not been established by those kings. Even though its kings lost their empire for the reasons and in the ways already discussed, *those who drove them out, having immediately established two consuls who took the place of the*

> *kings, nevertheless drove out of Rome only the title of king and not kingly power*, so that, since that republic had only the consuls and the senate, it came to be nothing more than a mixture of two of the three elements mentioned above, that is, the principality and the aristocracy. (I.ii.27; emphasis added)[37]

The "kingly power" (*potesta regia*) of the consuls that Machiavelli mentions included supreme command of the army as well as the highest juridical authority, though in practice consuls only rarely exercised certain judicial powers.[38] Machiavelli goes on to describe the tension between plebeians and patricians that the creation of the tribunes resolved:

> In order not to lose everything, the nobility was forced to concede to the people its share of power, but for their part, the senate and the consuls still retained so much authority that they were able to preserve their rank in that republic. In this manner the creation of the tribunes of the plebeians came about, after which the condition of the republic became more stable, since all three forms of government had their roles. (III.ii.27)

Though Plutarch's *Life* (rather than Livy's *History*, though he does draw on Livy at points) is his main source for the play, Shakespeare nevertheless quickly slides past Plutarch's account of creation of the tribunes, which occurs as a direct result of the corn riots that provide his opening scene.[39] Shakespeare retains little of the Plutarchan and Machiavellian accounts of their institution as a patrician concession that would avert a dangerous internal instability. Rather, his dramatic focus on the election for consul in effect supersedes the question of the origins of popular representation, transmuting the civic rituals of election into a personalist tragedy[40]—yet one that still retains the integrity of the civic unrest that prompts the rescinded election. Coriolanus's election and banishment, II.iii–III.iii, are the formal and dramatic crux of the play, and it is worth pausing to unpack this tense imbrication of events.

Cicero, in both *De re publica* and *De legibus*, discusses the office and the circumstances under which it was deemed necessary to select a dictator, as we see in this passage from *De re publica*:

> *Scipio*: Peace and tranquility are like a ship or a minor illness: you can be undisciplined when there is no danger. But when the sea gets rough or the disease gets worse, the sailor or the sick man calls for one person's help. So too, at home and in peace, our people give

> orders to the magistrates themselves—they threaten, refuse to obey, ask for one magistrate's help against another, and appeal to the people; but in war they obey their leaders as they would a king: safety matters more than one's own desires. And in major wars, our people wanted all the power to be in the hands of one individual without a colleague, *whose very title indicates the extent of his power: he is called dictator because he is appointed, but in our augural books, Laelius, you see that he is called "master of the people."* (I.63; emphasis added)[41]

Scipio thus defines the conditions for the potential reinstatement of both sovereign authority and the state of emergency as "major war." We might pause, though, over his etymological claim, which already postulates a conceptual split in the origins of dictatorship. On the one hand, the title "dictator," from *dicere*, suggests election—someone spoken for by the people. Yet the alternative title, *magister populi*, explicitly works against the previous sense, highlighting only the people's subjection to the consuls' sovereign decree. Consider, too, Scipio's account of the origins of the phrase "our augural books," which links the foundations of dictatorial power to the mystic authority of the banished kings.

During a state of military emergency, the power to appoint a dictator resided with the consuls. Machiavelli notes that during the early Republic the effectively dual status of the consulate—the highest elected officials, who must in times of emergency essentially nullify their own offices—presented something of a problem:

> Since the creation of the dictator brought some shame to the consuls, who from being the rulers of the city were reduced to obedience like everyone else, and since they assumed this would create contempt toward them among the citizens, the Romans decided that the power to elect the dictator would remain with the consuls, believing that when the circumstance came about and Rome needed this *royal authority* [*regia potesta*], they would do it willingly, and since they did it themselves, it would be less painful. *The wounds and all the other evils that men inflict upon themselves* ***by election*** [***per elezione***] *are far less painful than those which are inflicted upon them by others.*[42] Yet, afterwards in the later periods, the Romans were accustomed to granting such dictatorial authority to the consul, instead of a dictator, with these words: "that the consul shall see to it that the state takes no harm." (*Discorsi* I.xxxv.96; emphasis added and translation slightly modified)

Despite the fact that this passage occurs in a chapter that argues that "Dictatorial Authority Did Good, Not Harm, to the Roman Republic," Machiavelli's characterization of the election of a dictator as a self-inflicted "wound or evil" hints at a certain misgiving, and one that provides a useful opening for thinking about the problems of Shakespeare's play. Machiavelli's analogy of the wound inflicted voluntarily, "by election" (*per elezione*), points us directly toward the election scene in *Coriolanus*, which itself depends upon public display of the wounds the citizen-soldier has received in his country's service. Coriolanus himself, his civic identity simultaneously defined and ultimately effaced by his wounds,[43] perfectly represents this second or shadow threat of the citizen-turned-tyrant within the state of exception that already characterizes the transition to Republicanism. The citizen-soldier's wounds, the marks of his willing exchange of life for country, thus become signs of both "the gift of death" and its impossibility, and it is to the paradox of the gift that we now turn.

A Thing and No-thing: The Given Name

Martius's deeds at Corioles earn him a new name, a new identity as Rome's savior that he ultimately fails to fulfill. Like the honorific itself, Coriolanus's wounds signify both "arms and the man," but also like the honorific, which names only by erasing what it names (the patronymic), the citizen-soldier's wounds signify by syncope, marking by effacing their own marks. That is to say, in a sense, Coriolanus's suffering is marked primarily by *absence*: just as he is named by removing his name, so he is defined primarily by his missing flesh. In the kaleidoscopic political economy of the play, names, voices, wounds, words, occupy a shifting scale of value, emerging alternately as overdetermined "superfluity" or "surplus" (two terms that appear a great deal in the opening scenes of the play, always in contested form) of meaning and as its absolute negation or dearth.

Like *Timon of Athens* (with which it is occasionally linked by critics), *Coriolanus* constitutes a rather ambiguous tragedy: experimental, schematic, at times almost choric in nature, as Frank Kermode notes.[44] Kermode calls both plays "tragedies of ideas," and I would argue that *Timon* and *Coriolanus* must be read as Shakespearean "Parallel Lives." This is not only because Shakespeare derived much of the source material for each from Plutarch but also because the two plays represent, in a more profound sense, two sides of a Shakespearean meditation on political economy. If, as Ken Jackson has suggested, *Timon* depicts the exigencies of the gift economy,[45] *Coriolanus* provides its complement: an economy of pure exchange or pure means in which human life in its most basic form itself becomes the predominant counter.[46] Thus, even this play centered on a most *un-giving* protagonist contains, too, moments of grace that demonstrate what Derrida has called the impossibility of the gift.[47]

We might say that force always attends the gift, or in fact that every gift is a gift of force. Marcel Mauss noted that every gift carries with it a threat, for it enmeshes both giver and recipient in an economy of obligation: "To refuse to give, to fail to invite, just as to refuse to accept, is tantamount to declaring war; it is to reject the bond of alliance and commonality."[48] One such moment of subtended grace occurs at the end of act 1, after Martius has emerged, battered but victorious, from the gates of Corioles, to be renamed "Coriolanus" for his exploits. When his general commends his bravery in material terms—a horse, and a tenth of the spoils, "to be ta'en forth / Before the common distribution, at / Your only choice" (I.ix.34–36), Martius initially refuses any such honor. Cominius and Lartius refuse Martius's refusal, granting him "th'addition" of the honorific:

> COMINIUS: Therefore be it known,
> As to us, to all the world, that Caius Martius
> Wears this war's garland, in token of the which
> My noble steed, known to the camp, I give him
> With all his trim belonging; and from this time,
> For what he did before Corioles call him,
> With all th'applause and clamour of the host,
> Martius Caius Coriolanus.
> Bear th'addition nobly ever! (I.x.57–65)

Yet Cominius's "addition" also, inevitably, incorporates a subtraction: the name is a gift, but a gift that entails a certain sacrifice. Becoming "Coriolanus" means adopting a martial identity that is also a civic identity, but in the process, "th'addition" effectively cancels out the patronymic. *The giving of a name, the naming of a gift*: this chiasmic nominalism enacts in miniature one of the primary tensions of the play as a whole, that between ties of kinship and those of state.[49] In this moment, then, naming the gift simultaneously bestows and obliterates the name; the name of the soldier supersedes the name of the father (Martius), and even that of the soldier-god himself (Mars).

In Mauss's anthropological account, the gift gathers to itself the sense of being both a *thing* (an object or an occasion, such as a meal) and *no-thing*, a "super-thingly" aura or charge that accrues in the act of passage or exchange.[50] In the example of the Maori *taonga* and *hau*, Mauss describes this sacral accretion as a "spiritual bond" that both inhabits and exceeds the thingness of the gift: "What imposes obligation in the present received and exchanged is the fact that the thing received is not inactive. Even when [the gift] has been abandoned by the giver, it still possesses something of him."[51] Yet as the process of "becoming Coriolanus" shows, when the gift is itself an "unthingly thing"—such as a name, such as grace—it carries with it not only this "spiritual bond" that melds giver to recipient and thence to a larger community but also a sort of sinister or retroactive force that renders the recipient himself in some sense a thing, a creature simultaneously more and less than human. Hence Lartius's eulogy for Martius, before Martius's triumphant return, his becoming the thing that is Coriolanus:

LARTIUS: O noble fellow!
Who sensibly outdares his senseless sword
And when it bows, stand'st up. Thou art lost, Martius.
A carbuncle entire, as big as thou art,
Were not so rich a jewel. Thou wast a soldier
Even to Cato's wish, not fierce and terrible
Only in strokes, but with thy grim looks and
The thunder-like percussion of thy sounds
Thou mad'st thine enemies shake, as if the world
Were feverous and did tremble. (I.iv.57–66).

"Thou art lost, Martius. / Thou wast a soldier": Lartius's encomium encloses a eulogy within a eulogy, the four extra-syllabic lines (59–62) marked by two caesurae that carry all the weight of their subject matter. "Thou art lost, Martius," indeed: for these lines render Martius a martial thing: a jewel richer than a carbuncle, "fierce and terrible," whose "grim looks" and "thunder-like sounds" abstract the man even as they name his soldierly gifts. Just as the given thing draws to itself a spiritual charge or force that exceeds its objective nature, so, too, the one who receives the gift is translated, at that moment, into a thing simultaneously empty and full: a holder of the gift, a momentary nexus in the communal web that giving engenders.

In order to become Coriolanus, then, Martius must be "lost," must become a thing. Heidegger reminds us of the etymological correspondences between *thing* and Republic (*res publica, the public thing*).[52]

Heidegger's etymological linkage between the thing (*res*) and the legal, deliberative functions of the state (*res publica*) proves instructive when we think about Shakespeare's play, for Shakespeare gives us a dialectic of the thing, in which Coriolanus, now hailed as the *res publica*, or "public thing," par excellence, nevertheless cannot bear the burdens of his civic functions: the *res publica* threatens the Republic itself. A similar dialectic of the thing attends the scene's second moment of grace, when the newly named Coriolanus reneges upon his earlier refusal:

> CORIOLANUS: I sometime lay here in Corioles
> At a poor man' s house. He used me kindly.
> He cried to me; I saw him prisoner,
> But then Aufidius was within my view,
> And wrath o'erwhelmed my pity. I request you
> To give my poor host freedom.
> COMINIUS: O, well begged!
> Were he the butcher of my son, he should
> Be free as is the wind. Deliver him, Titus.
> LARTIUS: Martius, his name.
> CORIOLANUS: By Jupiter, forgot!
> I am weary; yea, my memory is tired.
> Have we no wine here?
> COMINIUS: Go we to our tent.
> The blood upon your visage dries; 'tis time
> It should be looked to. Come.
> *Exeunt* (I.x.81–93)

Coriolanus's call names both the possibility and the impossibility of the gift, the magniloquence of his gesture simultaneously enforced by the salvific sense of the verb "deliver" and undercut by the verb "used," which surreptitiously introduces the vocabulary of labor and commodity (and, potentially, usury) into the transcendent passage of this gift of martial grace. Coriolanus's first act as Coriolanus, to rescue his former host, even though that host was Rome's enemy, seems to bear out his desire "to undercrest your good addition / to th' fairness of [his] power." Yet Coriolanus recalls the hospitality of the "poor man" even as he forgets the name of his host, and the poor man's "deliver[ance]" remains suspended between intent and performance, will and action: in naming the gift Coriolanus forgets the name.

Coriolanus himself is caught between the name and the gift, in two ways. Addressed here as "Martius," his own nascent re-identity is momentarily checked: the gift of Coriolanus's name, like Coriolanus's gift of grace, is thwarted in the moment of its naming. Lartius's encomium, which I have already touched on, foreshadows Cominius's report of his attempts to plead with Coriolanus not to march on Rome:

> COMINIUS: "Coriolanus"
> He would not answer to; forbade all names.
> He was a kind of nothing, titleless,
> Till he had forged himself a name o'th'fire
> Of burning Rome. (V.i.8–14)

As with the nameless "poor man," so at first with Cominius, though eventually the hollowed thing that Coriolanus remains "one time call[s] [him] by [his] name," spurred on perhaps by "the drops / That [they had] bled together." Cominius thus assumes the mantle of the citizen-soldier that Coriolanus rejects, his civil policy framed by their shared bloodshed. In his report to the Senate of Martius's valiant deeds, Cominius had earlier likened him to "a thing of blood, whose every motion / Was timed with dying cries" (II.ii.103–104): already a military machine, Coriolanus now appears "a kind of nothing, titleless." In each of these scenes that turn upon the craving of a boon, the naming of a gift that in turn depends upon the giving of a name, "Coriolanus" slides between "thing" and "nothing," a creaturely identity consisting of only a hollowed-out "name" hallowed by bloodshed. Even as "the blood on [his] visage dries," hardening into a gory mask, so Coriolanus's rebirth as a martial thing precipitates a sort of congealing grace, in which he as recipient of the gift becomes the mirror of the thing, becomes the thing itself.

To fully appreciate Shakespeare's logic of the gift as it operates in the "poor man" scene we must momentarily turn to his source, Plutarch's *Life of Caius Martius Coriolanus*, to explore the ways Shakespeare works a variation on Plutarch's theme. There are two rather long passages from Plutarch to which I would like to draw attention:

> I. On the following day [after the battle at Corioles], when Lartius had come up, and the rest of the army was assembled before the consul, Cominius mounted the rostra, and after rendering to the gods the praise that was their due for such great successes, addressed himself to Marcius. . . . After the Romans had applauded [Cominius's] speech, Marcius came forward and said that he accepted the horse, and was delighted with the praises of the consul, but that he declined the rest, holding it to be pay, not honor, and would

> be content with his single share of the booty. "But I do ask one special favour [*kharin*]" he said, "and beg that I may receive it. I had a guest-friend [*xenos kai philos*] among the Volscians, a man of kindliness and probity [*epieikês kai metrios*]. This man is now a prisoner, and from wealth and happiness is reduced to subjection. Since, then, many evils have befallen him, let me at least free him from that one, that of being sold into bondage." (X.2–3)

First, a few philological remarks on the linguistic economy of the name and the gift in this passage. *Xaris*, the noun Marcius employs to "beg" what Perrin translates as "a special favour," can also be translated as "grace," equivalent to the Latin *gratia*—the root of the New Testament's *to xarisma*, "a grace, favour; a free gift, gift of God's grace."[53] *Xaris* can designate either a gift given freely, with no expectation of any return, or it can mean a kindness or boon done "to oblige" someone or *to return a previous favor*—in other words, it registers senses of both gift and exchange.[54] It is, too, like the words "favor" or "boon" in English that translate it, always an abstraction, and one often requiring an attendant action: we *do* someone a favor or we *grant* a boon, just as we *give* a gift. Plutarch's "wealthy man . . . reduced to subjection" provides a standard tragic trope (the Aristotelian *peripeteia*), yet Shakespeare turns Plutarch's "wealthy man" into a "poor man," emphasizing not the minor character's reversal of fortune but the conqueror's beneficent gesture to a supposed enemy. Whereas Shakespeare's Timon perhaps provides the best parallel for Plutarch's "wealthy man" whose fortunes reverse, we might also see Plutarch's nameless "wealthy man" as something of a proleptic foil for the renamed Coriolanus himself. This sense of a doubled namelessness begins with the term *xenos*, "stranger" or "guest-friend," that Coriolanus uses to describe the wealthy man in Plutarch's account. This term designates a curiously paradoxical bond: to the Roman Coriolanus, the wealthy Volscian is both *xenos* (a stranger, a foreign soldier) and *philos* (a beloved friend).[55] Both terms express a strong sense of obligation, the duty to reciprocate in the giving of gifts—Priam in the tent of Achilles is also a guest-friend. At the very moment in which he is rechristened or reforged as the citizen-soldier, Coriolanus confronts his double, but as is the way of confronting doubles, he does not know whom or what he confronts, and he forgets the name. So, too, by the end of the play Coriolanus himself stands as both *xenos* and *philos*, the banished stranger simultaneously the beloved savior, Rome's scourge and her deliverer.

In order to consider this dynamic, let us return to a somewhat later moment in Plutarch's account of the "Life" of Coriolanus, the passage that Shakespeare drew from and modified in the passage from I.v I discussed earlier. Plutarch's story of Martius's "addition" runs as follows:

> II. When the multitude had ceased shouting their applause, Cominius took up the word again and said, "Ye cannot, indeed, my fellow-soldiers [*sustratiôtai*], force these gifts [*dôreas*] of yours upon the man, when he does not accept them and is unwilling to take them; but there is a gift which he cannot refuse when it is offered [*hên de ouk estin epi toutô didomenêen apôsasthai*]. Let us give him this gift [*dômen autô*], and pass a vote that he be surnamed Coriolanus, unless, indeed, before such act of ours, his exploit has itself given him this name [*autê touto dedôken*]." Thence came his third name of Coriolanus. (XI.1)

Plutarch's second passage displays the binding of the gift (*to dôron*) with force (*bia*, present here in the verb *biazo*) but complicates this inextricable pairing by introducing a third term, "election," to the economy of exchange. The passage begins with a noun (*dôron*). *Dôron*, unlike *xaris*, is a concrete noun: the gift as thing, not as abstraction or idea. Yet then Cominius's terms shift, circling around various forms of the verb *didômi*, "to give," coupled with pronouns (e.g., *dômen autô—we give it* [*the thing itself, which has already been named*]). In this passage, "to give" replaces "the gift," and Plutarch's grammar doubly elides the gift, replacing the *thing* of the gift with the action of giving, and the noun with the pronoun. Thus we witness the grammatical withdrawal of the gift even in the very act of its naming—this rhetorical double-handedness becomes, in effect, shorthand for the economy of the gift itself, which never remains purely a thing but entails a perpetuation of actions and exchanges.

Yet the gift as thing remains, perhaps, in the concrete possibility of *election*, for in Plutarch's account—unlike in Shakespeare's—the gift of the name depends not upon the decision of the generals but with Coriolanus's *sustratiôtai*, his fellow soldiers (literally, "co-planners" or "co-campaigners"). Here the promise of election (*psêphisômetha*), a vote to be cast by equals or comrades, co-campaigners, stands against the specter of force (*ou dunasthe biazesthai*, *you are not able to force*)—and the call for election also places the name somewhat outside the realm of the gift, re-locating it in a civic sphere juxtaposed with the natural law of force, a politics formulated according to reciprocity and mutual exchange of benefits. In Plutarch's account, this is perhaps one of the most truly Republican moments in the nascent Republic, and the soldiers' election exemplifies the new political model. *The election of the name thus stands over and against both the gift of the name and the "force" of the name*—yet even as the election supersedes the possibility of "forcing the gift," "force" itself remains present in the passage (*biazesthai*). This residual notion of "force" behind both gift and the possibility of "election" returns in the election scene itself (II.iii), to which we now turn.

Sacred Life and Sacrificial Economy I: Election

Like yet unlike naming and gift-giving, election stands at the center of the play. In the election scene, the play's focus shifts from renominalizing (and phenomenalizing) Coriolanus to what is first termed the people's "voices" (in II.ii–II.iii) but by III.iii has become "the people's name." If Coriolanus's figure is *syncope*, *synecdoche* provides the figure for election—something we have already seen in act 1, as Menenius and the citizens debate the parable of the belly. Etymologically, both "election" (from *ex* + *legare*, "to ordain or appoint") and "exception" (*ex* + *capere*, "to take, seize, choose") describe a process of selection, a taking out.[56] Yet election also carries the register of unbinding or unmaking, (*ex* + *ligere*, "to bind or tie") and in Shakespeare's play the civic rituals of election that should constitute a central ligature in the Republic are themselves unbound, unmade—election becomes the paradigm for exception, particularly when we consider the strange scene of *de*-election (the decision to *rescind* the election) Coriolanus is subjected to in act 3. As a lead-in to the scene of election, though, we must first consider Coriolanus's wounds, the signs or tokens that enable him to stand as candidate:

> VOLUMNIA: There will be large cicatrices to show the people when he shall stand for his place. He received in the repulse of the Tarquin seven hurts i'th'body.
>
> MENENIUS: One i'th'neck and two i'th'thigh—there's nine that I know.
>
> V: He had, before this last expedition, twenty-five wounds upon him.
>
> M: Now it's twenty-seven. Every gash was an enemy's grave. (II.i.123–28)

This interchange between Volumnia and Menenius before Martius's triumphant return to Rome, his re-entry as Coriolanus, points up the ways his wounds, the inscription of his status, also serve as a perverse currency. In an earlier exchange between Volumnia and Virgilia, Volumnia, the martial Roman matron, has already equated the soldier's wounds with mother's milk.[57] In both instances, soldier's blood and mother's milk symbolize the cycle of life and death, in connection with the cycle of commodities and exchange. Martius's wounds mark his superhuman greatness as well as his mortal fallibility and, in Marxist terms, his use-value as well as his exchange-value.[58] To summarize Marx's argument very loosely, we might say that the commodity fetish replaces human labor—and, more explicitly, the *pain* of human labor, "the expenditure of human brain, nerves, muscles, and sense organs"—with an abstract value.[59] Marx tells us that the products of human labor exist fundamentally as a "residue" of human pain and must be understood in terms of "congealed labor-time" (130). Shakespeare's play depicts the reversal of this "congealing" process that leads to the fetishization of the commodity, viscerally reducing exchange to its bare minimum, a human body in pain. Bearing Marx's definitions in mind, we might say that for the citizen-soldier Coriolanus, wounds (both psychic and bodily) serve as both the *sign* of the labor he has performed and the *commodity or product* that he exchanges—for life itself has become the object of an exchange.

The election scene foregrounds this crossing, staging the exchange of the citizens' "words" or "voices" (the power of representation) for Coriolanus's wounds. In the *Life*, Plutarch describes the ritual of soliciting the vox populi as follows:

> Now it was the custom with those who stood for the office to greet their fellow-citizens and solicit their votes, descending into the forum in their toga, without a tunic under it. *This was either because they wished the greater humility of their garb to favour their solicitations, or because they wished to display the* ***tokens*** *of their bravery, in case they bore wounds.* It was certainly not owing to a suspicion of the dispensing of money in bribery that the candidate for the votes of the citizens was required to present himself before them without a tunic and ungirt. For it was long after this time that the buying and selling of votes crept in and money became a feature of the elections. But afterwards, *bribery affected even courts and camps, and converted the city into a monarchy* by making armies the utter slaves of money. For it has been well said that he first breaks down the power of the people who first feasts and bribes them. (XIV.i–iv; emphasis added)

Plutarch's long aside on what the custom is *not* (a reminder of previous bribery and corruption scandals) proves instructive, the quasi-paralipsis here underscoring rather than omitting any connection to bribery and ironically foregrounding what it supposedly seeks to deny. The passage thus underhandedly emphasizes two possibilities that would mean the ultimate contamination of the Republican ideal, bribery facilitating a return to corrupt monarchy. Perhaps more important, though: the word translated as "tokens" here is the Greek *sumbola*, which carries a variety of senses that it is useful to bear in mind. In English, too, "token" can denote either a sign or something to be exchanged for a good or service—these are both derived from Greek senses. But in Greek, *sumbolon* carries a couple of other registers.[60] Its primary sense is of contract, referring to an object that the two parties (*xenoi*, "guest-friends" or "strangers") break, each party keeping one half to signify their agreement; the term also refers to treaties between states. In Aristotle's *Politics*, the symbol is "a permit or licence to reside, given to aliens," thus it both partially incorporates and inevitably divides the alien from the true citizen. It is also an "identity-*token* given to Athenian dicasts [jurists] on entering the courts, entitling them to vote." Finally, in Ecclesiastes 12, it is "the distinctive mark of Christians," the sign of the covenant. In each of the senses that I have highlighted, the *sumbolon* is a sign of exchange and of citizenship, entitling bearers to certain rights but also inevitably marking them, sealing them either as or *not* as members of a polis or nation. Coriolanus's wounds, the symbols or "tokens" of his willing exchange for life or country, recall each of these senses—and, too, point us toward the originary definition of the sacred.

Though Shakespeare followed Plutarch closely for many episodes in the play, he diverges markedly from the *Life* in the election scene. Whereas in Plutarch Coriolanus is perfectly content to exhibit himself in the forum and display the wounds earned in Rome's service, Shakespeare's Coriolanus resists the custom and never does show his wounds (a fact the tribunes later use to incite the citizens against him). Coriolanus is reluctant enough "to hear [his] nothings monstered" before his fellow patricians (II.ii.70), so it is perhaps unsurprising that he positively rebels at the thought of displaying himself in the traditional garment of humility before the plebeians. Though he finally acquiesces to the patricians' demand and agrees to "fit [himself] to the custom" (II.ii.137), the meeting between Coriolanus and the citizens whose "voices" he solicits in spite of his loathing for "their breath" provides one of the more telling intersections between the metaphors of body politic and politicized bodies. As with the final crowd scene, which culminates in Coriolanus's death (V.vi), act 2, scene 3 demonstrates the uneasy balance that exists between Coriolanus, the people, and the state that supposedly incorporates all of them. Repeated images of bodies diseased and mutilated or grown monstrous underscore the dialogic tension, as do tropes for speech distorted or muted; all of these metaphors are intercut and intertwined with the reiterated motif of exchange.

The scene opens with a colloquy among seven or eight citizens in the Roman marketplace—an appropriate site for the exchange, which also bears certain parallels to the space of the theatre itself. As with the "mutinous members" of the body politic in I.i, the citizens in II.iii feel they bear legitimate grudges against Coriolanus and do not hesitate to make them known, mainly that he "[has] not indeed loved the common people" (II.iii.83). However, in spite of their misgivings, the citizens are willing to indicate their "noble acceptance" (II.iii.8) by "giving their voices heartily" (II.iii.92–93).[61] Thus, the "common" render themselves "noble" in the exchange between voices/esteem and wounds/consulship:

> FIRST CIT: Once if he do require our voices, we ought not to deny him.
>
> SECOND CIT: We may, sir, if we will.
>
> THIRD CIT: We have power in ourselves to do it, but it is a power that we have no power to do. For if he show us his wounds and tell us his deeds, we are to put our tongue into those wounds and speak for them; so if he tell us his noble deeds, we must also tell him our noble acceptance of them. Ingratitude is monstrous, and for the multitude to be ingrateful were to make a monster of the multitude, of the which we, being members, should bring ourselves to be monstrous members. (II.iii.1–11)

The citizens' dialogue sets up an exchange, voices for wounds; "speech for" the power to "speak for" as consul; a united body politic miraculously conjured from the ruins of the excoriated body natural. Second Citizen's play on "will" and Third Citizen's play on "power" indicate what this exchange is really about: the will to power, the power to enforce one's will.[62] Third Citizen's grotesque depiction of the spectacular aspect of the exchange is crucial: "For if he show us his wounds and tell us his deeds, we are to put our tongues into those wounds and speak for them" (II.iii.5–7). In this catachrestic exchange, the putting of tongues to wounds obliquely recalls the apostle Thomas's need to place his fingers in Christ's wounds, an analogy that would render Coriolanus a sacrificial victim.[63] Yet like the medieval images that link Christ's wounds with Mary's breast, Third Citizen also suggests a potentially cannibalistic kind of feeding, the citizens suckling from the soldier's wounds—a suggestion that, in its turn, evokes and torques the plebians' initial complaint against the patricians' usurpation of the stores of the "belly politic." The terms of the exchange that the citizens contemplate forge an analogical chain, linking voices-wounds-power or words-wounds; and also, of course, spectacle ("display") and power. Recall here that "noble" must always be read as a pun, for it is a type of coin, and the exchange motif becomes even more complex, removing both the fragmented body politic and the wounded body natural from the scene and replacing them with two abstractions: the commodity fetish and the *virtus* it can supposedly purchase. The noble was the first English gold coin minted in quantity, thus the pun punctures its own sense—if *virtus*, like gold, represents an absolute value, the large-scale production of the noble renders gold increasingly common, thereby metaphorically placing *virtus* itself on the market. Yet as the play repeatedly emphasizes, true "exchange" remains a phantasm.

Sacred Life and Sacrificial Economy II: Exception

In his introduction to *Homo Sacer*, Agamben argues that the idea of the sacred resists or exceeds religion, or at least a religious valuation of sacrifice:

> The protagonist of this book is bare life, that is, the life of *homo sacer* (sacred man), who *may be killed and yet not sacrificed*, and whose essential function in modern politics we intend to assert. An obscure figure of archaic Roman law, in which human life is included in the juridical order [*ordinamento*] solely in the form of its exclusion (that is, of its capacity to be killed), has thus offered the key by which not only the sacred texts of sovereignty but also the very codes of political power will unveil their mysteries. At the same time, however, this ancient meaning of the term *sacer* presents us with the enigma of a figure of the sacred that, before or beyond the religious, constitutes the first paradigm of the political realm of the West. (8–9)[64]

Agamben thus distinguishes between *bare life*, which is also *sacred* life, and *sacrificial* life: while the former is utterly abandoned by the polis, the latter may be constituted as such precisely because it retains an exchange value in the human community. Yet as we shall see, Agamben's decoupling of "bare life" from sacrificial violence erodes part of his Benjaminian foundation.

For Benjamin, I will argue, sacred or natural life is not bare life, as it is for Agamben. Rather, Benjamin's slippery designation comes closer to Jean-Luc Nancy's reminder of the etymological origins of the sacred as that which is "distinct," not analogous to the religious:

> The sacred, for its part, signifies the separate, what is set aside, removed, cut off. In one sense, then, religion and the sacred are opposed, as the bond is opposed to the cut. In another sense, religion can no doubt be represented as securing a bond with the separated sacred. But in yet another sense, the sacred is what it is only through its separation, and there is no bond with it. There is then, strictly speaking, no religion of the sacred. The sacred is what, of itself, remains set apart, at a distance, and with which one forms no bond (or only a very paradoxical one). It is what one cannot touch (or only by a touch without contact). To avoid this confusion, I will call it *the distinct*. . . . The *distinct*, according to its etymology, is what is separated by marks (the word refers back to *stigma*, a branding mark, a pinprick or puncture, an incision, a tattoo): what is withdrawn and set apart by a line or trait, by being marked also as withdrawn [*retrait*].[65]

Nancy's characterization of the sacred as what is *distinct*—stigmatized, marked out—suggests both Cain (about whom I shall say more below) and Coriolanus: each, in his way, abandoned and excoriated, "withdrawn and set apart by a line or trait, by being marked also as withdrawn." Coriolanus's wounds, like Cain's mark, in some ways save him from mob violence, inscribing his military service to Rome on his body even as the body politic abjects him in the initiatory scene of emergent popular sovereignty.

In his "Critique of Violence," Walter Benjamin argues that "all violence as a means is either law-making or law-preserving. If it lays claim to neither of these predicates, it forfeits all validity. It follows, however, that all violence as a means, even in the most favorable case, is implicated in the problematic nature of law itself" (287).[66] In this last portion of this argument, then, I will be drawing on Benjamin's distinction between "law-making" (*rechtssetzend*) and "law-preserving" (*rechtserhaltend*) violence as these processes appear in Shakespeare's play to think about the ways in which both forms inevitably decay until, as Benjamin has it, they "forfeit all validity." If we think of both law-making and law-preserving forms of violence as, at least in their idealistic origins, *generative*, we must then think of the inevitable corruption and decay of these nominally generative functions as *degenerative*, even anti-generative: willfully set against the perpetuation and preservation of life. It is this process of degeneration or decay in which the initial "ends" of law or of the state collapse into the perpetuation of acts of violence for its own sake that I am calling an "economy of pure means"—a cycle of violent exchange in which the perpetrators can no longer hide behind even a nominal claim to engage in acts of violence as a means to some (always deferred, or disputed) lawful end.

Violence thus becomes a self-perpetuating machine, and wounded bodies mount up in an endlessly unfolding vista of means without end. It is on this tragic stage that we witness the emergence of what Benjamin calls "mere life," the creaturely life deprived of the sacred remnant that characterizes the life of man even when it has been stripped of all external attributes of humanity (CV 299).[67] While I draw on Beatrice Hanssen's phrase and her cogent analysis of Benjamin's reconsideration of the Aristotelian dialectic of means and ends here, I want to insist that we consider Benjamin's argument not just in the light of a *politics* of pure means but also as an *economy* of pure means. Though Benjamin describes his own project as belonging to a "philosophy of history," I would assert that thinking of it as a certain analysis of *political economy* takes into account the underlying idea of a perhaps impossible *exchange* that precipitates out of Benjamin's conception of generative versus degenerative violence, and the "divine" or "sovereign" violence that obliterates even this distinction. The impossible exchange that Benjamin's critique circles around, contemplating but never addressing head-on until the very last sentence, is precisely that of sacrifice, the "gift of death."

While the first part of his Kantian critique parses the territories of law-making and law-preserving violence, it is only in the final few paragraphs of Benjamin's analysis that the residues of this untenable exchange can appear. In order to contemplate sacrificial violence, Benjamin introduces a third term, the Hegelian *Aufhebung* of his own dialectic: "divine" or "sovereign" violence, which entirely exceeds the juridical realm and ultimately becomes "law-destroying" (300, 297). In this it is distinguished from what Benjamin calls "mythical violence" (exemplified by the destruction visited on Niobe's children),[68] which ultimately emerges as "law-making," in which the manifestation of divine will (in the form of punishment) enjoins obedience. Of the distinction between mythical and divine violence, Benjamin writes, "If the former sets boundaries, the latter boundlessly destroys them; if mythical violence brings at once guilt and retribution, divine power only expiates; if the former threatens, the latter strikes; if the former is bloody, the latter is lethal without spilling blood" (297).[69] It is this last statement, and specifically Benjamin's insistence on spilled blood as a signifier, that concerns us here, for later in this paragraph Benjamin claims that "blood is the symbol of mere life" (*Denn Blut ist das Symbol des bloßen Lebens*). Divine violence, which is "lethal without spilling blood," both exceeds and ultimately defines the limits of "mere life" itself.

Whereas Benjamin exemplifies the bloody core of mythical, lawmaking violence by turning first to Greek myths (Niobe), divine violence as he defines it here seems most closely linked to the God of Mosaic law, the God of Leviticus, who allows the killing of animals yet prohibits the eating of creaturely blood:

> Therefore I said unto the children of Israel, No soul of you shall eat blood, neither shall any stranger that soujourneth among you eat blood. And whatsoever man *there be* of the children of Israel, or of the strangers that sojourn among you, which hunteth and catcheth any beast or fowl that may be eaten; he shall even pour out the blood thereof, and cover it with dust. For *it is* the life of all flesh, the blood of it is for the life thereof: therefore I said unto the children of Israel, Ye shall eat the blood of no manner of flesh: for the life of all flesh *is* the blood thereof: whosoever eateth it shall be cut off. (Leviticus 17:12–14)[70]

Note here that the prohibition turns on the punishment of banishment; "whosoever eateth [bloody flesh] shall be cut off." Benjamin's statement, "blood is the symbol of mere life," acquires a more complex shading when considered in conjunction with this passage from Leviticus. Benjamin reiterates the claim that blood "*is* the life of all flesh," or, we might also say, blood is the life of all *creatures* (human and animal). At the same time, recall that Benjamin introduces the concept of mere life in a passage in which he defines "divine violence" as "law-destroying"—yet his echoes of Leviticus here covertly reintroduce the specter of law at the very moment he seeks to pin down a violence that utterly escapes the juridical sphere. Divine violence escapes the human scene as well, for as Benjamin renders it here it exists as a force that operates between two absolutely non-human elements, proceeding from a divine origin to a bloodless annihilation that obliterates all traces of the human in its "expiatory" (or, perhaps we might say, "grace-giving"?) ends.

After invoking this hidden scene of Mosaic law, Benjamin continues,

> The dissolution of legal violence stems, as cannot be shown in detail here, from the guilt of more natural life [*natürlichen Lebens*], which consigns the living, innocent and unhappy, to a retribution that "expiates" the guilt of mere life—and doubtless also purifies the guilty, not of guilt, however, but of law. *For with mere life the rule of law over the living ceases. Mythical violence is bloody power [Blutgewalt] over mere life for its own sake, divine violence pure power [reine Gewalt] over all life for the sake of the living. The first demands sacrifice, the second accepts it* (297; emphasis added).[71]

Juxtaposed with "mere life" or creaturely life, then, Benjamin introduces the notion of "natural life"—yet "natural life" here hardly seems differentiated from the "mere life" it supposedly exceeds—"consigned" to legal violence.[72] As Derrida notes, Benjamin's introduction of sacrifice as a common term complicates an otherwise strict distinction between the two modes of violence he addresses; about this I shall say more presently.[73] But "guilt" becomes the condition of possibility of "natural life," and "natural life" thus emerges as, though outside or "purified" of positive law, nevertheless abandoned—vulnerable precisely because it hovers in an extra-juridical zone. "Natural life" thus constitutes one avatar of the state of exception, yet the task of tracing the precise lineaments of its distinction from "mere life" remains.

"With mere life the rule of law over the living ceases," Benjamin continues: mere life, the creaturely life of blood-things, seems too to be both separable and intrinsic to human life itself, the bodily life shared by humans and animals alike. Yet, Benjamin remarks, the bodily life of man is itself excepted from creatureliness, marked by a certain undefinable and equivocal sacrality:

> Man cannot, at any price, be said to coincide with the mere life in him. . . . However sacred man is (or that life in him that is identically present in earthly life, death, and afterlife), there is no sacredness in his condition, in his bodily life vulnerable to injury by his fellow men. What, then, distinguishes it essentially from the life of animals and plants? . . . Finally, this idea of man's sacredness gives grounds for reflection that what is here pronounced sacred was according to ancient mythical thought the marked bearer of guilt: life itself. (299)

Here, then, in Benjamin's final statement, we arrive at a crux: the sacredness of human life attends "the marked bearer of guilt." Guilt, then, becomes the possibility for the "sacred" life that exceeds the "mere life" of creatures, blood-things. This condition recalls Benjamin's previous remarks surrounding "natural life," and we can thus formulate something like an axiomatic proof: if guilt is the condition of "natural life," and guilt is the condition of "what is here pronounced sacred," then we may in a sense equate "natural life" with "sacred life." Guilt, paradoxically, becomes the mark or stigma of the human condition itself; or, perhaps we might say, *the possibility of guilt, and hence the possibility of atonement or rapprochement, becomes the marker of the human condition.*[74]

For this "Benjaminian postulate," natural life = sacred life, doubles back upon itself, turning on the axis of a biblical allusion. "The marked bearer of guilt": to whom can Benjamin refer here but Cain? Cain, not Niobe, thus becomes the exemplar of "the life that what is here pronounced sacred." Cain, marked with blood, guilty of the first blood crime, punished with exile:

> And now art thou cursed from the earth, which hath opened her mouth to receive thy brother's blood from thy hand; When thou tillest the ground, it shall not henceforth yield unto thee her strength; a fugitive and a vagabond shall thou be in the earth. And Cain said unto the Lord, My punishment is greater than I can bear. Behold, thou hast driven me out this day from the face of the earth; and from thy face shall I be hid; and I shall be a fugitive and a vagabond in the earth; and it shall come to pass, that every one that findeth me shall slay me. And the Lord said unto him, Therefore whosoever slayeth Cain, vengeance shall be taken on him sevenfold. And the Lord set a mark upon Cain, lest any finding him should kill him. (Genesis 4:11–16)

The Lord's condemnation casts the crime itself not just as the killing of a person, a creature among creatures, but also against the very earth itself: Cain who had tilled the earth has betrayed the earth; the earth, swallowing Abel's blood, vomits forth Cain's labor. Yet Cain is, as it were, marked for *life* rather than death, the antithesis of *homo sacer*: the Lord's mark saves him from mob violence. The first murderer, Cain's own end is never specified: he "went out from the presence of the Lord, and dwelt in the land of Nod, on the east of Eden," then has a son (Enoch) and builds a city (Enoch).[75] Builder of a city, father of a son: Cain thus becomes a sort of *Herr der Kreaturen*, a ruler, if not a sovereign—like Adam in this, "he is the lord of creatures, but he remains a creature."[76] Infinitely "fugitive and vagabond," he becomes the exponent of a "natural life" bound by an as-yet-unencoded law (the prohibition against murder), preserved yet excepted from the absolute expiation of a divine violence that is also a gift of divine grace.

Each of these biblical scenes that Benjamin covertly invokes thus turn on the violation of prohibition, whether latent or explicit, whose punishment is banishment—yet in the transition from Genesis to Leviticus "banishment" itself acquires new valences, a new absolutism. Cain's exile constitutes an infinitely delayed substitution, an exchange of banishment for death: the mark of Cain thus becomes a cipher of that transaction, the mark of the perpetual exile. Yet though the glyph saves Cain, allowing him to continue existing as a man among men, it forever separates him from the community of his birth—in effect, it becomes a sort of *symbolon*, the token of the exchange of exile for death. In each of these scenes, too, the "natural" life that is also "sacred" life emerges as, though excepted from law, nevertheless covertly bound by law.

In introducing "sacrifice" as an ends for both mythical and divine violence, Benjamin writes that "the first demands sacrifice, the second accepts it" (*Die erste fordert Opfer, die zweite nimmt sie an*) (CV 297; KG 200). "Sacrifice" (*Opfer*) becomes a common term that binds the two modes even as it separates them, yet Benjamin does not elaborate on what he might mean by sacrifice until the final lines of his "Critique"—and even then he does so only obliquely. "Divine violence, which is the sign and seal but never the means of sacred execution, may be called sovereign violence":[77] these are Benjamin's last words (CV 300).[78] "*Heiliger Vollstreckung*": this phrase, rendered by Jephcott as "sacred execution," contains one last ambiguity, a final unresolved point of law. "Sacred execution" suggests sacrifice, that which (we are reminded) divine violence accepts as its due while nevertheless preserving life. Yet *Vollstreckung*, "execution or enforcement," seems to refer us once again to a specifically human scene of law-making and law-preserving, the juridical theatre par excellence. And, too, the bloodless annihilation that is "the sign and seal but never the means of sacred execution"—this exsanguinous expiation seems a sign that remains perpetually withheld, except as it appears in the human realm of law as *exile*, if I have read Benjamin's allusion to Cain aright.

Let us now turn to Agamben's treatment of bare or sacred life. "The protagonist of this book is bare life," Agamben announces in his introduction to *Homo Sacer*, drawing on Benjamin's formulation and aligning it with the Greek term *zoê*. Agamben strictly distinguishes between *zoê* and one other Greek word for life, *bios*, arguing that while the former "expressed the simple fact of living common to all living beings (animals, men, or gods)," *bios* "indicated the form or way of living proper to an individual or a group" (*HS* 1).[79] Agamben, like Nancy, regards sacred life as that which is separate, distinct, "before or beyond the religious" (9). *Homo sacer*, the figure from archaic Roman law that Agamben takes as the exemplar of "bare life," is bound by the paradox of the sovereign decision that suspends law in the name of the law; it is life denuded of even the most basic of political forms, and also the most basic of *religious exchanges*. For *homo sacer* is defined (according to Pompeius Festus, Agamben's source) as life that "is situated at the intersection of a capacity *to be killed and yet not sacrificed*, outside both human and divine law" (73; emphasis added).[80] It is this "intersection"—itself a word that suggests decision and the potential, if not the actual act, of exchange—of the "capacity to be killed and *yet not sacrificed*" that Coriolanus inhabits.

Shakespeare again works certain changes on his source material at a crucial moment, and his variations concern another exchange of death for exile. In Plutarch's account of the "de-election," the citizens (under the leadership of Sicinius in particular) initially condemn Coriolanus to death by being cast from the Tarpeian rock, a form of punishment generally reserved either for the grossest political insurrection or for slaves (XVIII.iv–v.160–63).[81] And in Plutarch's account, the exchange of exile for death—the gift of exile?—occurs only after yet another piece of political theatre, an admixture of trial (*krisis*) and popular election (*psêphos*).[82] Indeed, the primary sense of the Greek *krisis* already incorporates a certain sense of election, or at least selection; it already carries a certain political flavor.[83] Etymologically, *krisis* also suggests the state of exception or emergency and the decision that governs it; the noun derives from the verb *krinein*, the primary sense of which is "to separate, part, put asunder, distinguish" (cf. *caedo* in *decision*).

In Shakespeare's reimagining of this Republican scene Coriolanus himself solicits either ritual death or exile, marking himself out as a potential sacrifice to the city. Though the tribunes pronounce his banishment, Coriolanus's retaliatory abjection lays claim to his own exile:

CORIOLANUS: Let them pronounce the steep Tarpeian death,
Vagabond exile, flaying, pent to linger
But with grain a day, I would not buy
Their mercy at the price of one fair word,
Nor check my courage for what they can give,
To have't with saying "Good morrow." . . .
SICINIUS: —in the name o'th'people
And in the power of us the tribunes, we,
Ev'n from this instant, banish him our city,

In peril of precipitation
From off the rock Tarpeian, never more
To enter our Rome gates. I'th'people's name,
I say it shall be so.

PLEBEIANS: It shall be so, it shall be so! Let him away!
He's banished, and it shall be so! (III.iii.94–114)

At this moment, then, of de-election, de-selection, Sicinius's chiasmic pronunciation of the sentence "in the name o'th'people" / "i'the'people's name" forms a crux, the two caesurae marking time, marking out this reiterated moment of popular ventriloquism. The popular voice is thus disarticulated at its moment of juridical articulation, the chiasmic reversal already partially suggesting Coriolanus's own twist on the sentence:

You common cry of curs, whose breath I hate
As reek o'th'rotten fens, whose loves I prize
As the dead carcasses of unburied men
That do corrupt my air, I banish you.
. . . Despising
For you the city, thus I turn my back.
There is a world elsewhere. (III.iii.128–31, 141–43)

In reappropriating the possibility of a sacrificial death and reclaiming his own exile, Shakespeare's Coriolanus emerges from the scene clothed in yet another new guise, that of "the wolf alone," abandoned, condemned like Cain to seek a stranger's hearth. Banishment thus becomes the condition of possibility for a state of suspended grace, an as-yet-uncertain "world elsewhere." Like Cain "in the land of Nod, on the east of Eden," who begins and begets anew, Coriolanus cannot be called a type of *homo sacer* at this moment: his life retains its sacrificial value even to those who pronounce his exile.

Homo Sacer at the Hearth? Coriolanus's "Elsewheres"

I began this argument by claiming two possibly contradictory things: first, that Coriolanus exemplifies Homer's "tribeless, lawless, hearthless one"; second, that Shakespeare holds out the sense of a potentially or becoming-political "world elsewhere," symbolized by Aufidius's hearth. In this last section, I would like to reconsider these claims, and in so doing to close the circle between "sacred life" and "sacrificial economy."

Let us pause, then, to consider locations. Most of the scenes in Shakespeare's play take place in recognizably public spaces: the battlefield; the marketplace; before the gates of the cities Rome and Corioles. In juxtaposition stands the "domestic" space exemplified in the cozy sewing scene of the women's colloquy in act 1, scene 3. The hearth, though, complicates this apparent distinction between domestic and public spaces, for it is both the avatar of the domestic (personified by the Greek goddess Hestia, or by the Roman Vesta) and a site of potentially public ritual as the refuge of the supplicant. "Tribeless, lawless": when Coriolanus turns his back on Rome and seeks out his sworn enemy, Aufidius, his "world elsewhere" begins in the great hall of Aufidius's house in Antium, and specifically at the hearth. When officious servingmen attempt to hustle him away, Coriolanus rejoins with "Let me but stand. I will not hurt the hearth"; in the meeting with Aufidius, he remarks that "extremity / Hath brought me to thy hearth" (IV.v.24, 75–76). Yet in his riddling play with the two comic servitors, Coriolanus renders this harboring hearth something far more rich and strange. In his initial claim that he "will not hurt your hearth," Coriolanus's consonantal phrase couples together "hurt" and "hearth," turning the refuge of the vulnerable exile itself into a body that can, like the exile himself, be wounded. A few lines thereafter, the hearth becomes "the canopy" (a possible allusion to both the theatre itself or to the canopy over the sovereign's throne—recall Hamlet's "excellent canopy of air"), and the liminal space Coriolanus has inhabited since his exile a "city of kites and crows" (IV.v.36, 40). Coriolanus's reference to "kites and crows," two types of *alites* (birds whose patterns of flight were considered augural indicators), rhetorically relocates him in a public religious sphere even as it indexes his abandonment. Thus Coriolanus brings into the hall, to the very hearth itself, an open and ambiguous space "under the canopy," a sky stitched by the potentially ominous flights of "kites and crows." Even when he has found a temporary "world elsewhere," it seems, Coriolanus remains, in a sense, "hearthless."

Shakespeare himself closes the circle between Rome and Corioles by relocating Coriolanus's death from Antium (where it occurs in Plutarch) to Corioles, and the city that provides Coriolanus with what Aufidius calls his "stol'n name" also proves the site of his ultimate undoing. Yet for Coriolanus "undoing" itself, as James Kuzner notes, constitutes a perverse form of "doing," of potentially-political action.[84] It is in these final moments that I think the now-unnamed Coriolanus truly brings together sacred and sacrificial orders. Even in this extremity, Coriolanus retains a peculiar grace, and it takes the form of a decision. For Aristotle, the capacity for rational choice, *proairesis*, separates the "political animal" from the apolitical realm of "other gregarious beasts" (I.1253a.10–18). Strangely, the only way Coriolanus can truly inhabit a "world elsewhere" is through another act of naming, one that is also a decision: he must lay claim to his own death as he has laid claim to his exile. Hence his heartrending command: "Cut me to pieces, Volsces. Men and lads, / Stain all your edges on me" (V.vi.114–15). In the frenzied carnage that erupts with the cry "Tear him to pieces! Do it presently!" we witness not a scene of ritual sacrificial violence or "sacred execution" but a depraved form of what Benjamin might pronounce "law-preserving violence," a state-sanctioned death pronounced by sovereign decree as soon as Aufidius declares Caius Martius "traitor" and strips him of his given name. But, doubled in death as they have been doubled in Aufidius's dreams, "fisting each other's throat, / and wak[ing] half-dead with nothing," at the very moment of Coriolanus's undoing it is Aufidius who becomes the beast, who renders himself an apolitical animal. Shakespeare's final stage direction reads, "The Conspirators draw and kill Martius, who falls; Aufidius stands on him" (V.vi.132., stage direction 2).[85] This suggestion that Aufidius tramples the corpse of an honored enemy casts him, rather than Coriolanus, utterly outside the bonds of political life, much like Achilles when he drags Hector's body through the dust before the gates of Troy. In this final exchange, the killer becomes the fallen, the sacred becomes profane, *xenos* and *philos* share one face.

The play, like *Hamlet*, closes with a dead march; Aufidius, having recollected himself, pronounces the Fortinbras-like final lines: "Yet he shall have a noble memory. / Assist" (V.vi.156–57). The play closes, but it has left an opening, a momentary glimpse of Rome's "elsewheres"—and what do we make of them? Is Shakespeare's political economy one of sacrifice—that is to say, the *only gift possible*? But as we have seen, there is no gift possible—unless it is the gift of grace, which would depend upon a "divine" or "sovereign" violence, a divine annihilation/expiation—in effect, a deus ex machina.[86] And the only god both inside and outside Shakespeare's Rome, in this play, is Coriolanus himself—the soldier-god, the warlike thing upon whose "grace" Rome's fate depends. The terms "grace" and "graced" occur six times in the course of the play, two of them in Volumnia's speeches (V.iii.121, 150)—yet it is perhaps an earlier usage of the term that is most instructive. Describing Coriolanus's power over Aufidius's men, Aufidius's Lieutenant remarks: "Your soldiers use him as the grace 'fore meat, / Their talk at table, and their thanks at end, / And you are darkened in the action, sire, / Even by your own" (IV.vi.3–6). The Lieutenant's anachronistic analogy (of communion) reminds us of Coriolanus's thingness, and so too of his exchange value: even as he is likened to "grace," it is a grace to be "used" in military service, one linked to both consumption ("'fore meat") and exchange—Coriolanus "darkens" Aufidius in his own men's esteem, his name replacing Aufidius's in their mouths. Rome's "elsewheres" thus seem to me in the end not to lie in the physical, staged space of Aufidius's household, or the not-very-different-from Roman political order seemingly exemplified by the Volscians, but in the much more indeterminate space "under the canopy": a spaceless space we might say accrues to itself the sacred and ultimately unintelligible resonance of "grace" in the play's final act. The election's clamorous reiteration of "voices" and "peace!" sublate, in the last scene, in Volumnia's call for "mercy," for "grace"—both terms that, in their simplest forms, must be considered extrinsic to the human economy of the gift. Those who read Coriolanus's death as "sacrificial"—either effective or failed—posit him as something like Hegel's "world-historical individual," whose demise brings about a new order. In this reading, grace assumes concrete, political form.[87] Yet, I would argue, in the end we are not to be allowed this palliative: what Coriolanus represents, finally, remains a *suspended* grace, a token withheld, a sign never fully either inscribed or understood, even as we are called upon to "assist" in his remembrance.

Chapter Four

The Aesthetics of Messianic Time

Gravity and Grace in *King Lear*

Eskhaton de pantōn hōsperei tō ektrōmati ōphthē kamoi.

—1 Corinthians 15:8

If then, in order to be time at all, the present is so made that it passes into the past, how can we say that this present also "is"? The cause of its being is that it will cease to be. So indeed we cannot truly say that time exists except in the sense that it tends towards non-existence.

—Saint Augustine, *Confessions* XI.xiv.17

Time does us violence; it is the only violence. . . . Time's violence rends the soul: by the rent eternity enters.

—Simone Weil, "Affliction"

[God] comes at his own time.

—Simone Weil, "The Love of God and Affliction"

The weight of this sad time we must obey,
Speak what we feel, not what we ought to say.
The oldest hath borne most; we that are young
Shall never see so much, nor live so long.

—Shakespeare, *King Lear*

What does the question of *aesthetics* have to do with *the politics of exception*, as I've defined it thus far, and what does it have to do with *temporality*? Or to turn the second question around, somewhat: what does temporality have to do with aesthetics, particularly dramatic aesthetics? The philosophical term "aesthetics" derives from the Greek term *aisthêsis*, "perception by the senses"—originally etymologically opposed to *mimesis*, it later comes to incorporate *mimesis* at its very core. At this level, the answer to my first (though doubled) question, seems clear: what *doesn't* aesthetics have to do with temporality? Sense perceptions must of course always be mediated by time. Yet it really is the more complex, post-Kantian sense of the term I want to consider here: to think of aesthetics not just as sense perception but also as the philosophical examination of questions of the beautiful (or of course the sublime)—and most properly, though again simply, the question of *representation*—of aesthetics carrying with it the sense of *mimesis*. Thus my opening question becomes "what does dramatic representation have to do with temporality?" Yet the temporality that concerns me here is not quite the "time" we think of when we think of what can (or can't) be experienced by the senses but what Giorgio Agamben, in his reading of Paul's letter to the Romans, has called "the time that remains": the messianic sense of a "now" both insistently present and insistently looking beyond its own immediacy, to that which is to come.[1]

In his reading of Paul, Agamben argues that the "contracted" time of the now is *unrepresentable*, though not *unthinkable*—this is one of the ways he distinguishes between *ho nun kairos* (the time of now) and the *eschaton* (the end of time), which is representable but *unthinkable* (64).[2] It's precisely this tension between what can be thought and what can be represented (or not) that the "end scenes" in *Lear* open out—yet in Shakespeare's play, even the thought *of* the unrepresentable is split, between rhetorical, textual, and aesthetic figurations. Simone Weil, not unconcerned with questions of temporality and aesthetics, is my touchstone here, for it's her dense, epigrammatic remarks on gravity and grace that I consider in conjunction with Shakespeare's *King Lear* in order to work through the implications of the questions I tentatively pose. Weil herself was fascinated by Shakespeare's play. In one of her last letters to her parents before her death in 1943, Weil wrote of a performance she'd seen in England, comparing herself to the play's fools, whose tragedy lies in the misrecognition of their positions *as* tragic, even as they are the only figures who speak "pure unadulterated truth—luminous, profound, and essential."[3] That is, the fools represent what seemingly lies beyond comprehension; their "truth" brings them closer to what Weil considers all truth.[4]

And there's this:

> All the natural movements of the soul are controlled by laws analogous to those of physical gravity. Grace is the only exception. We must always expect things to happen in conformity with the laws

> of gravity, unless there is a supernatural intervention. . . . Lear, a tragedy of gravity.[5]

So Weil, in the opening pages of the book that her friend and intellectual executor, Gustave Thibon, collected under the title *Gravity and Grace* (published in French in 1947 as *La pensateur et la grâce*).[6] In Weil's argument, only the "ascendant" movements of grace (which she defines as a "supernatural" force opposed to the physical forces of nature, even as she uses the language of physical force to describe it) can work against "gravity," here given both physical and metaphysical properties. "Gravity," for Weil, describes not simply Newton's experience with the apple but the spiritual burdens that attend physical suffering—and, more properly, human life. Suffering, though Weil does not conceive it as entirely redemptive in the sense of *tô pathê mathos*, also maintains a value in her spiritual economy: "We should seek neither to escape suffering nor to suffer less, but to remain untainted by suffering. The extreme greatness of Christianity lies in the fact that it does not seek a supernatural *remedy* for suffering, but a supernatural *use* for it."[7] This question of the use-value of suffering, how it might correlate with the "free gift" of grace, preoccupies me, for it is also a question raised by Shakespeare in *Lear*.[8] It is also the dialectical movement of "gravity *and* grace"—the copula points out that for Weil there's no separating the two, even at their seemingly most distinct—within the play that concerns me here.

On the one hand, borrowing Jonathan Gil Harris's formulation, I want to say that both Weil and Shakespeare offer up images of "palimpsested time"—a metaphor that anchors temporal abstraction via a material artifact, the overscripted text.[9] On the other, though, I would argue that the stratification of aesthetic and textual registers might pressure that formulation. I also want to retreat from Harris's focus on materiality, "objects as the new subjects" of Renaissance studies—a scholarly shift Harris critiques yet also engages in. This is not to suggest a return to apocalyptic readings[10]—the "time" I focus on is not simply the end of time but rather a stratified, punctuated "now" that remains insistently present even in the moment of its passage. Zoning in on *Lear*'s aesthetics—in particular, the differences between texts, the ways the multiple texts rub against the drama they depict, and the gendered valences of spectacle—draws Harris's complex notion of palimpsestic time back toward the *unrepresentable*, that which exceeds or resists mimesis even as it leans most heavily on materialist tropes.[11]

For Weil, "affliction" (*malheur*) provides the most insistent sense of materiality, the reminder of our fleshly presence in the world; yet, paradoxically, affliction also bears within itself the capacity to draw us toward grace. Like Paul's "now," Weil's *malheur* incorporates both a sense of fate, or doom—of that which is to come—and also folds itself around the *heur*, the punctual sense of a specific time, a now.[12] Connecting aesthetics with affliction and messianic time presents a dangerous proposition: a lingering around the potential beauty of suffering, a fetishizing of wounds.[13] *Lear* confronts this hazardous constellation, but *Lear*'s anatomization of the problem works differently from, for example, Marcus's blazon of the raped and mutilated Lavinia in *Titus Andronicus*. In that play, as in *The Revenger's Tragedy*, rhetoric simultaneously aestheticizes and anaesthetizes, creating emotional distance as well as an eerie temporal lapse between what is described and what is experienced. Yet aestheticizing suffering also brings the sufferer *closer* to the viewer or audience, even as it creates a gap between the sufferer and those who consume the suffering—as we shall see when contemplating Goneril's and Regan's deaths, Edmund's subsequent conversion. This doubled paradox itself leads us back to both messianic time, which also depends on the synesthetic sense of presence and absence, living "now" as well as "to come," and to the problems of representation, particularly the gendered representation of affliction.

In the argument that follows, I present Cordelia as a figure for this simultaneous passing away and passing on, both "now" and "to come" in the Pauline sense, whereas Lear stands for the ultimate suspension of either passage. In his *Confessions*, Augustine gnomically remarks of time, "The cause of its being is that it will cease to be. So indeed we cannot truly say that time exists except in the sense that it tends towards non-existence."[14] We might say something similar about art, which works to capture a present and render it into the future. And when it comes to drama, Augustine's remarks warrant special consideration. On the one hand, drama exists primarily *now*—in *this* performance, this immediacy, these bodies moving on a stage saying these words. Drama is also always "ceasing to be" in performance. On the other hand, however, the play *text* (or texts) means that the drama isn't "tending towards non-existence" in the Augustinian sense of time—merely moving toward a different mode, and different audiences—thus we arrive at the different texts of *Lear*, and the question of textual versus dramatic figuration. But in the intersections between Weil's thought and Shakespeare's play, a different problem of figuration emerges: the textual and aesthetic construction of both Weil and Cordelia as saints, and particularly (obvious though it may seem to point this out) as female saints. So, while on the one hand Weil helps us to understand how Shakespeare's treatment of bare life once again exemplifies its gendered underpinnings and consequences, on the other hand, Shakespeare points the way toward a reading of Weil that takes into account repressed elements of her own thought that continue to shape her textual afterlives.

Conversion and the Ends of Aesthetics: *Lear*, Caravaggio, Paul

I begin this analysis with a scene of conversion, in its strict etymological sense of a turning *with*—a radical torsion that nevertheless entails a strange sense of accompaniment or new fellowship (and not always in a comfortable or entirely settled way). Near the end of Shakespeare's *King Lear*, the moment of what we might call Edmund's conversion occurs after the metatheatrical display of Goneril's and Regan's bodies. The scene turns upon a series of spectacular revelations and subsequent obfuscations, beginning with the entrance of the Gentleman bearing (in the Quarto) "a bloody knife" (Q 24; F 5.3).[15] In a play much concerned with the distinction between what constitutes true affliction and what might be considered only "an image of that horror," the bloody knife conflates the two, both implement and image of horror. A phenomenalized version of Macbeth's phantom dagger, the Gentleman's knife serves as both material reminder and metaphysical cue, pointing both back to the bloody deeds it synecdochically recalls and forward to what lies ahead (or beyond). "'Tis hot, it smokes, / It came even from the heart of—O, she's dead!" (F 5.3.222–23): the broken lines culminating in the Gentleman's indeterminate proclamation don't really culminate at all, except in a further suspension of knowledge. We don't yet know who's dead, and Albany's testy demand, "Who dead? Speak, man" (F 5.3.224) draws out the delay.[16]

It's a scene of what we might term extreme spectacle, though not in the same way as Gloucester's blinding, one that shifts and resettles around Albany's command "Produce the bodies, be they alive or dead" (F 5.3.228; Q 24.225), and the stage direction about the display of Goneril's and Regan's bodies. In the Quarto, the now-undisguised Kent breaks in upon Albany's meditations on "the judgement of the heavens" and "the time [that] will not allow / The compliment that very manners urges." In the Folio, Kent's entrance is delayed, and Albany's lines are followed by the stage direction *Goneril's and Regan's bodies brought out*. The Quarto version makes somewhat more sense in terms of staging, for Albany's "O, 'tis he; the time will not allow / The compliment that very manners urges" can only refer to Kent, who in the Quarto enters before his lines (Q 24.228–29). I want to pause a moment on Albany's lines, particularly his suggestion that "the time will not allow / the compliment"; that is, the exigencies of the situation don't permit ordinary courteous behavior. Of all the normative acts omitted or suspended during the state of emergency, the proper greeting of Kent perhaps shouldn't strike us as particularly important—yet, like the Gentleman's bloody knife, this suspension of courtesy points toward something more. Homophonically, the line may also sound as "the time will not allow / *the complement*"—and it's precisely this sense of the potential *complement* of time, time added to itself yet also always doubling back on itself, suspended in a shocking instant yet pushing beyond that instant to contemplate "the object" at its core, at which Albany's line already hints.

The metadramatic momentum is also more pronounced in the Quarto, where Albany's "Seest thou this object, Kent?" (l. 235) occurs immediately after the bodies are returned to the stage. *This* object: despite their distinct modes of death, Regan and Goneril "contract" into one body, echoing Edmund's horrified recognition of a temporally disjunctive ménage à trois when the knife is brought in: "I was contracted to them both; all three / Now marry in an instant" (Q 24.223–24; F 5.3.227–28). The display of Regan's and Goneril's bodies representationally enacts the contraction or conflation that Lear's misogynistic rants and curses rhetorically suggested since the beginning, rendering one woman's body indistinguishable from another's. In the Quarto, the stage direction occurs after Albany demands of Edmund what's become of Lear and Cordelia: *The bodies of Goneril and Regan are brought in*. "The instant" Edmund contemplates, then, stretches to encompass the display of the bodies: "the object" becomes the *true* "instant," but the inertia of the sisters' bodies is immediately superseded by Edmund's conversion, his turning *with* that is also a *turning away*, an apostrophe. This apostrophe begins with an act of obfuscation that counters the initial acts of display, or at least with the suggestion that this will occur: Albany, again, gives the order to "[c]over their faces" (Q 24.238). Albany's line returns "*this* [singular] object" or vignette to its plurality, "*their* faces"—yet this plurality may be reasserted only in the very act of covering it over. Cover their faces, not their bodies: their bodies remain "contracted," a singular effigy of monstrous femininity, now rendered doubly indistinct by the draping of their individual features. These doubled movements—revelation and obfuscation, singularity and pluralism, suspension and conversion—shape the rhythms of the play throughout, but it is in the end scenes that both the textual variants and the multiple valences of spectacle become increasingly insistent, and in which the now-dead bodies of Lear's three daughters provide a locus for thinking about the problems I identified earlier.

The covering of the sisters' faces (presuming Albany's order is obeyed) slides immediately into Edmund's turn, which is also a doubled turn: toward "some good," away from the audience (the first line and a half seemingly spoken as an apostrophe or aside, though no stage direction indicates it):

> I pant for life. Some good I mean to do,
> Despite of my own nature. Quickly send,
> Be brief in't, to th'castle; for my writ
> Is on the life of Lear and on Cordelia.
> Nay, send in time. (Q 24.239–43; F 5.3.241–45)

Throughout the scene, Edmund has been focused on time compressed, contracted: "all three / Now marry in an instant" here turns to his frenzied attempts to head off the letter that dooms Lear and Cordelia. The erotic "contract" that Edmund imagines binding him to both Regan and Goneril dissolves in the very "instant" he announces it, and the contract he's now concerned with is the "writ"—that is, the death warrant for Lear and Cordelia (the "note" he had sent with them to prison). Yet how is it that Edmund, of all figures perhaps the least likely to be accounted king, except according to the "natural" sovereignty he proclaims, has the juridical authority to subscribe the death warrant?[17] In the muddled end time of the play, the question of sovereignty is of course even more complicated by the textual differences (in both Quarto and Folio, Albany orders Kent and Edgar to "[sustain] this gored state," and Kent refuses the office; yet the last lines of the play are spoken by Edgar in the Quarto, Albany in the Folio). Edmund, both before and after his dual turn, acting as shadow sovereign, with the right to punish or pardon, gives way to Kent's sovereign decision to renounce sovereignty, in his famously ambiguous final couplet "I have a journey, sir, shortly to go: / My master calls, and I must not say no" (Q 24.316–17; F 5.3.320–21).[18] The problem of vexed sovereignty that began the play also ends it, and the question of who's in charge at the end remains entangled with the question of conversion—but what do we make of this?

I want to answer this question by returning to the juxtaposition of temporality and aesthetics I posed initially, reapproaching both Weil and *Lear* by way of a reading of a painting by Caravaggio, one of two visions of the conversion of Saint Paul. Caravaggio completed both works, *The Conversion of Saint Paul on the Road to Damascus* (at the Odescalchi

Balbi Collection, Rome) and *The Conversion of St. Paul* (in the Cerasi Chapel of Santa Maria del Popolo, Rome), between 1600 and 1601 (see plate 4). The Cerasi painting is generally taken to be later in composition, simultaneously more enigmatic and somehow more complete, the more interesting to art historians—particularly because it does not include the summoning presences of Christ and the angel.[19] In Caravaggio's distinctively propulsive way, each painting depicts an example of what Alain Badiou has called "the Event," a literal "enlightenment" or moment of conversion, a moment suspended in time that, in turn, becomes the defining moment in the Pauline conception *of* time.[20] Any painting must of course choose its moment, but Caravaggio's insistent juxtapositions of stasis and frenetic motion exemplify the paradox of the Event, which simultaneously locates itself in an instant of fractured time and reorders the subsequent conception of time accordingly. In Caravaggio's works, this temporal dislocation manifests itself spatially—for example, in the contorted figure of the horse (in both), or the nearly "orthogonally foreshortened" figure of Saul,[21] in the Cerasi version.

But I would like to consider the more crowded Odescalchi painting, which depicts a man of seeming middle age thrown violently to the ground. This Saul/Paul appears nearly naked, his military garb oddly flesh-toned but for the crimson pool of his cloak, blinded by and bathed in a strange sourceless light as his companions reach out to assist him while his oddly distorted horse struggles to escape this apparent disaster. Here the thrusting lines of the fallen Saul's sword, his companion's spear, and the supplicating angel's arm intersect with the lines of the horse's right hind leg, his companion's strongly planted left leg, the companion's raised shield, and the curving branch that apparently floats, trunkless, across the painting's upper quarter. This line, in turn, oddly bisects the horse's body, so that the head, impossibly contorted on an absent neck, turns to gaze outside the painting's frame, toward yet beyond the source of the illumination that paralyzes Saul.

The horse's calm gaze (despite the straining mouth and agitated hindquarters) presents, in effect, the only stable point of reference in the painting, contrasting with Saul's tormented movement, his momentary blindness.[22] In this the horse perhaps resembles the ram whom Saint John caresses in a nearly contemporaneous painting. Walter Friedlaender reminds us that Saul's horse enjoys an important place in the Renaissance pictorial tradition (e.g., Michelangelo and Raphael), though there's no mention of him in the various accounts of Saul's conversion in the Acts.[23] The horse sees what the man cannot, yet at the same time appears decapitated (never forgetting Caravaggio's self-referential severed heads, such as Goliath,

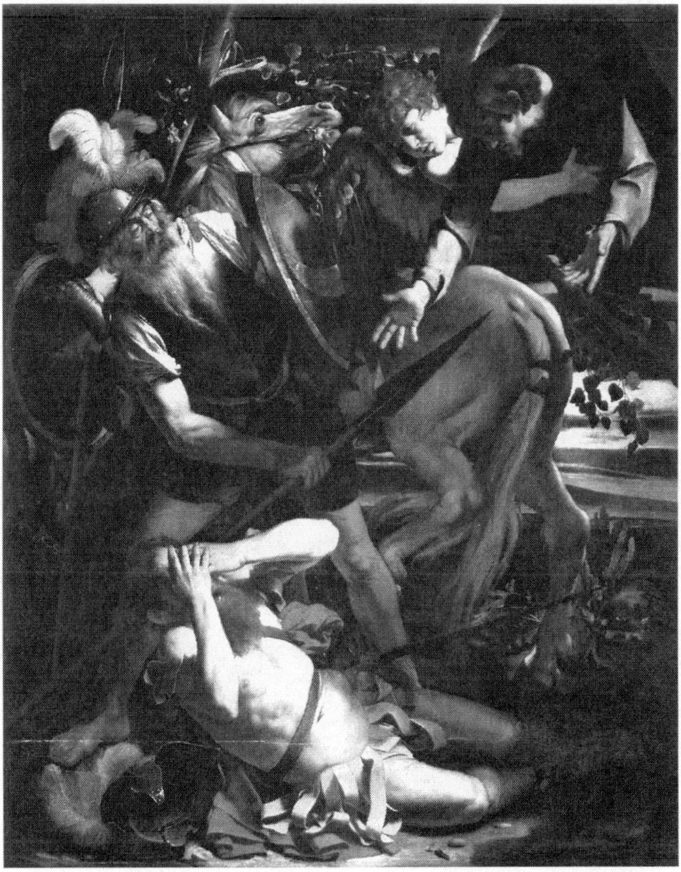

Plate 4. Michelangelo Merisi da Caravaggio, *The Conversion of Saint Paul* (ca. 1600/1601). Coll. Odescalchi Balbi di Piovera, Rome, Italy. By kind permission of Scala/Art Resources, NY.

Medusa, or Holofernes),[24] his shadowed head floating in the same plane as the heads of Christ and the angel. The horse's head perhaps thus represents the fallen Saul's conversion, the upward-thrusting movement that severs him from his past—yet *he's a horse*! What would it mean to say that the horse is the one who's really converted here? That all the fallen Saul depicts is, precisely, that blindness, that fall?

Or, perhaps, more precisely: that both the horse and Saul are converted, that the stallion's simultaneous strain and elevation, the violent contortions resolved in the serenely lifted gaze, give us the moment *after* the moment of conversion—the instant of the shift from Saul, Persecutor, to Paul, Apostle—yet, again, *he's a horse*! The moment after the moment, then, is still a moment of uncertainty, of disequilibrium, in which enlightenment reveals first, perhaps, the profoundly inhuman or bestial nature of the instant of intense doubt or self-erasure that must attend (or precede?) conversion.

Caravaggio's vision of conversion, then, offers up a representational split—for it is the stallion, that trope of the pictorial and not the textual tradition, who most clearly recalls Paul's oblique reference to his own conversion, his straining toward yet against the engulfing call, in Philippians 3:13–15: "One thing I do, forgetting what lies behind and straining toward [*epekteinomenos*] what lies ahead, I press on toward the goal for the prize of the upward call of God in Christ Jesus. Let those of us who are mature [*teleioi*] be thus minded; and if in anything you are otherwise minded, God will reveal that also to you." Paul's term *teleioi*, translated here as "mature," itself means "ended, finished, complete, perfect"; the claim reworks his own assertion in 1 Corinthians, "Last of all, *as to one untimely born*, he appeared also to me [*Eskhaton de pantōn hōsperei tō ektrōmati ōphthē kamoi*]. For I am the least of the apostles, unfit to be called an apostle, because I persecuted the church of God" (15:8–9). *As* to "one untimely born" (*tō ektrōmati*): the converted Paul's simile rhetorically distances himself from his prior incarnation even as he most recalls it, offering himself as an example of conversion. Yet this brief account of Paul's conversion—what might be said to be the *beginning* of the story he tells—also offers a truncated, proleptic rendering of the universal experience of the end (*eskhaton*). In typical Pauline fashion, even his personal *eskhaton* appears only indirectly, *as* appearance (*ōphthē*)—in passive voice no less (a clunkily literal translation of the phrase *ōphthē kamoi* might rather be "and to me also appeared him").

Paul figures the moment of conversion as a rending of both temporal-spatial perception and the self, which we see most clearly in the analogy "as to one untimely born [*tō ektrōmati*]." Paul's conversion, the moment of birth, incorporates a lexical doubleness, for *ektrōma* can reference either a living child, born before its time, or an abortion or miscarriage. The analogical violence Paul describes is deepened when we consider the etymological origins of the term he employs: he approaches his indirect end literally "out of trauma," out of a wound or hurt.[25] In this way Paul's "untimely birth" both articulates and complicates his "straining toward what lies ahead," a double movement we can see even in the paradoxical prefix (*epi* + *ek*, "*on*" but also "*out of*"[26])—the moment of conversion, of certainty, of coming to rest anew, incorporates always its own potential for movement *away from* certainty, away from the perfected appearance of the end.[27]

In his reading of the letter to the Romans, Agamben defines messianic time as, in his eponymous phrase, "the time that remains." Agamben distinguishes thus between *chronos* and *kairos*:

> First, you have secular time, which Paul usually refers to as *chronos*, which spans from creation to the messianic event (for Paul, this is not the birth of Jesus, but his resurrection). Here time contracts itself and begins to end. But this contracted time, which Paul refers to in the expression *ho nun kairos*, "the time of the now," lasts until the *parousia*, the full presence of the Messiah.[28]

Agamben translates Paul's *ho kairos sunestalmenos* (1 Corinthians 7:29) as "contracted time"—a phrase elsewhere translated as "*time is straitened*," or, prosaically, "the appointed time has grown very short."[29] *Ho nun kairos*, "the time of the now," directly links with Paul's representation of the traumatically unrepresentable or "untimely" sense of his own conversion, for both remain infinitely split, poised and quivering, impaled by what is (in Paul's literal term, in any case) first perceived as a *wound*, yet simultaneously passed through the trauma, into whatever unknown lies beyond. My point here is not to quibble with Agamben's rendering of *sunestalmenos*, which seems to me admirably suited to both the context of Paul's remarks and his own argument. It is perhaps interesting to note, however, that the verb *sustellô* often denotes a sense of contraction or coming together, even "huddling together" (or, in a nautical context, "drawing sail"), that specifically implies a perceived threat or trauma—hence we return, once again, to the perhaps inevitable sense of a rift or wound that attends conversion.

It is Paul's linked metaphors, the simultaneous "contraction" of time and the "stretching out" of the convertant, that raise for me the question of the aesthetic—or, perhaps more properly, the question of representation, and its limits. And, too, it is the stratification of time and timelessness that leads me to connect Paul with Shakespeare's play, itself probably written less than five years after Caravaggio's Paul paintings (ca. 1605, though not published in quarto until 1608). Later in 1 Corinthians, Paul returns to the *telos*: "Brothers, do not be children in your minds[;] in evil be as infants, but be mature [*telioi*] in your minds [*Adelphoi, mē paidia ginesthe tais phresin, alla tē kakia nēpiazete, tais de phresin teleioi ginesthe*]."[30] With Paul's focus on the new "maturity," the sense of ending or perfection, offered by conversion we might also proleptically recall Lear's last lines, and the question of "maturity" (age plus experience) in the play: "The oldest hath born most; we that are young / Shall never see so much, nor live so long" (F 5.3.324–25). These lines also end on the difficulty that attends "seeing": here, experience, with of course the attendant reminder of the blindness both literal and metaphorical that scores the play—but it also raises, for the last time, the play's difficulty coming to terms with its own aesthetic ideology—but about this I'll say more presently. Back to the horse for a moment: the horse, not yet the fallen Saul, most fully figures the becoming-Paul's *epekteinomenos*, his "straining forward to what lies ahead." And just as the stallion stretches himself out, gazing beyond the frame of the painting and attenuating into the light, while Saul/Paul remains, baffled and blinded, on the ground, so the moment-after-the-moment that the stallion represents becomes an infinite moment, a suspended movement that yet suggests the moment and the movement to come.

"How soon is now?": Distending Lear's "Promised Ends"

> The end is but a moment only of death.
>
> —Emmanuel Lévinas, *God, Death, and Time*

In her apothegmatic late writings, Simone Weil uses the language of physics and mathematics ("laws," "forces") as analogies for the indefinable. In some ways, both "gravity" and its apparent opposite, "grace," always elude definition—where "forces" can be pinned down or at least rendered recognizable (and thus, to a certain extent, conceptually manipulable) by "laws," neither gravity nor grace submits to human cognition. Hence "gravity" itself, she writes, "is, as it were, a symbol of" the difficulties of suffering, particularly suffering Weil describes as "base" (46). Yet it's *grace* she wants to approach via gravity, which itself remains intangible, unapproachable, merely a "symbol" for the profound unrepresentability of suffering. Grace, doubly displaced by the "symbol," the "as it were" of suffering, remains forever outside the limits of representation.

Yet suffering is also "superflux," for Weil as for Lear. Consider, for example, Lear's "prayer" on the heath:

> Poor naked wretches, whereso'er you are,
> That bide the pelting of this pitiless storm,
> How shall your houseless heads and unfed sides,
> Your looped and windowed raggedness, defend you
> From seasons such as these? O, I have ta'en
> Too little care of this. Take physic, pomp,

> Expose thyself to feel what wretches feel,
> That thou mast shake the superflux to them
> And show the heavens more just. (F 3.4.28–36; Q 11.25-33)

These lines align the deprived king with both biblical and classical antecedents. Like Job, like Philoctetes, Lear is "naked," houseless, exiled—like Job, and unlike Philoctetes, though, his friends attend him in his sufferings, allowing for a civil company, a "naked fellowship" that effectively rescripts political bonds. Even and perhaps especially in this moment of extremity, Lear's language assumes a poetic intensity, most apparent in the question he asks his fellow "naked wretches": "How shall your houseless heads and unfed sides, / Your looped and windowed raggedness, defend you / From seasons such as these?" Piti-less, un-fed, house-less, raggedness, super-flux: in this pileup of neologistic verbal prostheses, Lear's lack becomes "superflux"—he clothes his nakedness of condition in a gorgeous excess of words.[31] Yet if we scan the lines, Lear's superflux partially negates itself in the very moment of enunciation, or at least it must if the lines are to be forced into any sort of regular meter—the line "Your looped and windowed raggedness, defend you," in particular, would contain at least one extra-metrical syllable without spoken elision. "Thus plenty makes me poor," the old saw goes—and in these lines, the "plenty" of Lear's rhetorical *copia* simultaneously enforces and is subsumed by the "poverty" the lines express.

Lear's experience of the storm provides an example of what Weil terms the violence of time, for affliction produces an artificial infinity—the sense that pain knows neither beginning nor end: "There is a point in affliction where we are no longer able to bear either that it should go on or that we should be delivered from it," she writes.[32] Weil wants to use this artificial infinity to come closer to *the* infinite—to God, the "supernatural intervention" or "help" that allows the sufferer to pass corporeal and temporal limits.[33] Hence her insistence at the end of "Gravity and Grace": "Creation is composed of the descending movement of gravity, the ascending movement of grace, and the descending movement of the second degree of grace. *Grace is the law of the descending movement*" (48; emphasis added). The paradoxical notion of the "second degree of grace"—grace taken to its highest power, to use a different algebraic metaphor—as *descendant*, rather than transcendent, motion—offers a corollary for Lear's oft-remarked transformation.

Weil distinguishes between purely corporeal suffering and affliction, which strikes not just at the body but assails and deadens life at its very core:

> Affliction is an uprooting of life, a more or less attenuated equivalent of death, made irresistibly present to the soul by the attack or immediate apprehension of physical pain. If there is complete absence of physical pain there is no affliction for the soul, because our thoughts can turn to any object. Thought flies from affliction as promptly and irresistibly as an animal flies from death. . . . There is not real affliction unless the event that has seized and uprooted a life attacks it, directly or indirectly, in all its parts, social, psychological, and physical. The social factor is essential. There is not really affliction unless there is social degradation or the fear of it in some form or another.[34]

In Weil's insistence on the *social* element of affliction we can almost see Lear (as well as Job, Weil's exemplar for what she calls this "acute state" of affliction) standing within the lines—perhaps the most clear parallel would be his impassioned speech to Regan and Goneril, just before he casts himself into the storm (F 2.2.453–75):

> O, reason not the need! Our basest beggars
> Are in the poorest things superfluous;
> Allow not nature more than nature needs,
> Man's life is cheap as beast's. Thou art a lady;
> If only to go warm were gorgeous,
> Why, nature needs not what thou gorgeous wear'st,
> Which scarcely keeps thee warm. But for true need—
> You heavens, give me that patience, patience I need!
> (F 2.2.453–60)

As with the rhetorical "superflux" that characterizes his prayer on the heath, the repetition of Lear's naked "need" melts into the superfluity it apparently stands against. Lear's plea plays upon a series of syntactic and poetic parallels: "reason not"/"allow not"; "basest beggars"/"poorest things"; finally, perhaps, the two caesurae, "Thou art a lady / But for true need," and even a third, "patience I need." These negatively accretive phrases frame two seemingly contrasting central conceits: the beastly life of pure necessity versus the feminine excess of Regan's "gorgeous" apparel (line 456). Yet the line itself links the bestial and the feminine; the missing "as" in the first comparison makes its ghostly appearance in the caesura coupling the beast and the lady.[35]

In Weil's aesthetic schema, which bears the marks of both Plato and Kant, the beauty of the world serves as both sign and signified—that which has the potential to bring us closer to God yet also that which might obscure our attempts to focus on a divine removal rather than a fleshly present.[36] In this she also comes close to Paul's overlapped dialectics of flesh and spirit, letter and spirit, and to Paul's call for patience in the face of suffering, waiting in the now: "For I account the sufferings of the present time [or "the time of now," *ta pathêmata tou nun kairou*] not comparable with the splendors to be revealed to us in the future. . . . For all of creation groans together and travails together until now."[37] In the space of a few verses, Paul's "now" is temporally split: while we are suffering "in the now" (*ta pathêmata tou nun kairou*), we are also "groan[ing] and travail[ing] *until* now [*arxi tou nun*]." Now remains simultaneously present and passing away. Indeed, Weil's *attente* seemingly points toward Paul's *hupomonês apekdexometha*,[38] an almost redundant phrase that reduplicates its own attenuation (Romans 8:25). But when Paul speaks of waiting here he employs yet another metaphor of birth—or, in this case, not of birth but of "adoption," *huiothesian*—specifically, "adoption as sons."[39] This term proleptically sediments Paul's distinctions between "children of the flesh" (*tekna tês sarkos*) and "children of the spirit" (*tekna tês epaggelias*, better translated as "children of the promise") in Romans 9:8. The attendant metaphor of spiritual filiation, "adoption as sons" (*huiothesian*), in Romans 8:23 recalls the earlier "sons of God" (*huoi theou*) in Romans 8:15. Paul's analogy argues that the fleshly sign of living under the law (i.e., circumcision) no longer matters, that children of the promise (of hope, of grace) require no such corporeal inscriptions, though those who bear the mark of the law—the mark of the missing, of the remnant, of the detached flesh—are of course fundamental to the newly grafted *ekklesia*. So his argument about "children of the promise" rhetorically erases the mark of the law. Yet his attendant claims that all who heed the call will be "adopted as sons" performs a ghostly reinscription of the law, reasserting gendered differences and the potential for exclusion at the very moment he is describing the utter inclusiveness (the universality) of grace.

This transition between "children" and "sons" disappears from view in Badiou's treatment of Paul's "universal" call,[40] yet I want to insist on retaining that difference. In contrast to Badiou's claim that "for Paul, one is either a slave or a son" (49), I am arguing that for Paul one must be *both* a slave and a son. That is, despite the fact that unlike *pais*, which usually means "a human child" (whether boy or girl) and is a word Paul rarely uses, *teknon* is more truly a *zoêpolitical* term, for it can refer to either a male or a female child, or to the young of animals. It just means "that which is born," though it is most often translated "son." It indexes creatureliness, a common vulnerability, as well as the unfolded possibilities of gender that *huios* will foreclose. However, Paul's "adopted sons" may not be circumcised, but they are circum*scribed*, rewritten as masculine subjects (or, to use Paul's own introductory phrase, "slaves to") the undead Christ.

Paul's waiting, then, assumes an explicitly gendered cast that Weil's seemingly does not—a sense that is profoundly relevant when we think about Shakespeare's play. *Lear*'s focus on unnatural versus natural orders encompasses both monarchic and familial lineages, as well as a complex of other senses (natural as idiot, e.g., Edgar as Poor Tom). Thus "adoption" profoundly plays into the question of what constitutes natural orders of succession—father to sons, father to daughters, king to king—within the play, particularly the question of Edmund's "natural" birth as a bastard, Gloucester's "adoption" of Edmund when he repudiates Edgar, Lear's dispossession of Cordelia, "new-adopt[ing her] to [his] hate" (1.192). Paul's focus is also on the visible, or rather the invisible—on what we cannot *see* (*blepō*) but must expect and hope for anyway. Waiting is thus tied to the invisible, the unseen—or, we might also say, the unrepresentable, even as it is also metaphorically bound to "adoption"—for Paul, "hope" means that we must wait for this "adoption as sons" without being able to see what we are waiting for.[41]

But is it fair to connect Lear with Weil's, and Paul's, *attente de dieu*, especially here? That is to say, *is* Lear "waiting for God"? This of course is a version of the redemptive versus apocalyptic reading question, but it is also a way of reading skepticism itself skeptically. Lear's initial desire to "unburdened crawl towards death" (F 1.1.39–40) does not have any messianic expectation attached to it—precisely the opposite. But perhaps this is the connection, because God is in some sense a *burden*, for Weil. The word *attente* itself, the drawn-out, endlessly progressive "waiting," leads us back to Lear, for the play's "end time" ends up infinitely distended,[42] a temporal and dramatic attenuation figured at the end by Lear's suffering body, stretched upon the rack of the world:

> LEAR: Break, heart, I prithee break.
> EDGAR: Look up, my lord.
> KENT: Vex not his ghost. O, let him pass. He hates him
> That would upon the rack of this tough world
> Stretch him out longer.
> [*Lear dies*]
> EDGAR: O, he is gone indeed. (Q 24.305–9)

Or, in the Folio,

> KENT: Break, heart, I prithee break.
> EDGAR: Look up, my lord.
> KENT: Vex not his ghost. O, let him pass. He hates him
> That would upon the rack of this tough world
> Stretch him out longer.
> EDGAR: He is gone indeed. (F 5.3.288–90)

"Break, heart, I prithee break. / Look up my lord": The broken line, distributed between Lear and Edgar (Quarto) or Edgar and Kent (Folio), formally enacts the break it solicits (and if Lear in fact dies on the line, we could even call it a performative speech act), while Kent's "He hates him / That would upon the rack of this tough world / Stretch him out longer" is on one level supremely ironic, read as a rejoinder to the "stretched" and broken line that precedes it. And the heartrending final image of Lear stretched upon the rack, suspended between beats and breaks, offers only an *image* of horror, Kent's rhetorical approximation of Lear's profoundly unrepresentable suffering. Kent's metaphor renders up Lear's unrepresentable, onomatopoeaitic "Howl, howl, howl, howl!" which opened this final tableau, *figuring* it. Lear's reiterated "howl," like the iterative "image of that horror," mimetically depicts the limits of representation—precisely because it is neither mimetic nor diagetic. In a strange way, then, these rhetorically distended yet unrepresentable moments become the play's corollary of the non-representable in Caravaggio's painting. Just as conversion can be depicted only *indirectly*, split between the moments of prequel (Saul striving *not* to see) and sequel (the stallion's calm gaze beyond the frame of the painting itself—toward that which *exemplifies* the unrepresentable), so the play's simultaneously "stretched" and "contracted" poetics of the end (even without considering the textual variants) enacts the representational crises it foregrounds.

The play's closing lines, we recall, begin with an invocation of time: "The weight of this sad time we must obey / Speak what we feel, not what we ought to say" (F 5.3.322–23). Necessity calls, in other words—we who remain must make something of this mess, reknit ourselves in some way, despite the bodies of our loved ones littering the stage. It's a moment of textual instability (in the Quarto, the lines are spoken by Albany, in the Folio, by Edgar), thus also a call for editorial or directorial interpretation. This ultimate call to heed the pressure of impending time is at its most basic level a political one, but we must also connect it to an earlier moment of questioning—one that is arguably both theological and aesthetic: "Is this the promised end?" Kent wonders when confronted with the terrible spectacle of Lear bearing the body of Cordelia in his arms. "Or image of that horror?": Edgar responds by not responding, with a second question.[43] Kent's oddly jarring question, and Edgar's oddly aestheticized rejoinder, elicit a pause: a moment of questioning, a moment of doubt. The "promised end" for Paul is of course the resurrection, and Kent's question seems to invoke this messianic framing, something the closing call will do more explicitly. Yet both question and call remain uncertain, an unsettled "end" that reflects the skeptical impulse underlying the entire play, and it is to this moment that both *precedes* and *exceeds* a moment that I now turn.[44]

Misogyny and Messianic Time: "Woman" and Representation

> Beauty is a fruit which we look at without trying to seize it. The same with an affliction which we contemplate without drawing back. A double movement of descent: to do again, out of love, what gravity does. Is not the double movement of descent the key to all art?
>
> —Simone Weil, "Beauty" in *Gravity and Grace*

From the end to the beginning: like Paul's account of his conversion, *Lear* opens with a recollection of an untimely birth—Edmund's—and Gloucester's bawdy "do you smell a fault?" indexes the untimely in terms of the feminine grotesque (Q 1.1–16; F. 1.1.1–16). Gloucester's focus on his dead mistress's "fault" opens out the abyssal misogynistic logic that characterizes both the "now" of Paul's letters (particularly, perhaps, the letter to the Romans) and the play's own contorted messianic aesthetics, and this last section analyzes the peculiar conjunctions of these movements in Weil's thought as well as in the play. At the end I turn to Jacques Rancière, who reminds us in several recent works that the interconnection of aesthetics and politics cannot be ignored, today more than ever.[45] Though he argues against any "communitarian" conception of art's political potential in either utopian universalist or "micro-political" (i.e., identity-based) capacities, Rancière insists on a conceptual link between art and public life via their ability to rezone space and time, both physically and symbolically. Tracing the philosophical conjunctions between politics and aesthetics back to Plato's *Republic*, Rancière allows for drama's privileged place in this intertwined intellectual history, arguing that "theatre and assembly" constitute "two interdependent forms of the same distribution, two spaces of heterogeneity."[46] Moreover, Rancière's understanding of the radical *inoperability* of art in what he terms "the representative regime" grounds itself first of all in a reading of a play (Corneille's *Oedipe*). Though Rancière repeatedly insists on the non-periodicity of his schematic rendering of the three interpretive "regimes" of art he defines (ethical, representative, and aesthetic), again and again his examples *do* attest to the period-specific temporality of his claims—hence the "ethical" regime finds its example in classical tragedy; the "representative" incorporates both neoclassical and Romantic art; and the "aesthetic" (which, Rancière declares, founds itself on no "modern rupture") nevertheless might be located most clearly in what seems to be "our own" now, the now that is even now passing away. While Shakespeare and his contemporaries are (perhaps unsurprisingly) left out of this non-period-specific, highly periodic narrative about competitive interpretive regimes, I take up some of Rancière's terms in what follows.

Both Weil and Cordelia have been read as female saints.[47] Critics and lovers alike attribute to each both the usual martyrological qualities of sacrifice, suffering, and *deprivation*[48]—but also an always potentially erotic treatment of submissiveness in general, and female submissiveness in particular.[49] This returns us, yet again, to the question of *representation*—women as the most perfect aesthetic embodiment of suffering, perhaps sexualized in their abjection.[50] Famously, of course, we could point to Lacan's reading of Bernini's *Saint Teresa*—though this is visionary ecstasy, not the scene of suffering—yet what I am arguing here is that we can hardly separate the two, at least when it comes to reading Cordelia's place in *Lear*, and, correspondingly, though less obviously, when it comes to reading Weil. In an essay on Marlowe's *The Jew of Malta*, Julia Lupton argues that the twice-converted Abigail figures one face of the female "citizen-saint, who mortifies her previous tribal and local ties, her native particularism, in favor of naturalization and conversion to a general economy."[51] While this characterization does not fit Weil, precisely, as her religion and her politics are so intertwined, critics who castigate her as "anti-Jewish" rely on this sort of thinking, to a certain extent.[52] In a way these critical readings canonize Weil even as they decry her canonization, her own turn against her Jewish "roots": reiterating the scenes of suffering as well as her supposed betrayal.[53] Ironically, then, such readings ultimately offer up Weil as a sort of sacrament—not an erotic sacrament, to be sure, but a fragmented textual body deployed as a means of consolidating a critical community—in much the same way purely Christian readings seek to do. It is not my intention here to rehearse the question "was Simone Weil a good Jew or a bad Jew?"; rather, I seek to parse the ways both the suspended question of her conversion and the various critical responses to her ultimately undefinable religious sensibility correspond, in some sense, to the ways Shakespeare approaches the unrepresentable.[54]

While Cordelia begins the play under the sign of the unrepresentable—recall her reiterated, and much critically dissected, "nothings"—by the end she has become *nothing but* the representable, nothing but the image. This translation happens somewhat gradually, and I want to suggest that it is linked to the play's treatment of skepticism.[55] While Cordelia's "nothings" (which, like Ophelia's, are "more than matter"—though perhaps without the bawdy pun Hamlet activates) speak through the refusal to speak, by the end nothing speaks more clearly than her tears and her corpse. Two moments of transformation, one of which might even, perhaps, be called a moment of redemption, each of which turns upon truth revealed by tears: first, the Gentleman's report, to Kent, of Cordelia reading his letter (Q scene 16; F 4.3); second, Lear's awakening (Q scene 21; F 4.7).[56]

> KENT: Did your letters pierce the queen to any demonstration of grief?
> GENTLEMAN: Ay, sir. She took them, read them in my presence,
> And now and then an ample tear trilled down
> Her delicate cheek. It seemed she was a queen
> Over her passion, who, most rebel-like,
> Sought to be king o'er her.
> KENT: O, then, it moved her?
> GENTLEMAN: Not to a rage; patience and sorrow strove
> Who should express her goodliest. You have seen
> Sunshine and rain at once, her smiles and tears
> Were like a better way. Those happy smilets
> That played on her ripe lip seemed not to know
> What guests were in her eyes, which parted thence
> As pearls from diamonds dropped. In brief,
> Sorrow would be a rarity most beloved
> If all could so become it.
> KENT: Made she no verbal question?
> GENTLEMAN: Faith, once or twice she heaved the name of father
> Pantingly forth as if it pressed her heart;
> Cried "sisters, sisters, shame of ladies, sisters!
> Kent, father, sisters! What, i'th'storm, i'the night?

> Let pity not be believed!" There she shook
> The holy water from her heavenly eyes,
> And clamour mastered her; then away she started,
> To deal with grief alone. (F 4.3.9–33)

The irony here is almost comic, especially in Kent's flat-footed "O, then, it moved her?"—which triggers the Gentleman's multi-layered blazoning of Cordelia's tears. In his first, brief description, his martial metaphor seeks to overturn any political threat Cordelia poses. She *is* a rebel, at this point—a sense visually reinforced by the Quarto, when she returns at the head of the French army, "with her father in her hand" (Q scene 23; F 5.2, opening stage directions). The Gentleman's metaphor translates political dissent to affective rebellion, softening the queen even as he argues that she subordinates her "most rebel-like" passions.[57] Playing on tropes of seeing and speaking, the Gentleman's blazon, and Kent's responses, align Cordelia with Lear even as they also recollect her earliest moments in the play. While she "cannot heave [her] heart into her mouth" when Lear demands it, now "she heave[s] the name of father / Pantingly forth as if it pressed her heart." Speech becomes affliction, in both these moments, the labor expressed by the consonantal links between "heave" and "heart," "pantingly" and "pressed." Twinned opposite of Lear's unruly "mother," the *hytserico passio* that threatens to choke him, "the name of father" cuts between Cordelia and her own heart. But "the name of father"—curious phrase. Not the name of *her* father, not "Lear" or "father,"—"the name of father," abstract, uncoupled from its referent. Much has been made of Kent's ambiguous "my master calls me" in the play's final moments; the Gentleman/messenger's phrase already sets up this ambivalent messianism (what Benjamin might call "weak messianism")—something even the Gentleman himself, who recalls here the messengers of Greek tragedy, might already be said to have done.

The terms of his blazon itself are tripled, shading from the military knell in the first two lines (recalled by the "clamour" of line 32) through Petrarchan and hagiographic topoi—the latter two condensed in the translation of Cordelia's tears. While her tears initially appear to the Gentleman "as pearls from diamonds dropped," the martyrological sense of "pressing" activates the blazon's quasi-sanctification of its object, who "[shakes] / the holy water from her heavenly eyes." Cordelia seems to deliquesce even as her tears do—or perhaps these three personae, the rebel-suppressing queen, the ever-distant beloved, and the holy hermit who hurries away "to deal with grief alone," cannot be separated. And just as Lear's broken speech before his flight into the storm peels back the skin of his suffering, so Cordelia's fragmented vocatives become the site of her own translation.

Cordelia's tears crystallize the play's skeptical crisis, which is also a crisis of representation—a crisis continually recalled in the second half of the play, through the reiteration of that most fundamental question, "Do you know me?" In the Gentleman's report, her tears initially prove doubtful signs (expressing by turns, or even all at once, patience, sorrow, clamor, grief), yet they are also the only legible tokens she offers. Beyond language, at this moment, her weeping testifies to that which eludes expression. Yet like the prophecies of the Pythia, which have first to be translated and then interpreted, at each stage in this transmission room for error creeps in. Cordelia is triply distant even as the Gentleman's blazon brings her most movingly present. By the time she greets Lear, after he awakens from what almost seems a magical sleep, her tears sign and seal her identity as his daughter, which he initially doubts—as he doubts all the evidence of his senses:

> LEAR: You do me wrong to take me out o'the grave.
> Thou art a soul in bliss, but I am bound
> Upon a wheel of fire that mine own tears
> Do scald like molten lead.
> CORDELIA: Sir, do you know me?
> LEAR: You are a spirit, I know; where did you die? [. . .]
> Methinks I should know you and know this man,
> Yet I am doubtful; for I am mainly ignorant
> What place this is and all the skill I have
> Remembers not these garments; nor I know not
> Where I did lodge last night. Do not laugh at me,
> For, as I am a man, I think this lady
> To be my child Cordelia.
> CORDELIA: And so I am, I am.
> LEAR: Be your tears wet? Yes, faith; I pray weep not. (F 4.7.45–49, 64–71)

Cordelia's tears facilitate a sort of skeptical epiphany, one that also turns on Lear's reassertion of a certain order. He remains "a man"—that is, presumably, still "naked man," "poor, bare, forked"—yet recognizes Cordelia first as "a spirit," next as "this lady," and finally as "my child." It's his first utterance that seems most sure: "You are a spirit, *I know*," before his certainty trickles into "doubt" and "ignorance," "know[ing] not." It is only when Lear gets to "I *think*" instead of "I know," to "*my* child" instead of "*this* lady," that he becomes certain, and this uncertain certainty once again takes tangible form in the wetness of Cordelia's tears.[58] In the Folio text, Cordelia's reiterated "I am, I am" seals Lear's knowing, her repetition now filling the evacuated space of her initial "nothings"—yet we must also note that the repetition highlights and prolongs the moment of uncertainty. As with the profound anguish of Lear's "howl, howl, howl, howl," this most fundamental ontological claim ends up curiously emptied of meaning—signifying only metrically.

The pietà-like tableau of Lear bearing the dead Cordelia has, in turn, attracted much artistic attention, and the redemptive treatment of Cordelia herself has seemed to some critics to salvage the play from its own misogyny. Alain Badiou's anti-misogynist reading of Paul as "the foundation of universalism" ends—or nearly ends—with what has sometimes been called "the woman question." Of course, since part of Badiou's project is to exculpate Paul from charges of misogyny that might be posed by "the tribunal of contemporary feminism" (104), he must necessarily conclude by reiterating Paul's inclusiveness. In a spectacularly ironic Hegelian reading (ironic, given Hegel's own insistence on Woman as sign of the particular), Badiou closes by asserting that Paul's "balanced" statements about women's and men's respective places in the coming community in effect *exemplify* the obliteration of particular difference in the light of a universal truth: "What matters, man or woman, Jew or Greek, slave or free man, is that differences *carry the universal that happens to them like a grace*. Inversely, only by recognizing in differences their capacity for carrying the universal that comes upon them can the universal itself verify its own reality" (106).[59] Badiou's lyrically enigmatic formulation of "carry[ing] the universal that happens to them *like a grace*" seems to me a possible point of connection to the image of Lear bearing Cordelia, the seeming reconciliation of his previous hatred with a final grace.

In the first quarto of 1608, the passage appears as follows:

> *Enter King Lear with Queen Cordelia in his arms* [*followed by the Second Captain*]
>
> LEAR: Howl, howl, howl, howl, howl! O, you are men of stones.
> Had I your tongues and eyes, I would use them so
> That heaven's vault should crack. She's gone for ever.
> I know when one is dead and when one lives.
> She's dead as earth.
> [*He lays her down*]

Lend me a looking-glass.
If that her breath will mist or stain the stone,
Why, then she lives.
KENT: Is this the promised end?
EDGAR: Or image of that horror?
ALBANY: Fall and cease. (Q 24.253–60)

Here are the lines as they appear in the Folio:

Enter Lear with Cordelia in his arms [followed by the Gentleman]

LEAR: Howl, howl, howl, howl! O, you are men of stones!
Had I your tongues and eyes, I'd use them so
That heaven's vault should crack: she's gone for ever.
I know when one is dead and when one lives;
She's dead as earth. [*He lays her down.*]
Lend me a looking-glass;
If that her breath will mist or stain the stone,
Why then she lives.
KENT: Is this the promised end?
EDGAR: Or image of that horror?
ALBANY: Fall, and cease. (F 5.3.254–62)

The moment's ambiguity deepens when we consider the lineation and textual variants, and Shakespeare's apparent invocation of the earlier anonymous play, *King Leir*, at this moment, as well as Edmund's "I have told you what I have seen and heard—but faintly; nothing like the image and horror of it" (F 1.2.172). Kent and Edgar's articulation of despair when they behold the pietà-like display of Lear bearing the dead Cordelia in his arms acquires a new sense if we think of it as a palimpsestic recryption of Edmund's earlier articulation—first, of course, in unconsciously echoing *Edmund*, their almost choral commentary perhaps leaches away some of the "horror" it strives to convey. Recall the context of Edmund's line: he's hinting at his father's supposed displeasure with Edgar. Edmund articulates his deception by sketching a scene of witnessing:[60] "I have told you what I have seen and heard, but nothing like the image and horror of it." Rhetorically positioning himself as witness to an event (however false) in the first part of the line, Edmund uses the language of the apostles—of the *other* apostles, not Paul, who inscribes his authority simply according to his singular calling, not according to what he has seen and heard.[61]

Yet the second part of the line immediately undercuts the certainty he's constructed: while the first half of the line presents him as a credible witness, the second half works against this sense. His language becomes increasingly abstract, moving from the immediacy of sensory impressions (seeing and hearing), to "the image" (a representation of sensory impressions), to "the horror" (a possible response to sensory impressions). While the syntactic parallelism of the first and second clauses seems to counterbalance "seeing and hearing" with "the image and the horror," the single line effectively telescopes cause and effect—"seeing and hearing" collapse into "horror," and the "image" effectively drops out of this cognitive play. Describing failed mimesis, the sentence itself enacts this failure, leaving the impossible "image" hovering between representation and reality, bound to neither. Yet the "image" itself is merely a possible gloss on unrepresentable "horror"—much as, for Weil, "gravity" stands as a symbol for the unrepresentability of suffering.

Jacques Rancière's critique of Badiou's "inaesthetics" also lends itself to a critique of his reading of Paul. In *Aesthetics and Its Discontents*, Rancière distinguishes three "regimes for the identification of art": the ethical, the representative, and the aesthetic. Taking as his starting point and prime example Schiller's analysis of the *Juno Ludovisi*, Rancière argues that to the first category belongs perception of the statue merely as an image of divinity; to the second category, perception of the statue as both product of a specific art and an imitation, not just of a divine ideal but also of an overlapping structure of meaning coding particular attributes of femininity, divinity, and sculpture. Yet it is the third category, the aesthetic, that most interests Rancière.[62] Though he takes Schiller as his primary example, the aesthetic regime, as Rancière defines it here and elsewhere, is explicitly post-Romantic, for the Romantics exemplify what Rancière calls the "representative regime."[63] While Corneille's *Oedipe*, with its blasted and blinded hero, typifies both the representative regime and its failures, perhaps we might name Shakespeare's play about blindness and insight *not* as a second example of the representative regime but as a "representative" of the aesthetic regime. It's precisely the play's "suspension" of an ending, the poised, infinitely drawn moment of *attente*, that moves it in this direction. I have already touched on Lear's own ending and begun a reading of Cordelia's final appearance—or, rather, her non-appearance, but the way her lifeless body, simultaneously sanctified and abjected, becomes a stage property. Of course we might say that this is true of, say, Macbeth's head, as it is for Mortimer's, at the end of *Edward II*—but what makes Cordelia's body any different from these severed heads? It isn't simply gender, or the reversal of the decapitation as castration topos we get when we confront the full female body. It's not "Diana described," as it was in the blazoning of her tears. Rather, when Cordelia's body becomes a prop (that is, a stage property) physically weighing Lear down even as it restores him to his proper status as both father and king[64]—at this moment the play shifts into hyper-representative mode, in the sense that it shifts into *a mode where representation becomes impossible*. Hence Lear's "howl"—hence the pathos of his search for breath, the material pathos of the "button" that impedes him.

At this same moment, though, Cordelia's body propels the play into the aesthetic regime. The latter, Rancière argues, is not "non-figuration" but rather "the emancipation of resemblance from the triple constraint" of the representative regime, which he defines as follows:

> The representative regime in art is not one in which art's task is to fashion resemblances. It is a regime in which resemblances are subject to the triple constraint that we have noted: a model of visibility of speech that at the same time organizes a certain restraint of the visible; an adjustment of the relations between knowledge-effects and *pathos*-effects, governed by the primacy of the "action" . . . and a regime of rationality peculiar to fiction, which exempts its speech acts from the normal criteria of authenticity and utility of words and images, subjecting them instead to intrinsic criteria of verisimilitude and appropriateness.[65]

Here it might help to recall another scene of Caravaggio's, his *Death of the Virgin*, painted around the same time as the first performances of Lear (ca. 1605–6). Let us leave aside the famous controversy surrounding its rejection by the priests who had initially commissioned it, on the basis that the Virgin looked "too much like the corpse of an ordinary dead woman," "swollen up and with bare legs."[66] What is interesting here is, as others have so elegantly demonstrated, the contrast between the dead weight of the Virgin's strongly lit upper body and the mysterious levitation of her darkened lower body, particularly her feet, linking her to the crimson drapery swathed across the painting's upper right quarter.[67] As the straining stallion seems to metonymically represent the moment of Saul's conversion, here the cloth prefigures the Ascension the emphasis on the Virgin's inert flesh explicitly seems to deny. In the same way the painting translates this possible Ascension, so too the play congeals itself around the moment Lear enters bearing Cordelia: in a way, this terrible vignette constitutes its true end, yet it doesn't end—the play goes on, and also, I suggest, the vignette symbolically ejects Cordelia's body outside its own dramatic frame, into the space of "free appearance" that characterizes the aesthetic regime.

Even as Lear's focus on Cordelia's chthonic immobility rhetorically emphasizes corporeality, the *visual* composition of the scene works against this overdetermined materialism. And like Paul's simultaneous insistence on living "now" and "to come," Cordelia's body bridges these times, much as it also creates a representational vortex. Lear's description and his frantic attempts to revive her both emphasize materiality—earthiness, stoniness—things that can't be mistaken, at least as Lear sees it at this moment. But the questioning exchange between Kent, Albany, and Edgar undercuts even this most terrible and final certitude, holds off the earth and the inevitable end. The *image* of Lear bearing Cordelia collapses aesthetic and temporal registers—hence the oddness of the question-answer exchange: just as the line empties out its own "horror" by recollecting Edmund's scheming, it offers a sort of proximal palliative by alluding to the "promised end" of the Lear story Shakespeare's audience would have been familiar with, even as the staging betrays the expectation the lines conjure. In the pause engendered by their broken lines, Kent, Albany, and Edgar conjure a space of messianic indeterminacy, a rhetorical uncertainty that works against what the audience thinks they see and know.

If Lear is "a play of gravity," then it is only by realizing that for Weil gravity equals "the second degree of grace" that we come to see the twinned paradox at its core: the impossibility and crucial necessity of representing the sufferings of life and the cruelly permeable division between beauty and horror. In his own meditations on time, Emmanuel Levinas writes,

> In pain, sorrow, and suffering, we once again find, in a state of purity, the finality that constitutes the tragedy of solitude. . . . The content of suffering merges with the impossibility of detaching oneself from suffering. And this is not to define suffering by suffering but to insist on the *sui generis* implication that constitutes its essence. In suffering there is an absence of all refuge. It is the fact of being directly exposed to being. It is made up of the impossibility of fleeing or retreating. The whole acuity of suffering lies in this impossibility of retreat. It is the fact of being backed up against life and being. In this sense suffering is the impossibility of nothingness.[68]

An acute reader of Weil, Levinas here comes close to her thinking but remains simultaneously far more hopeless and far more romantic in his remarks. Levinas, like Arendt, reminds us that the loneliness of suffering contributes to it, that the utter impossibility of community leads to "a state of purity" that nevertheless also constitutes a tragic isolation. While Levinas' "tragedy of solitude" means lived rather than dramatic tragedy, these lines shed a reflected light on tragic art.[69] For Weil, there must always be a *calculus* of pain, and the impossibility of retreat is precisely what she would have us seek—annihilation of the self as a true coming-to-being of the self, through coming to God. In this twist on the Pauline concept of *kenosis* lies the only pure form of beauty, and Weil's aesthetics founds itself in such a primary abnegation: "A double movement of descent: to do again, out of love, what gravity does. Is not the double movement of descent the key to all art?"[70]

Chapter Five

Paul's Call; *Cymbeline*'s Calling

Touto logizesthō ho toioutos, hoti hoioi esmen tō logō di' epistolōn apontes, toioutoi kai parontes tō ergō.

—2 Corinthians 10:11

The absence within the particular field of writing will have to be of an original type if one intends to grant any specificity whatsoever to the written sign.

—Jacques Derrida, "Signature Event Context"

Once again taking Paul as a starting point, this final chapter also returns to questions of the undead letter, in conjunction with *Cymbeline*'s treatment of sleeping and dead bodies. My main intertext here is 2 Corinthians, for it may be said to be Paul's "letter of the letter"—his most profound meditation on the status and the symbology of the letter, in its now dual status as epistle and *gramma*. There are no dead letters, in Shakespeare—or perhaps, there are only dead letters, but their signifying capacity lies precisely in their apparent inanimation. The undead letter paradoxically inscribes itself as its own absence, inviting reflection, conjecture, further inscription. Reading Shakespeare's play alongside Paul loosens the apparent dichotomies between flesh and spirit, letter and spirit, letter and law, presence and absence Paul initially sets forth. At the same time, reading Paul's epistle alongside the play highlights the political potential of Shakespearean romance.

The Letter and the After-Eye

Cymbeline is a play shaped by absences.[1] The titular character himself really has only a supporting role, but my topic here is not so much an absence as an obscurely proximal presence. Shakespeare's main source, the chronicler Raphael Holinshed, begins his account of Cymbeline by stating, "Little other mention is made of his doings, except that during his reign the Saviour of the world, our Lord Jesus Christ the only son of God, was borne of a virgin about the twenty-third year of the reign of this Cymbeline"[2]—yet Shakespeare does not treat this. Many critics have addressed the fantastical combination of Roman and Celtic Britain and early modern Italy that serve as the play's setting, and some have wondered why the play never seems to make anything of Holinshed's claim that Christ was born during Cymbeline's reign.[3] Early in Shakespeare's play, Innogen chides her banished husband Posthumous's servant, Pisanio, for not watching his master's withdrawal as attentively as she would have, in his place:

> INNOGEN: Thou shouldst have made him
> As little as a crow, or less, ere left
> To after-eye him.
> PISANIO: Madam, so I did.
> INNOGEN: I would have broke mine eye-strings, cracked them, but
> To look upon him till the diminution
> Of space had pointed him sharp as my needle;
> Nay, followed him till he had melted from
> The smallness of a gnat to air, and then
> Have turned mine eye and wept. (1.3.14–22)

Innogen's words play on the fallibilities of sense perception and perspective, and she insistently locates perception in the body, in the "eyes": "after-eye"; "eye-strings"; "have turned mine eye and wept." Despite seeming to follow the expected paths of faculty psychology and cognition, though, Innogen takes metaphysical detours. "After-eye": her physical phrase conjures the ability both to eye (see) Posthumous after he's already gone and to recall him to memory once he's left. Isolated from its context, and with, admittedly, some homophonic stretching, "after eye" also suggests both "after-aye," after all, a messianic pull, and "after-I," both a temporal and an ontological questioning that sits uneasily in this already most uneasy opening act.

The play begins with an exchange that calls into question the status of knowledge and report: the two Gentlemen's recitation of the histories of Posthumous, Innogen, and her banished brothers, and Britain's so-far accord with Rome. Simon Forman, whose breathless "remembering" of the play is the first written mention of it in performance (probably in 1611), begins his account as follows:

> Remember also Cymbalin King of England in Lucius' time, how Lucius came from Octavious Caesar for tribute, and being denied, after sent Lucius with a great army of soldiers who landed at Milford Haven, and after were vanquished by Cimbalin, and Lucius taken prisoner, and all by means of 3 outlaws, of the which 2 of them were the sons of Cymbaline, stolen from him when they were but 2 years old, by an old man whom Cymbalin banished, and he kept them as his own sons 20 years with him in a cave.[4]

Forman's "remembering" proceeds curiously backward in terms of the play's chronology: he begins with the end and focuses first on the "historical" events that lead to tribal Britain's clash with Rome. Like the two Gentlemen's chorically retrospective exposition in I.i, Forman's account fuses the *retrospective* act of looking back with the *perspectival* rerendering of plot points. Recent criticism of the play tends, to a certain extent, to favor this same focus, reading the play in terms of its treatment of emergent nationalism.[5] I would like to suggest, however, that while always bearing both political and historical questions in mind, we also consider the various ways the play glosses both retrospective and perspective acts of viewing, knowing, and reporting. Such a consideration, in turn, lends itself to a focus not just on how the play reflects on nationalism but also on how it treats (or refuses to treat) grace.

Innogen and Forman (and the play in its entirety) make us think about what makes "after-eyeing" impossible: absence; death; doubt; shifts in perception; chronological gaps. In a way, Innogen's agonized desire to "after-eye" is, like Forman's, a call to "remember"—and not just to remember but also to reconstruct, to call back time. This chapter draws on the double sense of "calling" deployed in Max Weber's 1919 essay "Politik als Beruf" in order to read between Shakespeare's late play and Saint Paul.[6] Generally translated as "vocation," the German term *Beruf* implies a supernatural as well as a worldly "calling," a voice that is more than a voice (think here of the theological sense of a "vocation" as a call from God). It also carries the decidedly worldly sense of "business" or "profession." Peter Lassman and Ronald Speirs translate the essay's title as "The Profession and Vocation of Politics" in order to convey this doubleness. Yet we must note that "profession" too carries a dual sense—the business-like or economic connotation we're probably most accustomed to every day (especially when hearing the latest unemployment figures) but also the religious sense familiar to scholars of the Reformation—profession as *con*fession, a statement of faith. The translators' attempts to preserve the term's doubleness, then, introduce a split that in fact returns to the "vocational" sense of calling, and I want to remain attentive to these polyvalent meanings in what follows. Ultimately, I will argue, the play's "calling" is simultaneously erotic, political, and poetic in a way that recollects yet reconfigures the Pauline notion of *ekklesia*.[7]

For Weber, "charisma" is a key political term—only a charismatic leader can embody, inspire, and sustain a truly political calling. While Weber's *das Charisma* retains its roots in the Greek *charis*, though, speaking to the religious underpinnings of *Beruf*, tracing the term throughout his works ultimately finds it more grounded in the "business" side of calling. Grace is thus superseded or folded into political economy, and part of Weber's task seems to be to recover this fragile element that he nevertheless seems to regard as, finally, unsustainable, or at least insufficient for modern governance. In this Weber, who figures in this book chronologically as the first thinker but the last to be treated, may perhaps be termed *proto*– but also, to a certain extent, *anti*–political theological.[8] So too might Shakespeare's play, in its very lack or absence of anything approaching charismatic leadership, be termed both proto- and anti-Weberian.

Paul begins his "second" letter to the Corinthians by referencing yet another past letter of his own, the so-called letter of tears (2:4), and we shall return to both this and to the famous distinction between the spirit and the letter of the law in 3:3–6.[9] I want to begin somewhat later, almost at the end, of Paul's meta-epistle, with the first epigraph opening this chapter. I would translate the verse as "This let some person figure out, that what we are in the words of our letters when we are absent, so when we appear we will be in our works." I give this bad translation for a reason; there are much more fluent ways to render Paul's rhetorical parallelism.[10] Yet a few things strike me about this passage in Greek, one of which is that while it is logically parallel, it is not syntactically parallel. Whereas elegant translations invariably contrast absence and presence, letters and (variously) "works," "deeds," or "action," and of course the Greek word *forms* bear out these seeming binaries, the word *order* is not quite so rigid. The difference turns on the relative positions of *apontês* and *parontês* versus *logô di'epistolôn* and *ergô*. In Paul's Greek, the first clause ends with *apontês*, "absence," while the second ends with *ergô*, which I am translating "works," though of course it can also be "deeds" or even "actions." I choose "works" because of the sense of *technê*, of craft, that the word incorporates—here I try to come close to Jerome's "*in facto*," which captures the making as well as the doing present in *facere*.[11] Thus Paul syntactically draws a shadowy contrast between absence and works, and this contrast helps to unsettle or soften the apparently rigid distinctions he carves between absence and presence, words (of a letter) and works.

Letters constitute the supplement in this passage. Though the previous two verses have concerned letters—in particular, a potential fear of the letter—here letters are secondary, the bearers of words. Hence we arrive at a second shadowy distinction between absence and presence, symbolic and corporeal: letters give words bodies.[12] They may be misleading in this sense, as Paul has (somewhat jokingly) remarked in verses 9 and 10: "I do not want to seem to be trying to frighten you with my letters. For some say, 'His letters are weighty and forceful, but in person he is unimpressive and his speaking amounts to nothing.'" These fanged letters, and this unimpressive speaker! In verses 9 and 10, the dichotomy Paul introduces is not just absence versus presence but also written versus spoken words. Yet by the verse that concerns us, the speaker has retreated from view; it is the potential worker or doer or actor who *appears* (*parontês*) on the scene, and who in fact ends the scene.

The second thing that strikes me about this verse is a sense of uncertainty, marked by the opening pronouns: the thing to be understood, the person or persons to whom understanding must come, are both initially abstract. The "understanding" is of course that of the correlation between the words of the letter and the physical presence of the writer, but the rhetorical promise of that understanding is, to a certain extent, held in abeyance by the vague *ho toioutos*. "Let some person," "let such a person": these diverse renderings point up the pronomial ambivalence. In making its claims about the potency of words in the writer's absence, the verse rhetorically models that absence: there is no person, at first, either writer or reader, only the initially incorporeal, dislocated words of the letter. But what I am here calling "uncertainty" might also be read as *potentiality* or possibility, the *dunamis* Paul writes of elsewhere.[13] Paul, who repeatedly insists on "waiting in the now" (as we have seen in the previous chapter), once again models for us what that waiting must be—we must even wait for the true meaning of his sentence to reveal itself. That is to say, it is precisely *in* the figural uncertainty, in the "absence" standing as a fulcrum between the two main clauses and in the "appearance" emphasized by the preceding *kai*,[14] that Paul sketches for his audience a particular sense of faith.

The term Paul uses that comes closest to the vocational sense of Weber's *Beruf* is the Greek *klêtos*.[15] Readers of Agamben's book on the letter to the Romans might be especially attuned to the resonances here: while *klêtos* means "selected" or "chosen," it is often translated "called" or "having been called" since it derives from the verb *kaleô*. From *kaleô* also derives *ekklesia*, literally those who have been "called out" but also, by extension, those who have been called *together*. Both *Beruf* and *klêtos* bridge the gap between what may be, however eventually, known and practiced in the world, the *business* of living and all it entails, and what must remain perpetually withheld. Perhaps, then, the sense of a nostalgia, an echo, a voice both pre- and post-leptic, also attends the word "call" as I use it here. For Paul, as we saw in chapter 4, the messianic call endlessly recollects its own trauma, yet it also becomes the basis for what Agamben terms "messianic time" (Paul's *ho nun kairos*), the "time that remains"—the interval between Incarnation and *eschaton* (the end of time) to act and do and be as neighbors, a community of faith that looks to the end of time but exists, always and ever, in the now.

Shakespeare's play shares this ambivalent messianism, which we see most clearly, and most literally, in the treatment of Cloten. It's easy to dismiss Cloten, who's often played as a clown—the pronunciation of his name may pun on this sense (Cloten/clod/clown[16]). After all, Cloten assumes real importance only as a headless body, a "trunk" that recalls the "trunk" in Innogen's chamber, in a scene that plays a grotesque fantasia on that earlier scene of sleeping and *not* waking. But I want to suggest that we take him more seriously than either the other characters in the play or critics generally do,[17] as a potential sacrifice that makes us question the very efficacy of sacrifice, and especially the religious and political valences sacrifice acquires when tied to treason (as it is for Cloten).

When Cloten enters with two mocking companions in 1.2, the First Lord's first words to him are "Sir, I would advise you to shift a shirt. The violence of action hath made you reek as a sacrifice" (1.2:1–2). Two things to remark here: first, the "shirt" that the Lord recommends he "shift"; second, the analogy to a reeking sacrifice. Cloten later takes great exception to Innogen's withering comparison of him with Posthumous's "least garment," and of course he later "shifts" his garments for Posthumous's, leading to the most tragic scenes in the play. But the consonantally linked "shift" and "shirt" suggest both "shriving" and a more profound shifting, a transformation more unsettled than a simple change in garments, which recollects Paul's use of clothing or reclothing as a metaphor for conversion, "putting on" (*endunô*) Christ.[18]

Posthumous, who doubles for Cloten as the headless Cloten doubles for him, later appears "dressed as a Roman, carrying a bloody cloth" (5.1., stage direction). If Cloten's reeking shirt marks him as a sacrifice, and obliquely recalls Christ, Posthumous's Roman garb (though a disguise) and the "bloody cloth" align him with the dicing Roman soldiers at Golgotha—but with a twist, for the "bloody cloth" also recollects both Cloten, the "bloody man" Innogen awakens beside in the cave, and the marriage sheets he thinks Innogen has re-stained by being unfaithful.[19]

Hence, the cloth also ties us back to Innogen, whose apparent death and nightmarishly magical reawakening reorient us to the play's intertwining strands of fairy tale and underlying messianism, in the person of one who has reinscribed herself as "faithful." Though the play makes much of Cloten's foolishness (culminating in Guiderius's reference to "Cloten's clodpoll" in 4.2), reading the play retrospectively means that it ultimately insists we take his death as a form of sacrifice that acquires a strangely Pauline resonance, in contrast with the generally pagan images of sacrifice that occur elsewhere in the play. Yet Cloten as substitute or shadow sacrifice (to employ René Girard's term) will never be enough—though in death he acquires a dramatic vitality and poetic significance denied him in life. Only Innogen's substitutions and sacrifices (first as Fidele, later as quasi double for the dead Euriphile[20]) point the way toward *being* and *acting* here and now, insisting on a Pauline sense of what is to come.

The language of sacrifice permeates the play, linked with both political and erotic strife, as when Innogen begs Pisanio to kill her when first reading Posthumous's condemnation of her virtue (3.4.64–98).[21] Cloten's death occurs offstage; like Macbeth's, his severed head stands in for the action that has already occurred. Here the retrospective act of viewing assumes a newly grotesque literalness. Belarius is perhaps the first to take Cloten seriously, though he does so too late. Reflecting on Guiderius's and Arviragus's "native" royalty and likening it to natural growth, Belarius passes on to wondering what Cloten's death might mean:

> BELARIUS: 'Tis wonder
> That an invisible instinct should frame them
> To royalty unlearned, honour untaught,
> Civility not seen from other, valour
> That wildly grows in them, but yields a crop
> As if it had been sowed. Yet still it's strange
> What Cloten's being here to us portends,
> Or what his death will bring us.
> GUIDERIUS: Where's my brother?
> I have sent Cloten's clodpoll down the stream
> In embassy to his mother. His body's hostage
> For his return. (4.2.177–87)

Guiderius's savage punning on Cloten's newly acquired political efficacy (or at least potential—"embassy" reads one way, "hostage" quite another) covers over one other important register, the poetic, which his wordplay only glancingly invokes. "Cloten's clodpoll" undergoes a sea change: like the dismembered Orpheus, whose head also floats down a stream,[22] his decapitation acquires poetic as well as political significance.

If Cloten stands for sacrifice in the play, though, the question of how, or even whether, this sacrifice *matters* carries us back to Paul. Paul's living letters, whom he urges to follow him in his own *imitatio Christi* to become "poured out like a drink offering on the sacrifice" (Philippians 2:17), are in a sense *fluid*, signifying the transformative potential of the new faith. Cloten, on the other hand, figures both blood and earth, the "clot" or "clod" whence his name derives, and which Guiderius's pun highlights. In a way he resembles Caliban, whose "creatureliness" indexes romance's links with creation, and also with creativity.[23] *The Tempest* is a play preoccupied by "art" (Prospero's term for his magic, which can be extended to encompass his domestic and political machinations), and *Cymbeline* shares this concern. Yet whereas "art" in *The Tempest* signifies distance, delegation, spectacle—the prosthetic operations of patriarchal sovereignty[24]—*Cymbeline*'s preoccupation with the corporeality of letters reorients this consideration around the relationship between *technê* and *poiesis*. Cloten, like Caliban, is a "thing of darkness" who nevertheless sheds light on the play's treatment of absence, precisely *because of* his thingness, his materiality—his status as the ultra-corporeal "clot" who enters "reeking as a sacrifice." On the one hand, "Cloten's clodpoll" suggests coagulation, stagnation—sacrificial blood congealed, perhaps inefficacious. On the other hand, though, Cloten's dual ends (trunk and head) undergo a series of new modifications and migrations. This series of movements, in turn, highlights the problems of not just inscribing but also deciphering the undead letter.

Untimely Reading: Touching on Roots

In 2 Corinthians 1:23–2:9, Paul speaks of his absence from Corinth, and of a letter "[written] out of great distress and anguish of heart and with many tears" (*ek gar pollēs thlipseōs kai sunokhēs kardias egrapsa humin dia pollōn dakruōn*) (2:4). This "letter of tears" must in turn be linked with Paul's later metaphor of the converted as the undead letter, in 3:2–3: "You yourselves are our letter, written on our hearts, known and read by everyone. You show that you are a letter from Christ, the result of our ministry, *written not with ink but with the Spirit of the living God, not on tablets of stone but on tablets of fleshly hearts*."[25] This is shortly followed by the famous distinction of 3:6: "For the letter kills, but the Spirit gives life" (*To gar gramma apokeinei, to de pneuma zôopoiei*). In chapter

2 Paul recalls the infamous "circumcision of the heart" passage from his letter to the Romans (2:25–29). Once again, he describes the passage between Mosaic law (that "written on stone tablets") and the new covenant, the law of love, graven "on fleshly hearts." And here, again, it is in the strange doubling of corporeality and removal that we must seek Paul's message. *Inscribed by the spirit of the living God / on fleshly hearts* (*Pneumati theou zôontos / en plaxin kardias sarkinais*): in these lines coupling "the spirit of the living god" with "fleshly hearts" we witness the birth of the undead letter (epistle), which in turn contrasts with the dead letter (*gramma*) of the law in the subsequent chapter.

Both epistle and *gramma*, and the contrasts Paul draws in these passages, turn on concepts of LIFE (*zôon*) as they relate to SPIRIT (*pneuma*). And as the LETTER is the supplement in 10:11, here it is LIFE, or a form of life, that becomes the supplement to the neat parallels Paul sketches. *Zôopoiei* is the most poignant encapsulation of Paul's true letter about the letter, for it combines *zôon* with *poieô*, "to make"—thus it is etymologically closer to "to make life" than "to give life," as most translations would have it. Yet the translations preserve or, perhaps, add, something else, in incorporating the notion of the *gift* at this moment—for, after all, it is *grace* that Paul speaks of when he writes that "the spirit makes living." At the same time as they add this resonance of grace, however, they subtract the poetic element of *poiesis*, the graphological element of making that stands out as we turn back to Shakespeare's play, which is so concerned with letters and bodies, quick and dead.

Innogen's association with reading and writing appears first in the chamber scene (II.ii), which opens with Innogen noting that she has stayed up too late: "I have read three hours, then. Mine eyes are weak" (3–5). Time is both *metatextual* and *textured* in this scene, a fractured surface on which both Giacomo and the complicitously voyeuristic audience imaginatively project the actual rape that the text denies. The deep layering of allusions is what allows Giacomo's interval its power, even as it strips Innogen of hers. As with Posthumous's departure, her focus on *eyes* here bears remark, but here eyes are the instrument of knowledge not through seeing but through reading. Reading and sleeping are both *timed* (she has read three hours, she begs Helen to wake her at four) and *untimely*, for it is during the "interval" of Innogen's sleep that Giacomo deciphers her surroundings (including the ekphrastic tapestry and Ovid's *Metamorphoses*) and body as so many more texts. The polytextual play begins with Shakespeare's allusion to his own *Rape of Lucrece*, *Titus Andronicus*, and, latterly, *Macbeth*; by the end of Giacomo's speech, as he "writes in his tables," he's shadowing Hamlet as well as Tarquin. Innogen's "weak" eyes prefigure her vulnerability, as does "the leaf turned down / Where Philomel gave up" (2.2.43–46). Giacomo is, it seems, a good reader, even if he is also a potential rapist (who recasts Philomel's rape as her "giving up"). The scene ends, of course, with the striking clock: "One, two, three. Time, time!" (2.2.51). Like the increasingly menacing, physical sense of time in act 2 of *Macbeth*, Giacomo's interval reminds us of both time's suspension—its dreamlike entanglings, its impossible loops—and its propulsion.

In this short scene, then, Giacomo occupies the overlapping interstitial zones between presence and absence, sleeping and waking, signifying and deciphering. Innogen's awakening in the cave repeats this scene with variations. Before her strange interment (an interment that becomes the play's most potent interval, in Agamben's Pauline sense—this time, perhaps, retrospection as projection?), Arvarigus and Guiderius catalogue Fidele's virtues. Guiderius remarks that "he cut our roots in characters" (4.2.51). Roger Warren notes that "characters" means "letters of the alphabet (as in modern 'alphabet soup,' given to children to make the food more interesting and so tempt them to eat)" (line 51n). Yet the "roots" of Innogen/Fidele's "neat cookery" grow to signify "character" as not just demeanor but also as familial lineage—an unnatural or grafted image of lineage that returns us, once again, to Paul and the famous passage on being "grafted" into the Church: "For if you have been cut from what is by nature a wild olive tree, and grafted, contrary to nature, into a cultivated olive tree, how much more will these natural branches be grafted back into their own olive tree" (Romans 11:24).[26] Arviragus's retort to his brother, "Grow patience, / And let the stinking elder, grief, untwine / His perishing root with the increasing vine" (4.2.60–62), solders the popular emblematic image of a tree choked by parasitic vines onto the trope of patience as an "increasing vine," where grief is the tree that the vine strangles.[27] In a strange transmutation, then, the normally deathly vine becomes salvific, life-giving, recollecting the common trope of Christ as a fruitful vine (e.g., John 15:1–2), while the tree, which usually represents strength and stability, stands for corruption.[28]

Both Guiderius and Arviragus, then, don't seem to speak of Pauline grafting, at least transparently so, but Guiderius's initial metaphor of "spurs" that "mingle" their growths can suggest grafting—"spur," whose own root is probably the Old English *spora*, whence also derives *spore*, is also a horticultural term, at least by the early eighteenth century.[29] While Shakespeare uses it to mean "roots" in *The Tempest*,[30] here "spur" seems to mean not roots but branches or offshoots, grafted ("mingled") together to form Fidele's hybrid character. Arviragus's continuation of his brother's metaphor shifts from a covert scene of grafting to an overt scene of parasitic growth, the monstrous mingling "untwine[d]" by the "increasing vine." The brothers' conjoined consonantal phrases ("grief and patience," "grow patience") flower into Arviragus's couplet, "untwine/vine"—yet poetically, the couplet rebinds grief and patience even as Arviragus claims that the "increasing vine" will overcome the "perishing root." The brothers' exchange moves from the "characters" the disguised Innogen carves in roots to the grafted roots of her own character—linking *poiesis* (in its etymological sense of "making," as well as the literary sense) with moral fiber, the "roots" of the soul.

Innogen's "cut[ting their] roots into characters" invokes the etymological origins of "graft," the Greek *graphein*, "to write"[31]—thus while Arviragus and Guiderius play on the "mingling" sense of grafting, of making two one, Innogen's initial graft stands as a solitary act of writing. Solitary, despite its social ends, because ultimately, as much as Innogen stands for faith in this play, so she stands for *faith alone*—a faith that must withstand multiple tests; most significantly, a faith that must persevere, and even grow stronger, despite absence and overt rejection. Innogen's awakening curse—"To read and write be henceforth treacherous!" (4.2.317–18)—fuses the acts of inscription and deciphering with political upheaval, the state turned inside out.[32] This concatenation of reading, writing, and solitary faith might seem, on its surface, Protestant—*sola scriptura, sola fides*, exemplified—but I don't think it is. The ethical significance of both reading and writing already teased out in the brothers' play on grafting acquires new resonances in the closing scenes of the play.

If Innnogen presents one face of faith, that which never doubts, Posthumous, finally filiated in a dream vision, gives us another—Posthumous is Saul to Innogen's Paul, the becoming-faithful subject. Innogen's imagined vision of the vanishing Posthumous is bookended, in acts 4 and 5 of the play, by a series of dreams: her own symbolic rebirth; the Soothsayer's vision of the flight of the Roman eagle; and, finally, Posthumous's vision of his family. The disoriented, clinging sense of "dream" when Innogen awakens to find "Posthumous's" headless body beside her becomes another version of "after-eying":

> I hope I dream,
> For so I thought I was a cavekeeper,
> And cook to honest creatures. But 'tis not so.
> 'Twas but a bolt of nothing, shot at nothing,
> Which the brain makes of fumes. Our very eyes

> Are sometimes like our judgements, blind. Good faith,
> I tremble still with fear; but if there be
> Yet left in heaven as small a drop of pity
> As a wren's eye, feared gods, a part of it!
> The dream's here still. Even when I wake it is
> Without me as within me; not imagined, felt. (4.2.298–308)

The synesthetic tangibility of the dream that is *not* a dream is linked here with both faith and judgment. Innogen's piteous cry to the gods, damning writing and reading, the acts that have brought her here, invite speculation about her *mis*reading of Cloten's body as corporeal text, the letter *beyond* the letter. Dramatically, the scene is probably the most important in the play, but in her conflation of flesh and letter we might say she is profoundly un- or even anti-Pauline, though this chapter has focused on his testaments to "calling." In this reading, Innogen figures the deep sense of faith exemplified in the famous *noli me tangere* episode in the gospel of John (20:17): like yet unlike Mary Magdalene meeting the risen Christ, forbidden to touch and confirm but bidden to speak of what she has seen, Innogen must bear witness without having been called to do so.[33] Though she remains "faithful" to her husband even in death, Innogen's calling must remain secret. Yet the coupling of Posthumous and Innogen also gives us a profane analogue to those who accept Paul's calling—though perhaps only if we adhere to the most misogynistic reading of the troubling passages on gender in Romans, which I am not suggesting we do.[34] I spoke in the beginning of the play's absences, and Posthumous, we recall, is described first of all only as a reflection of Innogen's estimation, by the Gentleman who "cannot delve him to the root" (1.1.16–53).[35]

In this reading, the graft represents a particular sort of *ekklesia*, in which Posthumous and Innogen's marriage and the tributary arrangement between Britain and Rome mirror one another,[36] but neither fully "delve[s] to the root" of grace—because it isn't possible. Grafting, after all, requires at least one cut—like Paul's metaphors of conversion as traumatic birth and inscripted flesh, the graft always reminds us of the wound that gives it life. And while the graft yields a new form of life (Paul's *dunamis*, Arendt's natality, incarnate), it also means a scar, a reminder that two might become one, but also that the hybrid growth maintains its roots in gashed flesh,[37] with the insertion and binding of an initially foreign object (the "scion," in horticultural terms). As Guiderius and Arviragus's dialogue points out, the fruitful graft presents the flipside of a parasitic guest/host relationship. The analogy here is medical rather than horticulatural, suggesting graft versus host disease,[38] in which the grafted tissue mutates into what is not quite an autoimmune disorder—the implanted cells turning against the body they are meant to save.[39] This ever-present specter of danger and disease, the wound mutating to engulf the entire body (or body politic) reconnects the play's treatment of grafting to Paul's meditations on the letter, for it is only in recalling the "letter of tears," that previous cut, that he arrives at the metaphor of corporeal *re*scription, the "writing on fleshly hearts" that seals the old wound only through perpetually incising a new one.

Oneiric Ontologies, "Senseless Speaking"

While both Giacomo's interval and Innogen's drugged sleep suggest—or, in the latter case, even recall—dreams, a Roman Soothsayer and Posthumous experience the only "true dreams" the play recounts. The Soothsayer's dialogue with Lucius (whom Innogen is about to encounter, after her awakening) first points up what I am calling the play's *oneiric ontology*,[40] the somnolent, intangible counterpart of its obsession with the flesh of the letter, and the letters of the flesh. For Posthumous, in particular, dreaming allows not just *knowing* but also *being* in an entirely new way, one that takes into account both his buried past and his portentous future. Posthumous's dream thus exemplifies the duality of perspective and retrospective the play has treated all along. The unfolded, messianic resonances of the "after-eying" acquire overtly political significance with the second instance of perspectival stretching, the Soothsayer's dream:

> SOOTHSAYER: Last night the very gods showed me a vision—
> I fast, and prayed for their intelligence—thus:
> I saw Jove's bird, the Roman eagle, winged
> From the spongy south to this part of the West,
> There vanished in the sunbeams; which portends,
> Unless my sins abuse my divination,
> Success to th'Roman host.
> LUCIUS: Dream often so,
> And never false.
>
> *He sees Cloten's body*
>
> Soft ho, what trunk is here
> Without his top? The ruin speaks that sometime
> It was a worthy building. (4.2.346–60)

The Soothsayer's vision conflates several types of meaning and knowing: first, it is a dream vision, nocturnally linked with Giacomo in Innogen's bedchamber, Innogen's internment in the cave, and Posthumous's dream. Both oneiromant and augur, the Soothsayer again exemplifies the play's layering of retrospective (looking back to the dream) and perspective (the physical gaze projected forward, beyond the eagle's flight). While the Soothsayer of course interprets his dream as favorable, portending "success to the Roman host," we might also note that it is a dream in which the eagle, the symbol of Rome's imperial grasp, *vanishes* into the dawn; and that Rome itself, alluded to as "the spongy south," hardly seems a stable referent. Thus, the vision suggests not so much Rome's coming victory as it does Rome's coming dissolution. Just as Innogen envisions Posthumous "melt[ing]" into airy insubstantiality, so the Soothsayer's vision projects a Rome "vanish[ing]" into the light. Though the eagle's flight into the sun traditionally symbolizes a renewal of youth,[41] like the phoenix to which Innogen is compared, I think that here it can bear this dual interpretation. As an image of both rebirth and a vanishing, presence and absence, the eagle's flight into the sun returns us to the play's messianic calling. However, the seemingly stately "ruin" Cloten's corpse suggests to Lucian frets the edges of the ecclesiastical image: if Guiderius and Arviragus represent a "natural" growth in its most perfect form, the "trunk" without its top, the ruin without its head, hauntingly limns the potentially disjointed political-theological body.[42]

Posthumous, who stands for absence in the play, becomes fully present only in the space of his dream—and in the face of his bondage. In a pre-dream soliloquy, he figures life and grace in terms of an exchange economy,[43] a prayer/fantasy in which he might ransom Innogen from the death to which he had previously condemned her:

> Is't enough I am sorry?
> So children temporal fathers do appease; Gods
> are more full of mercy. Must I repent,
> I cannot do it better than in gyves
> Desired more than constrained. To satisfy,
> If of my freedom 'tis the main part, take
> No stricter render of me than my all.
> I know you are more clement than vile men
> Who of their broken debtors take a third,
> A sixth, a tenth, letting them thrive again
> On their abatement: that's not my desire.
> For Innogen's dear life take mine, and though

'Tis not so dear, yet 'tis a life; you coined it.
'Tween man and man they weigh not every stamp;
Though light, take pieces for the figure's sake;
You rather mine, being yours. And so, great powers,
If you will make this audit, take this life,
And cancel these cold bonds. O Innogen,
I'll speak to thee in silence. (5.3.105–23)

Perhaps it makes sense to begin thinking about this bargain simply by considering Posthumous's name. Like Paul, Posthumous is "untimely born," as the First Gentleman relates: after his brothers' and his father's death, "[Sicilius Leonatus's] gentle lady, / Big of this gentleman, our theme, deceased / As he was born" (1.1.38–40). The King takes him under his protection and names him "Posthumous Leonatus," granting him his dead father's honorific. In the undead world of his dream, his mother tells a slightly different tale: "Lucina lent me not her aid, / But took me in my throes, / That from me was Posthumous ripped, / Came crying 'mongst his foes, / A thing of pity" (5.3.137–41). The mother's recollection, more than the Gentleman's recounting, again points up the gendered valences of Pauline conversion. The line folds together the sovereign-gifted name and the mother's death, for "Posthumous" can refer to both the son and to the mother taken by Lucina in her throes. Simultaneously cognomen and living epitaph, "Posthumous" figures rescription, the "undead letter" incarnate. The "theme" of the two Gentlemen's opening colloquy, Posthumous is also "set down" or set forth as a figure for the *ambivalence* of law,[44] particularly the "natural" laws of succession the play will continually call into question. Physical proximity to the King grants the unparented favorite a certain protected but precarious status;[45] as Innogen's husband, Posthumous later acquires a reflected but juridically unacknowledged political status that, in turn, renders his position at court even more precarious. Given both life and name from death, he *is* the grace who escapes the grave yet remains shadowed by the grave. His banishment constitutes the undead counterpart to Innogen's sleepy internment.

As a foil for the now-dead Cloten, Posthumous, like Innogen, signifies a certain sort of resurrection, and his dream vision a certain sort of conversion. The spiritual and erotic economy he attempts to broker in the soliloquy closes with "silence" as the most perfect mode of speech. If the graft is a figure for grace that always recollects suffering, silence, the evacuated presence of sound, the blank slate of the dreaming mind, gives us the *space* for grace—precisely because it isn't a space. Projection rather than recollection,[46] the vision reanimates Posthumous's unknown family, repatriates him both filially and nationally.[47] "Sleep, thou hast been a grandsire, and begot / A father to me; and thou hast created / A mother and two brothers," Posthumous marvels upon awakening. Present though absent, the ghosts leave Posthumous not just with a new knowledge but also with the weighty signifier of Jupiter's prophetic tablet: "Senseless speaking, or a speaking such / As sense cannot untie" (5.3.241–42). This is not Paul's writing on fleshly hearts—and yet, it is, for the dream and the tablet precipitate Posthumous's acceptance of his coming death. Not the undead letter, but the turning letter: a Janus-faced, lithic script suggesting Mosaic law as much as pagan oracles.

Weber's Call; *Cymbeline*'s Calling

In his discussion of the "three grounds *legitimating* any rule," which takes place in the context of his argument concerning the state's monopoly on violence, Weber writes,

> Firstly, there is the authority of "the eternal past," of *custom*, hallowed by the fact that it has held sway from time immemorial and by a habitual predisposition to preserve it. This is "traditional" rule, as exercised by the patriarch and the patrimonial prince of the old type. Then there is the authority of the exceptional, personal "*gift of grace*," or charisma, the entirely personal devotion to, and personal trust in, revelations, heroism, or other qualities of leadership in an individual. This is "charismatic" rule, as exercised by the prophet or, in the field of politics, by the chosen war-lord or the plebiscitarian ruler, the great demagogue and leader of a political party. Finally, there is rule by virtue of "legality," by virtue of belief in the validity of legal *statute* and the appropriate [*sachlich*] juridical "competence" founded on rational devised rules. . . . Here we are interested above all in the second of the three types: rule by virtue of devotion to the purely personal "charisma" of the "leader" on the part of those who obey him. For this is where the idea of *vocation* [*Beruf*] in its highest form has its roots. (PVP 311–12; emphasis in original)[48]

In this context one thinks of Fortinbras, installed first by *custom* ("the rights of memory"), *elected* or legally sanctioned by Hamlet's "dying voice"—before any of this, though, it is the indefinable *charisma* that apparently draws his followers (the "lawless" [Q1, Q2] or "landless" [F] "resolutes") to him. But Cymbeline has little to do with charismatic leadership in Weber's sense—and the other two "grounds" for rule in the play are split between Cymbeline and Rome.[49] That is, *custom* pulls one way while *legality* or statute pull another, as we see in the dialogue between Cymbeline and Lucius in 3.1, particularly Cymbeline's argument concerning the origins of British sovereignty and British law.

If *charisma* adheres to anyone in the play, it would seem to attach to Guiderius and Arviragus, the "sparks of nature" whose "thoughts do hit / The roofs of palaces," who "prince it much / Beyond the trick of others" (3.3.79, 83–86). Act 5, scene 3, an expositionary window opening between the tainted pastoral of Wales and the stuttering movement back to Cymbeline's court, recalls the initial dialogue between the two Gentlemen. Here the Lord's report of the battle and its end suggests Guiderius and Arviragus's charismatic potential: "This was strange chance: / A narrow lane, an old man, and two boys" (5.3.51–52). Posthumous's mockery translates this charismatic trace into poetry:

> Nay, do not wonder at it: you are made
> Rather to wonder at the things you hear
> Than to work any. Will you rhyme upon't,
> And vent it for a mock'ry? Here is one:
> "Two boys, an old man—twice a boy—a lane,
> Preserved the Britons, was the Romans' bane." (5.3.53–58)

Posthumous's bitter commentary on the "strange chance" performs its own wonder, forging rhyme from its initial focus on making and working. In their transition from wonder through craft ("you are made / Rather to wonder at the things you hear / Than to work any") to poetry (doggerel though it is), Posthumous's lines do not so much invalidate "wonder" as underscore it—first in the repetition (which recalls Belarius's musings on the "wonder" of the brothers and the "strangeness" of Cloten's appearance in 4.2), then in the reiteration of the Lord's story. Encapsulating the "strange chance" in verse may be "a mock'ry," but it also seals it, sets it apart, as the encounter between Posthumous and the Lord is itself separated from the frenetic action their conversation glosses.

Posthumous's lines thus link the "business" of war (a.k.a. politics by other means) with the craft of poetry, and Weber himself does something similar at the end of *Politik als Beruf*. Weber closes his reflection on the impetus and responsibilities of politics by citing a Shakespearean sonnet:

It would be fine indeed if Shakespeare's Sonnet 102 fitted the situation:

> Our love was new, and then but in the spring,
> When I was wont to greet it with my lays;
> As Philomel in summer's front doth sing,
> And stops her pipe in growth of riper days.

> But that is not how things are. What lies immediately ahead of us is not the flowering of summer but a polar night of icy darkness and hardness, no matter which group wins the outward victory now. For, when there is nothing, not only has the Kaiser lost his rights but so too has the proletarian. (368)[50]

Throughout the essay, Weber's primary task has been to diagnose, but he also prescribes: he both lays out the historical contours of the contemporary German political landscape and seeks something beyond mere "officialdom." Why, then, does he end (or nearly end) with Shakespeare? While Weber expresses his desire for a political flowering that will somehow emerge despite the "polar night of icy darkness" that engulfs the present state, his "summer" is already marred, in the cited lines—Philomel is hardly a comfortable way to invoke pastoral joys. Considering the sonnet in its entirety yields further signs of disconnection:

> My love is strengthened though ore weak in seeming;
> I love not less, though less the show appear.
> That love is merchandized whose rich esteeming
> The owner's tongue doth publish everywhere.
> Our love was new, and then but in the spring,
> When I was wont to greet it with my lays,
> As Philomel in summer's front doth sing,
> And stops his pipe in growth of riper days:
> Not that the summer is less pleasant now
> Than when her mournful hymns did hush the night,
> But that wild music burdens every bough,
> And sweets grown common lose their dear delight.
> Therefore, like her, I sometime hold my tongue,
> Because I would not dull you with my song.[51]

The first quatrain's reference to love "merchandized" links back to the "business" side of *Beruf*, the "party boss" who lacks the passion or the vision to maintain faith with a cause (PVP 345–46). As for Philomel: like Giacomo, Weber turns away from the sexual violence at the heart of Ovid's tale while covertly calling attention to it. The sonnet links rape with silence, as it should, given Philomel's fate, but here it is not Philomel's silence that matters but the poet-speaker's, who voluntarily "holds [his] tongue." Protesting the lover who "merchandizes" his affection by "publish[ing it] everywhere," the poet-speaker nevertheless refers to lovers (presumably, himself included) as "owner[s]," revealing his complicity in the erotic economy he seeks to escape. And it is "the owner's tongue" that the speaker castigates—not the owner's words—shades of Paul on speaking versus writing! But also shades of Philomel, whose tongue Tereus cuts out to keep her from publishing the deed: the poet-speaker thus gifts the verbal agency reft from Philomel to the cheap speakers who publish their love too broadly, or too quickly, effectively merchandizing Philomel's wrenched-out "tongue" as well as the doubtful lovers'. The erotic and poetic double valence of the poem becomes more apparent in the second stanza, the one Weber quotes—"lay" of course means *lai* but also carries an unmistakable erotic charge, which the lover's/summer's "stopped pipe" underscores. By the time "the tongue" returns, in the couplet, it has become the speaker's own, which he chooses to hold.

Weber's turn toward Philomel but away from a full confrontation of her rape, mutilation, and silencing as part of his imagined vision of political calling stands as a symptom of the ways some modern political theorists draw on early modern works but apparently choose to underplay their explicitly gendered and sexualized import. Weber begins his essay by defining contemporary politics as, at its core, the state's monopoly on violence (in this, he prefigures Benjamin), and despite his critique of the correlation between violence and power he seems to accept it even when he decries it (e.g., at 310, 326, 360–61). His essay is, in some sense, an attempt to redefine this relationship, and he closes with a clear call about what we might, following Derrida, term a politics *à venir*:

> Politics means slow, strong drilling through hard boards, with a combination of passion and a sense of judgement. . . . The person who can do this must be a leader; not only that, he must, in every simple sense of the word, be a hero. . . . Only someone who is certain that he will not be broken when the world, seen from his point of view, is too stupid or too base for what he wants to offer it, and who is certain that he will be able to say "Nevertheless" in spite of everything—only someone like this has a "vocation" for politics. (369)[52]

The metaphor captures Weber's argument that only the bureaucracy of the state *can* safely harness violence, by turning it into a purely mechanistic exercise, a view for which he is often criticized. As we have seen, both Carl Schmitt (Weber's student) and Hannah Arendt later take up the cry against politics as bureaucracy[53]—Arendt's concept of the social essentially figures forth Weber's nightmare at the end of the piece. While Weber's "slow, strong drilling through hard boards" figures politics in terms of what Arendt's will call *work*, his vision of the charismatic "hero" who can truly accomplish this comes closer to Schmitt's definition of sovereignty (as well as to the Nietzschean *Übermensch* Weber overtly criticizes but also seems enamored of). And, too, the "slow, strong drilling" eventually results in what for Schmitt is an "eruption" that "breaks through the crusty mechanisms of everyday life."

Whereas Schmitt remains focused on the miracle, Weber is a materialist, though a vexed one. By the end of this statement we can see how Schmitt will be able to use Weber's own teachings against him, for Weber paves the way for Schmitt's dangerous romanticism in the search for a politician who is also a hero:[54] the leader "who is certain that he will be able to say 'Nevertheless' in spite of everything" presents, in its most basic form, another version of what will become, for Schmitt, the sovereign decider. Weber's fear, expressed in these final paragraphs, is that those involved in politics will descend to "embitterment and philistinism, sheer, dull acceptance of the world and of your job [*Beruf*],—or the third, and not the least common possibility, a mystical flight from the world on the part of those with a gift for it or—a frequent and pernicious variant—on the part of those who force themselves into such an attitude because it is fashionable" (368). Here again we return to the duality of *Beruf*, translated as "job" but also allusively present in Weber's reference to "a mystical flight from the world."[55]

But to return to Shakespeare, and to Paul: I have been arguing that the play's covertly messianic drive is, essentially, redemptive, though troubled. I have said little, thus far, about the mystic or miraculous elements of the play. Paradoxically, it is Weber who brings us back to the question of the miraculous. In the last paragraph of his essay, Weber (like Cassirer) recognizes that the "mystic" elements of politics that can potentially be monstrous (resulting in a Schmitt) can also be salvific. Walking the edge, then, is the problem—what Weber essentially calls for is not a politics of myth or without myth but what we might term a *politics of romance*.[56] Weber's hope for a political hero also seems to be his fear—the guise of a politics of romance might turn out to be a rape that ultimately leaves the people even more voiceless, like Philomel. Yet if romance remains hyper-aware of its own contingencies and vulnerabilities, it nevertheless maintains a sure sense of something to come.[57]

The play closes with a planned sacrifice, one that will formally seal Britain's acceptance of the Roman yoke, and that also knits together the play's various anachronisms:

> CYMBELINE: Laud we the gods,
> And let our crooked smokes climb to their nostrils
> From our blest altars. Publish we this peace
> To all our subjects. Set we forward. Let
> A Roman and a British ensign wave
> Friendly together: so through Lud's town march,
> And in the temple of great Jupiter
> Our peace we'll ratify, seal it with feasts.
> Set on there. Never was a war did cease,
> Ere bloody hands were washed, with such a peace. (5.4.477–84)

Cymbeline's call returns us to the redoubling strands of *Beruf* I outlined at the beginning of this chapter. On the surface, his intention seems to be to celebrate a purely Roman rite, "in the temple of great Jupiter," yet his reference to the washing of bloody hands might also recollect Pilate. We might expect the play to close with a couplet, but Cymbeline goes one better, ending with a rhyming triad, feasts/cease/peace, which in turn recalls the "peace" he calls to be published in line 479. This reiterated focus on "peace" and the cessation of battle, though, is marred by both its linkage to the "bloody hands" that have yet to be washed and by the general sense of untimely *enforcement*: Cymbeline's proclamation goes too far, tries too hard. The "ratification" he envisions has yet to come to pass: again, we return to the clash of perspective and retrospective, for Cymbeline looks both back (to the war, as well as to the Queen's patriotic speech in 3.1[58]) and forward, to religious, civil, and juridical unification, ordering what has yet to come to pass. Cymbeline's closing lines remain proleptic, and recollecting the play's uncertain treatment of Cloten as sacrifice causes us to question, again, what it means to end the play by calling for a ritual regeneration of the body politic.[59]

Alain Badiou is perhaps the most prominent of the recent theorists to read Paul's letters as a testament to "universal" truths that transcend differences and particularities.[60] While I think we can read Paul's "calling" as universal, both Weber and Shakespeare invite us to examine how a seemingly universal calling maintains, at its core, an unsettled sense of difference. While, for Paul, the "grafted" branches of the new *ekklesia* do indeed give rise to an entirely new, hybridized growth, Shakespeare's focus on lopped trunks and mingled spurs and Weber's distressed exploration of the dual dead ends of political myth-making and political bureaucracy call on us, above all, to remember Paul's sense of *epekteinomenos*: straining ahead toward what is to come but retaining a certain wariness about not just the beginnings but also the ends of "the profession and vocation" of politics.

Epilogue

Last Words

The Stakes of Reading / Political Life

What are "last words"? What do they say, and what do they do? Who speaks "last words," the last word? Perhaps we can think of "last words" in terms of a "last will and testament"—a considered allocation of property, a final statement of intent. Yet even that phrase "last will and testament" already incorporates a split between desire (will) and action (testament, a statement of belief or purpose). As such, "last words" are always already doubled, both a closing and an opening: a statement of intent and a relinquishment, a letting go, a disposition and a dispensation.

It is perhaps *Timon of Athens* that offers the most profound gloss on the radical openness of last words. The print history of the play itself presents something of an open-ended question.[1] Written collaboratively by Shakespeare and his young contemporary, Thomas Middleton, between 1605 and 1608 (most likely later rather than earlier in this span), it neither appeared in print nor was performed before Shakespeare's death in 1616, and it was not in the original list of plays to be included in the First Folio of 1623. At the last minute, Hemmings and Condell hastily jammed it into the catalogue of "Tragedies," where it nestled uneasily between *Romeo and Juliet* (one of the earliest plays) and *Julius Caesar*, in a place originally destined for *Troilus and Cressida*. Since the largely forgotten *Timon* was recruited at the last minute to fill a gap in what was already a set number of pages, and it was a shorter play than *Troilus*, it ended up generating even more textual gaps (most literally in the eight blank pages between the always-unwilling-to-mingle *Timon* and *Julius Caesar*, which followed).

These literal textual openings perhaps find their interpretive correlative in the play's famously vexed treatment of epitaphs. What, after all, are Timon's own last words? The play text offers at least three possibilities.

1. The last words he speaks on the stage, to the Senators:

> Come not to me again, but say to Athens,
> Timon hath made his everlasting mansion
> Upon the beached verge of the salt flood,
> Who once a day with his embossed froth
> The turbulent surge shall cover. Thither come,
> And let my gravestone be your oracle.
> Lips, let four words go by, and language end.
> What is amiss, plague and infection mend.
> Graves only be men's works, and death their gain.
> Sun, hide thy beams, Timon hath done his reign. (15.749–58)

2. The epitaph the Soldier apparently *reads*, at least in part, in the following scene:

> SOLDIER:
> By all description, this should be the place.
> Who's here? Speak, ho! No answer?
> What is this?
> "Timon is dead, who hath outstretched his span.
> Some beast read this; there does not live a man."
> Dead, sure, and this his grave. What's on this tomb
> I cannot read. The character I'll take with wax.
> Our captain hath in every figure skill,
> An aged interpreter, though young in days.
> Before proud Athens he's set down by this,
> Whose fall the mark of ambition is. (16.1–20)

3. Or, again, the "insculpture" the Soldier brings to Alcibiades, who, again apparently, reads it:

> *Enter Soldier, with a tablet of wax*
>
> SOLDIER:
> My noble general, Timon is dead,
> Entombed upon the very hem o'th'sea;
> And on his gravestone this insculpture, which
> With wax I brought away, whose soft impression
> Interprets for my poor ignorance.
> *Alcibiades reads the epitaph*

ALCIBIADES:

"Here lies a wretched corpse, or wretched soul bereft.
Seek not my name. A plague consume you wicked caitiffs left!
Here lie I, Timon, who alive all living men did hate.
Pass by and curse thy fill—but pass, and stay not here thy gait."
(17.66–74)

Each of these moments, in turn, generates a series of questions and problems, which lead both forward into interpretation and conjecture and back through the course of my arguments thus far. First last words, spoken: the incantatory couplets that seal Timon's final speech apotropaically enact the misanthropic *gestus* it articulates—yet, of course, Timon *doesn't* stop speaking, here, though we never see him on stage again. Positing his gravestone as "your oracle," Timon already tells us that his words will resonate beyond the tide-fretted "hem o'th'sea" where he's laboriously engaged in digging his own grave. And, of course, so they do: in the proliferation of epitaphs, in the Soldier's interpretive difficulties, in the very work of fabricating an "insculpture" of the words he doesn't know how to read.

This *labor* of Timon's, and of the Soldier's (who becomes a figure for the audience)—the labor of grave-making, of word-making, of meaning-making—recalls, again, Arendt's *Human Condition*. In the munificent panoply of the play's opening half, Timon presents the apolitical animal inasmuch as he's neither embedded nor interested in *oikonomia* in its most concrete sense, or in any form of civil exchange; in the play's closing (and unclosing) scenes he signifies his misanthropic stance by literally throwing himself headlong into his own labor. Like Hamlet, Timon plunges into the grave, but here it's a grave of his own *making*—unlike gold, unlike the "roots" that are perhaps the play's only true gift. In this most corporeal emphasis on the *labor* of living, and of dying, Timon's "everlasting mansion," precariously set upon the shoal, suggests not only Arendt's diagnosis of the profound "worldlessness" of the modern human condition but also Benjamin's remarks about the creatural landscape of ruins that characterizes *Trauerspielen*. The final irony, perhaps, is that Timon refuses this status (of the mourning play)—"pass by and curse thy fill," but do not mourn.

As befits so relentlessly material a play, perhaps, *Timon* offers us no ghosts—no intangible signifiers of what might lie beyond. And yet it does. The status of the ghost in *Timon*, I would argue, must be exactly the specter of the last word—which means, here, the specter of the labor of reading and writing, of passing the word properly, which demonstrates how reading and writing constitute a political act. The threat Alcibiades poses to Athens is not only military.[2] In the last scenes of the play, the threat is that *he will stop reading*, that he will refuse to interpret—that he will simply ignore Timon's most ambivalent last words. Instead, though, he keeps the ball rolling—he mourns, and he promises more:

> Dead
> Is noble Timon, of whose memory
> Hereafter more. Bring me into your city,
> And I will use the olive with my sword,
> Make war breed peace, make peace stint war, make each
> Prescribe to other, as each other's leech.
> Let our drums strike. (V.v.77–83)

It's more than a little strange to move from Timon's radical misanthropy to a call to arms for the humanities, but Alcibiades's final task is also our own. If our *work* as literary scholars today is to have any meaning beyond the page (or, increasingly, the computer screen), it needs to lead to *action*. This is Arendt's goal, and it is mine—to preserve the ancient civic impetus behind humanities education while looking forward to what that impetus means in the relentlessly transformational realms of new media, scarcer resources, casualized labor. "Let our drums strike"—not just in reading, writing, thinking, teaching but in acting. Timon inhabits the pause between labor and work. It is Alcibiades who speaks the last words, who returns to the polis and its problems—who *acts*. And his first act is that of a reader, a translator, a transmitter of someone else's words. It's a start.

NOTES

Introduction

1. I use the term here in its eighteenth- to nineteenth-century sense of the philosophical consideration of the beautiful, though aware of the problems associated with this ahistorical highjacking of a later philosophical category. Christopher Pye and Hugh Grady are among those whose recent work brings together aesthetics and political theology. See, by Christopher Pye, "Leonardo's Hand: Mimesis, Sexuality, and Early Modern Political Aesthetics," *Representations* 111, no. 1 (2010): 1–32 and "Against Schmitt: Law, Aesthetics, and Absolutism in Shakespeare's *Winter's Tale*," *South Atlantic Quarterly* 108, no. 1 (2009): 197–217, as well as Hugh Grady, *Shakespeare and Impure Aesthetics* (Cambridge: Cambridge University Press, 2009), particularly chapter 4, "*Hamlet* as Mourning Play," 133–92.

2. See *The Ideology of the Aesthetic* (Oxford: Blackwell, 1990), 13.

3. On political theology as a "turn to theory" rather than a turn (or return) to religion, see Graham Hammill and Julia Reinhard Lupton's introduction to *Political Theology and Early Modernity* (Chicago: University of Chicago Press, 2012), as well as Lupton's earlier essay "The Religious Turn (to Theory) in Shakespeare Studies," *English Language Notes* 44, no. 1 (Spring 2006): 45–49, and Ken Jackson and Arthur Marotti, "The Turn to Religion in Early Modern Studies," *Criticism* 46, no. 1 (Winter 2004): 167–90.

4. Much critical work addresses the conjunction of violence and eroticism via gender or queer theory, and my debt to these critics appears in the following pages. I am most indebted to those whose analyses take what Frances Dolan has termed a "presentist historicist" approach. In a recent book, Dolan writes, "I practice what might be called a *presentist historicism* that tries to denaturalize present arrangements by uncovering their roots in the past. . . . I dwell on the connections between present and past so as to estrange the present rather than domesticate the past" (*Marriage and Violence: The Early Modern Legacy* [Philadelphia: University of Pennsylvania Press, 2008], 17). Like Dolan, I want to think about the problems that might conjoin literary pasts with literal presents yet recognize that this approach risks flattening out the differences between the two and doing justice to neither.

5. See Hannah Arendt's *The Human Condition* (Chicago: University of Chicago Press, 1958), cited parenthetically as *HC* hereafter. For a reading of Arendt's conjunctions with early modern political philosophy and theatre, see Paul Kottman, *A Politics of the Scene* (Stanford, Calif.: Stanford University Press, 2008).

6. In *The Concept of the Political*, originally published in 1927, Schmitt argues that the ancient distinction between *friend* and *enemy* remains the foundation of political thought; thus war must be considered the horizon of political action. See George Schwab's translation (Chicago: University of Chicago Press, 1996). See also Jacques Derrida, "Hostipitality," trans. Barry Stocker with Forbes Morlock,

Angelaki: Journal of the Theoretical Humanities 5, no. 3 (2000): 3–18, and *The Politics of Friendship*, trans. George Collins (New York: Verso, 2006).

7. See Carl Schmitt, *Political Theology: Four Chapters on the Concept of Sovereignty*, trans. George Schwab (Chicago: University of Chicago Press, 1985). All quotations in English taken from this edition. Citations in German refer to the first German edition, *Politische Theologie: Vier Kapitel zur Lehre von der Souveränität* (Munich: Duncker and Humblot, 1922). Hereafter I will cite both works parenthetically as *PT*.

8. In a Heideggerian twist on Aristotle's *Metaphysics*, Agamben torques the statement "What is potential can both be and not be, for the same is potential both to be and not to be" to claim that Aristotelian potentiality must be conceived as "*potential not to be*," arguing that "the greatness of human potentiality is measured by the abyss of human impotentiality." See "On Potentiality," in *Potentialities: Collected Essays in Philosophy*, ed. and trans. Daniel Heller-Roazen (Stanford, Calif.: Stanford University Press, 1999), 182. On political and literary conjunctions between pleasure and pain, see Melissa Sanchez, *Erotic Subjects: The Sexuality of Politics in Early Modern English Literature* (Oxford: Oxford University Press, 2013). My arguments here are also indebted to Joseph Campana, *The Pain of Reformation: Spenser, Vulnerability, and the Ethics of Vulnerability* (New York: Fordham University Press, 2012), and James Kuzner, *Open Subjects: English Renaissance Republicans, Modern Selfhoods, and the Virtues of Vulnerability* (Edinburgh: University of Edinburgh Press, 2012).

9. See the Loeb parallel text edition of Aristotle's *Politics*, trans. H. Rackham (Cambridge, Mass.: Harvard University Press, 1932), hereafter cited parenthetically as *Politics* using book, chapter, and Bekker numbers. The passage in question: "Ho anthrōpos phusei politikon zōon, kai ho apolis dia phusin kai ou dia tukhēn ētoi phaulos estin, ē kreittōn ē anthrōpos: hōsper kai ho huph' Homērou loidorētheis 'aphrētōr athemistos anestios'hama gar phusei toioutos kai polemou epithumētēs, hate per azux ōn hōsper en pettois." Greek text taken from perseus.tufts.edu.

10. In the discussion that follows, I will continue to adopt Aristotle's "man" and the masculine pronoun, *not* as universal terms but because the political relationships Aristotle touches on here still carry the original (or at least Homeric) register of *phratrai* as blood brotherhood, though *phratrai* are no longer literal kinship groups for Aristotle.

11. See *The Beast and the Sovereign*, vols. 1 and 2, ed. Michel Lisse, Marie-Louise Mallet, and Ginette Michaud, trans. Geoffrey Bennington (Chicago: University of Chicago Press, 2009, 2011). On sexual difference as central to the sovereign/beast dialectic, see especially vol. 1, "Third Session," 63–68.

12. "Hoi polloi tôn anthrópon glikhómenoi tou zên, hôs enoúsês tinos eumerías en autô kai glukutêtos phusikês" (*Politics* III.1278b. 29–31).

13. "*Souverän ist, wer über den Ausnahmezustand entscheidet*" (*PT* 9).

14. See Tracy B. Strong's analysis of the opening sentence and the ambiguities of translation in the foreword to Schwab's translation (xi–xiv).

15. "Der Ausnahmefall, der in der geltenden Rechtsordnung nicht umschriebene Fall, kann höchstens als Fall äußerster Not, Gefährdung der Existenz des Staates oder dergleichen bezeichnet, nicht aber tatbestandmäßig umschrieben werden" (*PT* 8).

16. Unless otherwise noted, all citations from the *Nicomachean Ethics* refer to the Loeb parallel text edition, trans. H. Rackham (Cambridge, Mass.: Harvard University Press, 2003), hereafter cited parenthetically as *NE*.

17. See Giorgio Agamben, *Homo Sacer: Sovereign Power and Bare Life*, trans. Daniel Heller-Roazen (Stanford, Calif.: Stanford University Press, 1998), hereafter cited parenthetically as *HS*, and *State of Exception*, trans. Kevin Attell (Chicago: University of Chicago Press, 2005), hereafter cited parenthetically as *SE*.

18. Compare Bradin Cormack's reading of Agamben in the introduction to *A Power to Do Justice* (Chicago: University of Chicago Press, 2007), 6–10. In his account, jurisdiction provides "one symbol of the possibility of finding within the law the mobility that, subject as we are to a narrowed conception of sovereignty, we may too easily locate in the phantasm of a 'life' beyond law" (2). While I position my argument as political theological, something Cormack resists (9), I share some of his concerns about positing the limits of life and law.

19. See Hannah Arendt's introduction to Walter Benjamin, *Illuminations: Essays and Reflections*, trans. Harry Zohn, ed. Hannah Arendt (New York: Harcourt Brace Jovanovich, 1968), 49.

20. See Walter Benjamin, "The Storyteller: Reflections on the Work of Nikolai Leskov," in *Illuminations*, 83–109.

21. On Benjamin's natural history, see Eric Santner, *On Creaturely Life: Rilke, Benjamin, Sebald* (Chicago: University of Chicago Press: 2006), addressed more fully in chapter 1.

22. Benajamin, "The Storyteller," 89, 95–96.

23. See Walter Benjamin, "Theses on the Philosophy of History," in *Illuminations*, 253–64.

24. Benjamin, "Theses," 257.

25. See Hannah Arendt's *The Human Condition* (Chicago: University of Chicago Press, 1998); *The Origins of Totalitarianism*, new ed. with added prefaces (San Diego: Harcourt, 1976); "The Concept of History," in *Between Past and Future: Eight Exercises in Political Thought* (Harmondsworth, U.K.: Penguin, 1956), 41–90. Hereafter I shall cite these works parenthetically as *HC*, *OT*, and *CH*.

26. *Telos* (vol. 142, Spring 2008) contains several articles addressing the occasionally surprising conjunctions between Arendt's work and Schmitt's. See, especially, Christian J. Emden, "Carl Schmitt, Hannah Arendt, and the Limits of Liberalism," 110–34, particularly 112–16, where Emden provides a rundown of these disparate political thinkers' "elective affinities."

27. In a series of lectures delivered at the University of Toronto, Julia Kristeva explored this aspect of Arendt's work in detail. See Julia Kristeva, *Hannah Arendt: Life Is a Narrative*, trans. Frank Collins (Toronto: University of Toronto Press, 2001).

28. See Simone Weil, *First and Last Notebooks*, trans. Richard Rees (Oxford: Oxford University Press, 1970), 324.

29. See *The Shattering of the Self: Violence, Subjectivity, and Early Modern Texts* (Baltimore: Johns Hopkins University Press, 2002).

30. See *Frames of War: When Is Life Grievable?* (London: Verso, 2009), 101.

31. See Margaret Canovan, *The Political Thought of Hannah Arendt* (New York: Harcourt Brace Jovanovich, 1974), 2–3.

Prologue

1. "Hê de kômôidia estin hôsper eipomen mimêsis phauloterôn men, ou mentoi kata pasan kakian, alla tou aiskhrou esti to geloion morion. To gar geloion estin hamartêma ti kai aiskhos anôdunon kai ou phthartikon, hoion euthus to geloion prosôpon aiskhron ti kai diestrammenon aneu odunês." See Aristotle, *Poetics* V.1449a.30–36. The English translation is taken from Stephen Halliwell's Loeb edition (Cambridge, Mass.: Harvard University Press, 1995), 45.

2. See *Hegel's Philosophy of Right*, trans. T. M. Knox (Oxford: Oxford University Press, 1967); hereafter cited as *PR*.

3. *PR*, note to para. 255, p. 154 in Knox's translation.

4. For one cogent response to this question, see Natasha Korda, "Domesticating Commodities in *The Taming of the Shrew*," *Shakespeare Quarterly* 47, no. 2 (1996): 109–31, as well as Lena Cowen Orlin, "The Performance of Things in *The Taming of the Shrew*," in *"The Taming of the Shrew": Critical Essays*, ed. Dana L. Aspinall, 187–209 (New York: Routledge, 2002). Unfolding the possible senses of the pun on Kate/cate, Korda brilliantly demonstrates the ambivalent construction of Kate as a consumer of "cates" (luxuries), which both cements and unmoors her potential on the marriage market in patriarchal Padua. Korda traces connections between Kate's own ambiguous status, commodity fluctuations, and Shakespeare's language play. Most recently, Julia Lupton's brilliant analysis of the play's treatment of Arendt's conceptions of *bios* and *zoê* in conjunction with Gervase Markham's 1610 household manual reorients the question of domestic rule around the play's scenes of "husbandry," in both senses. See Julia Reinhard Lupton, "Animal Husbands and *The Taming of the Shrew*," in *Thinking with Shakespeare: Essays on Politics and Life* (Chicago: University of Chicago Press, 2010), 25–67.

5. Arendt's teaching notes on *The Nicomachean Ethics* from a 1962 seminar at Wesleyan are archived at the Library of Congress and can be viewed online.

6. Giorgio Agamben, *Homo Sacer: Il potere sovrano e la nuda vita* (Torino: Einaudi, 1995), trans. Daniel Heller-Roazen as *Homo Sacer: Sovereign Power and Bare Life* (Stanford, Calif.: Stanford University Press, 1998). All subsequent references will be abbreviated *HS* and cited parenthetically, with the English page numbers preceding the Italian (e.g., *HS* 10/12).

7. The nobleman, significantly, remains unnamed (as do many of Marie's characters); in their edition, Hanning and Ferrante note that once transformed, the article *Le* that had preceded *bisclavret* is dropped—he nominally becomes the beast. See Robert Hanning and Joan Ferrante, trans., "Bisclavret," in *The Lais of Marie de France* (Grand Rapids, Mich.: Baker, 1978), 95 TN. l. 125. Hereafter all references in French will be to Marie de France, *Lais*, ed. Alfred Ewert (Oxford: Blackwell, 1965); unless otherwise noted, all references in translation will be to Hanning and Ferrrante's edition.

8. "Bisclavret," l. 57.

9. See Carole Pateman, "The Fraternal Social Contract," chap. 2 of *The Disorder of Women: Democracy, Feminism, and Political Theory* (Stanford, Calif.: Stanford University Press, 1989) and *The Sexual Contract* (Stanford, Calif.: Stanford

University Press, 1988), as well as Sedgwick's introduction to *Between Men: English Literature and Male Homosocial Desire* (New York: Columbia University Press, 1985).

10. What Agamben casually terms "the encounter [*incontro*] with the ex-wife" refers to the following episode: "Oiez cum il est bien vengiez! / Le neis li esracha del vis. / Quei li peüst il faire pis?"

"Now listen to how well he [Bisclavret] avenged himself! / He tore the nose off her face. / What worse thing could he have done to her?" (ll. 234–36). At the instigation of one of his counselors, the king then tortures the wife to obtain an admission of her betrayal of her husband: "Kar metiz la dame en destreir, / S'aucune chose vus direit" (Out of fear and pain / she told all) (ll. 255–65).

11. The werewolf's "estimable wife," rather understandably wondering why her husband disappears for three days of the week, asks him about his absences, though she is "so afraid of [his] anger / that nothing frightens [her] more"; the *bisclavret* tells her the truth and that his clothing is what enables him to transform back to his human form from his bestial one. Upon hearing this, she "is terrified of the whole adventure" and turns to "a knight of that region / who had loved her for a long time," consenting to become his mistress and conspiring with him to steal the *bisclavret*'s clothing, trapping him in wolf form (ll. 21–22, 62–78, 98–120). This particular form of conjugal betrayal, as well as the changeling motif, are of course common folk topoi: compare, for example, the story of Llew Llaw Gyffes and Blodeuwedd in "Math the Son of Mathonwy," the oldest of the tales that make up the Welsh *Mabinogion* (quite possibly known to the Breton Marie), or the biblical Samson and Delilah, for the former. See AT types D113.1 (werewolf); D537 (transformation by changing clothing); D630 (periodic transformations); K2213 (treacherous wife); K2213.4.1 (secret of hero's vulnerability disclosed by hero's wife); K2213.3 (faithless wife plots with paramour against her husband's life), in Stith Thompson, *Motif-Index of Folk-Literature,* 6 vols. (Bloomington: Indiana University Press, 1955), cited hereafter as *MIFL*.

12. "Li reis l'en meine en sun chastel; mut en fu liez, mut li est bel, / Kar unke mes tel n'ot veü; / A grant merveille l'ot tenu / E mut le tient a grant chierté. / A tuz les suens ad comaundé / Que sur s'amur le gardent bien / E li ne masfacent de rien, / Ne par nul de eus ne seit feruz; Bien seit abevreiz e peüz. / Cil le garderent volenters; Tuz jurs entre les chevalers / E pres del re se alout cuchier."

"The king led him to his castle; / he was delighted with this turn of events, / for he'd never seen anything like it. / He considered the beast a great wonder / and held him very dear. / He commanded all his followers, / for the sake of their love for him, / to guard Bisclavret well, / and under no circumstances to do him harm; / none of them should strike him; rather, he should be well fed and watered. / They willingly guarded the creature; / every day he went to sleep / among the knights, near the king" (ll. 165–77).

13. "La femme ad del païs ostee / E chacee de la cuntree. / Cil s'en alat ensemble od li, / Pur ki sun seignur ot trahi. / Enfanz en ad asés eüz, / Puis unt esté bien cuneüz / [E] del semblant e del visage: / Plusurs [des] femmes del lignage, / C'est verité, senz nes sunt nees / E si viveient esnasees."

"[The king] banished the wife, / chased her out of the country. . . . She had several children / who were widely known / for their appearance: / several women of the family / were actually born without noses, / and lived out their lives noseless" (ll. 255–65, 305–14). Cutting off the nose is apparently a common folk punishment for treachery as well as adultery; see, in *MIFL*, AT types Q450.1 (torture as punishment); Q451 (mutilation as punishment), in particular Q451.5.1 (nose cut off as punishment for adultery) and 451.5.1.1 (mistress's nose cut off as punishment for faithlessness).

14. For a nuanced reading of Arendt's philosophical debt to her teacher, see Dana R. Villa, "The Anxiety of Influence," chap. 3 of *Politics, Philosophy, Terror: Essays on the Thought of Hannah Arendt*, 61–86 (Princeton: Princeton University Press, 1999), as well as Villa's more complete treatment, *Arendt and Heidegger: The Fate of the Political* (Princeton: Princeton University Press, 1996).

15. *Sunduazesthai*, the term Aristotle uses for the union between man and woman in the *Politics*, designates the "coupling" or binding of the marriage ceremony itself, not the married state. See H. Rackham, ed. and trans., *Politics* (Cambridge, Mass.: Harvard University Press, 1932); the reference is to 1252a.26–28. Aristotle later distinguishes between a man's "royal" (*basilikôs*) rule over his children and his "constitutional" (*politikôs*) rule over his wife (1259b.1–18).

16. Arendt refers specifically to the work of Jean-Jacques Rousseau here, but her comments on the "rebellion of the heart" (a philosophical position that she connects, usefully, to the rise of the novel as a literary genre) must also, I feel, be considered relevant to an examination of her remarks about pain, here and elsewhere.

17. See Aristotle, *Politics*, 1253a2–18.

18. Elaine Scarry, whose analysis of the "world-making" (e.g., relating to labor) and "world-destroying" (e.g., relating to war or torture) capacities of pain occasionally accords with Arendt's, concurs: "Physical pain—unlike any other state of consciousness—has no referential content. It is not *of* or *for* anything. It is precisely because it takes no object that it, more than any other phenomenon, resists objectification in language" (*The Body in Pain: The Making and Unmaking of the World* [Oxford: Oxford University Press, 1985], 4).

19. See Scarry's introductory comments on the two types of metaphors used to describe pain, which she classifies as "external agents" or "weapons" and "bodily damage pictured as accompanying the pain" (ibid., 15–17).

20. In this context, it is worth pointing ahead to the complicated structure of Shakespeare's play: the marriage plot and subplot are framed as the dream vision of the tinker Sly. Scholars have long speculated that earlier redactions of the text may have included a final scene that returns to the framing dream narrative, rendering the "now kiss me, Kate" closure of the play even more ambiguous. Despite Arendt's antipathy for Freudian psychology, it is perhaps also worth pointing out certain parallels between her ideas here and Freud's theory of the voiceless nature of melancholia. See Freud's "Mourning and Melancholia" (1917), in *General Psychological Theory: Papers on Metapsychology*, ed. Philip Rieff, 164–79 (New York: Collier, 1963), as well as Judith Butler's reading of Freud's essay in "Psychic Inceptions: Melancholy, Ambivalence, Rage" in *The Psychic Life of Power: Theories in Subjection* (Stanford, Calif.: Stanford University Press, 1997), 167–98.

21. On Arendt's account of the social, see, especially, Hannah Fennichel Pitkin, *The Attack of the Blob: Hannah Arendt's Concept of the Social* (Chicago:

University of Chicago Press, 1998), in which Pitkin notes the "feminine" nature of Arendt's social, likening it to a devouring "bad mother" (168–75).

22. Though some feminists, such as Adrienne Rich, have long castigated Arendt for her apparent failure to fully engage with what she called "The Woman Question," I would argue that she *does* do so—perhaps not overtly, but often, as she does here, rather more implicitly. While Rich argues (with some justice) that in *The Human Condition* Arendt "stare[s] straight through unseeing" issues such as "women as the laborers in reproduction . . . women as workers in production . . . the relationship of women's unpaid labor in the home to the separation between 'private' and 'public' spheres . . . the woman's body as commodity," Arendt was in fact more than aware of such issues, as attested by her 1933 essay "On the Emancipation of Women" (a review of Dr. Alice Rühle-Gerstel's *Das Frauenproblem der Gegenwart: Eine psychologische Bilanz*). I would agree with critics such as Bonnie Honig, Elizabeth Young-Bruehl, Mary Dietz, and Hannah Pitkin (among others) who attempt to ask, in Honig's words, "How does reading Arendt change the way we think about feminist theory?" See Adrienne Rich, "Conditions for Work," in *On Lies, Secrets and Silence: Selected Prose, 1966–78* (New York: Norton, 1979), 211–12; Hannah Arendt, "On the Emancipation of Women" (1933), in *Essays on Understanding, 1930–1954* (New York: Harcourt Brace, 1994), 66–68; Elizabeth Young-Bruehl, "Hannah Arendt among Feminists," in *Hannah Arendt: Twenty Years Later*, ed. Larry May and Jerome Kohn, 307–24 (Cambridge, Mass.: MIT Press, 1996); Bonnie Honig, "Introduction: The Arendt Question in Feminism" and "Toward an Agonistic Feminism: Hannah Arendt and the Politics of Identity" in *Feminist Interpretations of Hannah Arendt,* ed. Bonnie Honig (University Park: Penn State University Press, 1995), quotation on p. 3; Mary Dietz, "Feminist Receptions of Hannah Arendt," in Honig, *Feminist Interpretations of Hannah Arendt*, 17–50; Hannah Pitkin, "Conformism, Housekeeping, and the Attack of the Blob: The Origins of Hannah Arendt's Concept of the Social," in Honig, *Feminist Interpretations of Hannah Arendt*, 51–82; and Pitkin, *The Attack of the Blob*.

23. Critical wrangling over the generic designation of *The Taming of the Shrew* has been unusually lively. Recent interpretations have generally swung between reading it as a farce and, more often, a "problem comedy." See, for example, Richard A. Burt, "Charisma, Coercion, and Comic Form in *The Taming of the Shrew*," in *William Shakespeare's "The Taming of the Shrew,"* ed. Harold Bloom, 79–92 (New York: Chelsea House, 1988); Margaret Lael Mikesell, "'Love Wrought These Miracles': Marriage and Genre in *The Taming of the Shrew*," in *"The Taming of the Shrew": Critical Essays*, ed. Dana L. Aspinall, 106–29 (New York: Routledge, 2002); and Coppélia Kahn, "'The Taming of the Shrew': Shakespeare's Mirror of Marriage," *Modern Language Studies* 5, no. 1 (1975): 88–102.

24. Unless otherwise noted, all references to the play will be to Ann Thompson's edition (Cambridge: Cambridge University Press, 1984). *Shrew* presents a complicated textual history. The Stationers' Register of May 2, 1594 lists "A plesant Conceyted historie called the Tamynge of a Shrowe," which may or may not be another version of Shakespeare's play. *The Taming of the Shrew* did not appear in published form until the First Folio of 1623, in which it is one of the "Comedies," but it is thought to have been composed in June 1592 or for the previous season (Thompson 1–3). For a concise summary of the somewhat vexed

question of textual and performance history and dating, see Thompson's introduction; for more detailed analysis, see also G. I. Duthie, "*The Taming of a Shrew* and *The Taming of the Shrew*," *Review of English Studies* 19 (1943): 337–56; Richard Hosley, "Sources and Analogues of *The Taming of the Shrew*," *Huntington Library Quarterly* 27 (1963–64): 289–308; and M. Mincoff, "The Dating of *The Taming of the Shrew*," *English Studies* 54 (1973): 554–65.

25. My line of argument here draws something from Gary Schneider's reading of different rituals and forms of "shaming"; see his "The Public, the Private, and the Shaming of the Shrew," *SEL* 42, no. 2: (2002) 235–58.

26. On this topic, see Julia Reinhard Lupton, "Merchants of Venice, Circles of Citizenship," in *Citizen-Saints: Shakespeare and Political Theology* (Chicago: University of Chicago Press, 2005), 73–102.

27. In "Civilizing Subordination: Domestic Violence and *The Taming of the Shrew*," *Shakespeare Quarterly* 48, no. 3 (1997): 273–94, Detmer argues, "My point is not just that taming by policy can be violent but also that the wife-beating reformers' emphasis on 'blows' makes other coercive and threatening behavior appear to be outside the model for what counts as domestic violence" (282). For further historical and literary background on taming, see also Lynda E. Boose, "Scolding Bridles and Bridling Scolds: Taming the Woman's Unruly Member," *Shakespeare Quarterly* 42, no. 2 (1991): 179–213, and Frances E. Dolan, *"The Taming of the Shrew": Texts and Contexts* (Boston: Bedford, 1996).

28. See, in the *OED*, "man" (v), I.4, III.8, 9; the former carries an implicit sexual register. "Haggard" initially referred specifically to a wild female hawk, thence to "a wild and intractable person (at first a female)"; the second example given in the *OED* is from *Shrew* IV.ii.39. Thus "to man my haggard" can (admittedly with some stretching) suggest not just falconry but sexual domination.

29. The play experienced a somewhat troubled performance history even in its own day, as Ann Thompson and others have shown and as John Fletcher's 1611 "sequel," *The Woman's Prize; or, The Tamer Tam'd*, seems to attest. Thompson argues that the discomfort modern audiences feel with Kate's submission is hardly a new thing: "Despite a long and vigorous stage tradition, it has probably been played straight less often than any other play in the canon" (18).

30. The lecture is reprinted in Hannah Arendt, *Responsibility and Judgment*, ed. Jerome Kohn, 147–58 (New York: Harcourt Brace Jovanovich, 2003); the reference is to p. 147. The notion of "collective responsibility" is one to which Arendt returned often in her post–World War II writings and lectures. See, for example, her 1945 essay "Organized Guilt and Universal Responsibility," in *Essays on Understanding*, 121–32, as well as the posthumously published lectures now collected in *Responsibility and Judgment*.

Chapter One

The epigraph is from Löwith's closing remarks on "The Biblical View of History," in *Meaning in History* (Chicago: University of Chicago Press, 1949), 190.

1. See Eric L. Santner, *On Creaturely Life: Rilke, Benjamin, Sebald* (Chicago: University of Chicago Press, 2006), 17; emphasis added.

2. For a reading of this dynamic, see Julia Reinhard Lupton, "The Denouement of Martyrdom," in *Afterlives of the Saints: Hagiography, Typology, and Renaissance Literature* (Stanford, Calif.: Stanford University Press, 1996), 64–67.

3. On undead letters see also Jacques Derrida, *The Post Card: From Socrates to Freud and Beyond*, trans. Alan Bass (Chicago: University of Chicago Press, 1987).

4. See, by Irving Ribner, *The English History Play in the Age of Shakespeare* (Princeton: Princeton University Press, 1957), hereafter cited as *EHP*; "Marlowe's *Edward II* and the Tudor History Play," *ELH* 22, no. 4 (1955): 243–53, quotation on p. 243; and "The Tudor History Play: An Essay in Definition," *PMLA* 69, no. 3 (1954): 591–609.

5. See, for example, E. M. W. Tillyard, *Shakespeare's History Plays* (London: Chatto and Windus, 1944), hereafter cited as *SHP*. Tillyard's notion of the "Tudor myth" has been somewhat overturned by arguments such as Annabel Patterson's; see her *Reading Holinshed's "Chronicles"* (Chicago: University of Chicago Press, 1994).

6. See Aristotle, *Poetics*, trans. Stephen Halliwell (Cambridge, Mass.: Harvard University Press, 1995), and Sidney, *A Defence of Poetry*, ed. J. A. Van Dorsten (Oxford: Oxford University Press, 1966).

7. See Ernst H. Kantorowicz, *The King's Two Bodies: A Study in Mediaeval Political Theology* (Princeton: Princeton University Press, 1997), hereafter cited parenthetically.

8. Ribner, "Marlowe's *Edward II*," 244.

9. In a recent special issue of *Representations*, Richard Halpern addresses Kantorowicz's chapter on *Richard II*, arguing that Shakespeare's play is best understood as a form of *Trauerspiel*. While written before the article appeared, my own essay also treats history plays according to Benjamin's formulation, yet my focus on Marlowe's earlier, more experimental play will, I hope, add to our readings of both Shakespeare and Kantorowicz. See Richard Halpern, "The King's Two Buckets: Kantorowicz, *Richard II*, and Fiscal *Trauerspiel*," *Representations* 106 (2009): 67–76. See also Santner's most recent book, *The Royal Remains: The People's Two Bodies and the Endgames of Sovereignty* (Chicago: University of Chicago Press, 2011), which addresses the spectral remnants of sacral kingship in "the new bearer of sovereignty, the People," focusing on a psychoanalytically inflected consideration of flesh as the linchpin in this transformation (245).

10. See Ernst Cassirer, *The Myth of the State* (1946) (New Haven: Yale University Press, 1974). On Kantorowicz's treatment of and connection to Cassirer, see Joseph Mali, *Mythistory: The Making of a Modern Historiography* (Chicago: University of Chicago Press, 2003). More recently, Victoria Kahn, "Political Theology and Fiction in *The King's Two Bodies*," *Representations* 106 (2009): 77–101, focuses on Kantorowicz's links to both Schmitt and Cassirer; see also her earlier essay on Benjamin and Schmitt, "Hamlet or Hecuba: Carl Schmitt's Decision," *Representations* 83 (2003): 67–96.

11. See Carl Schmitt, *Political Theology: Four Chapters on the Concept of Sovereignty*, trans. George Schwab (Chicago: University of Chicago Press, 1985).

12. See Kahn's thorough reading of this dynamic in "Political Theology and Fiction," as well as Giorgio Agamben, *Homo Sacer: Sovereign Power and Bare Life*, trans. Daniel Heller-Roazen (Stanford, Calif.: Stanford University Press, 1998). Agamben, who draws the same connections between Kantorowicz, Benjamin, and Schmitt I will outline in the next section of this argument, puts this much more strongly than I do, arguing that *The King's Two Bodies* constitutes not just Kantorowicz's meditation on myths of state but also a repudiation of

his own earlier attempt to construct them. Though Agamben is quick to suggest Kantorowicz's own early investment in the emerging Nazi construction of myths of state because his first book was read and praised by Hitler and Göring, among others, this somewhat simplifies the complexity of both the very mixed contemporary responses to Kantorowicz's work and Kantorowicz's own politics. While Kantorowicz certainly takes up his own problematic legacy in *The King's Two Bodies*, it seems to me injudicious to read the second as an entire disavowal of the first—Kantorowicz is, after all, building on his own foundations in the later work. Joseph Mali offers a more nuanced perspective: "For even if one believes, as I do, that his biography of Frederick is defensible on methodological grounds, it is still disconcerting to recall what it meant to Hitler, Göring, and other Nazis. Karl Löwith's judgment on the George circle applies to Kantorowicz's book as well: 'They prepared paths for National Socialism which they themselves did not take' " (*Mythistory*, 214). See also Ralph Giesey's biographical essay about his teacher, "Ernst H. Kantorowicz: Scholarly Triumphs and Academic Travails in Weimar Germany and the United States," included in the Kantorowicz Archive at the Leo Baeck Institute and published in the institute's *Year Book* 30, no. 1 (1985): 191–202. Giesey discusses Kantorowicz's own response to the popular misreading of *Frederick II*, aligning *The King's Two Bodies* much more closely with Kantorowicz's *Laudes Regiae* (completed in 1938 but not published until 1946) than with Kantorowicz's first work.

13. See Ernst H. Kantorowicz, "Mysteries of State: An Absolutist Concept and Its Late Mediaeval Origins," *Harvard Theological Review* 48, no. 1 (1955): 69–91. Though Kantorowicz incorporated parts of the argument with *The King's Two Bodies*, in this earlier article he articulates the connection between medieval and modern forms of absolutism much more clearly: "It is from these strata of thought, I believe, that the absolutist concept 'Mysteries of State' took its origin and that, *when finally the Nation stepped into the pontifical shoes of the Prince, the modern ABSOLUTE STATE, even without a Prince, was enabled to make claims like a Church*" (91; emphasis added). On this topic, see David Norbrook, "The Emperor's New Body? *Richard II*, Ernst Kantorowicz, and the Politics of Shakespeare Criticism," *Textual Practice* 10, no. 2 (1996): 329–57.

14. On the sometimes indirect dialogue between Benjamin and Schmitt, see Jennifer R. Rust and Julia R. Lupton, "Introduction: Schmitt and Shakespeare," in Carl Schmitt, *Hamlet or Hecuba: The Intrusion of Time into the Play*, trans. David Pan and Jennifer R. Rust (New York: Telos, 2009); Jacques Derrida, *The Beast and the Sovereign, Volume 1*, trans. Geoffrey Bennington (Chicago: University of Chicago Press, 2009); Marc de Wilde, "Violence in the State of Exception: Refelections on Theologico-Politcal Motifs in Benjamin and Schmitt," in *Political Theologies: Public Religions in a Post-Secular World*, ed. Hent de Vries and Lawrence E. Sullivan, 188–200 (New York: Fordham University Press, 2006); Giorgio Agamben, *State of Exception*, trans. Kevin Attell (Chicago: University of Chicago Press, 2005); Julia Reinhard Lupton, *Citizen-Saints: Shakespeare and Political Theology* (Chicago: University of Chicago Press, 2005); Kahn, "Hamlet or Hecuba"; Horst Bredekamp, "From Walter Benjamin to Carl Schmitt, via Thomas Hobbes," trans. Melissa Thorson Hause and Jackson Bond, *Critical Inquiry* 25, no. 2 (1999): 247–66; and Sam Weber, "Taking Exception to Decision: Walter Benjamin and Carl Schmitt," *Diacritics* 22, no. 3/4 (1992): 5–18.

15. See Jonathan Goldberg, "Sodomy and Society: The Case of Christopher Marlowe," in *Staging the Renaissance: Reinterpretations of Elizabethan and Jacobean Drama*, ed. David Scott Kastan and Peter Stallybrass, 75–82 (New York: Routledge, 1991), and Stephen Orgel, "Tobacco and Boys: How Queer Was Marlowe?," in *The Authentic Shakespeare, and Other Problems of the Early Modern Stage* (New York: Routledge, 2002), 211–29.

16. See Park Honan, *Christopher Marlowe: Poet and Spy* (Oxford: Oxford University Press, 2005).

17. For a corrective, see Benjamin Griffin, "The Birth of the History Play: Saint, Sacrifice, and Reformation," *SEL* 39, no. 2 (1999): 217–35.

18. Tillyard, *SHP*, 108, 107.

19. Ribner, *EHP*, 131–32; emphasis added.

20. See Walter Benjamin, *The Origin of German Tragic Drama*, trans. John Osborne (London: Verso, 1998).

21. Ibid., 62.

22. Ibid., 63.

23. Ibid., 71, 81, 85–86, 138–142; quotation on p. 65.

24. Benjamin cites Schmitt here.

25. Benjamin, *Origin*, 65–66; emphasis added.

26. Schmitt, *Political Theology*, 1, 36.

27. See James VI/I, *The Trew Law of Free Monarchies*, in *King James VI and I: Political Writings*, ed. Johann P. Sommerville (Cambridge: Cambridge University Press, 1994), 75.

28. See Bredekamp, "From Walter Benjamin to Carl Schmitt," 249–51; Kahn, "Political Theology and Fiction," 79–80.

29. A point made by many previous critics; see notes 9–14, this chapter, as well as Lorna Hutson's critique of Deborah Shuger's reading of Kantorowicz in "Imagining Justice: Kantorowicz and Shakespeare," *Representations* 106 (2009): 120.

30. See Agamben, *Homo Sacer* and *State of Exception*.

31. Benjamin, *Origin*, 67, 137.

32. See Löwith's closing remarks on "The Biblical View of History," in *Meaning in History* (Chicago: University of Chicago Press, 1949), 190. Löwith's characterization of history as "a scene of the most intensive life, which ends time and again in ruins," points us toward drama. Bernhard Jussen, whose assessment of "*The King's Two Bodies* Today" also appeared in the recent special issue of *Representations* devoted to Kantorowicz (106 [2009]), begins by noting Löwith's meeting with Kantorowicz in 1941 (102).

33. The play was first published in quarto in 1594, identifying "Chri. Marlow *Gent.*" as the author; the title page of the first edition claims that the text is presented "As it was sundrie times publiquely acted in the honourable citte of London, by the right honourable the Earle of Pembrooke his servants." All citations of the play refer to the Martin Wiggins and Robert Lindsey New Mermaids edition (New York: Norton, 1997) (hereafter cited parenthetically), which preserves the quarto's division of the play into scenes.

34. Readings of Marlowe's play tend to exemplify the tragedy/history bifurcation, focusing either on questioning the conception of historical "truth" and Marlowe's fidelity to his chronicle sources or on defending this episodic drama

as a valid tragedy. For examples of the former, see Joan Parks, "History, Tragedy, and Truth in Christopher Marlowe's *Edward II*," *Studies in English Literature* 39, no. 2 (1999): 275–90; Denis Kay, "Marlowe, *Edward II*, and the Cult of Elizabeth," *Early Modern Literary Studies* 3, no. 2 (1997): 1–30; and Georgia E. Brown, "Tampering with the Records: Engendering the Political Community and Marlowe's Appropriation of the Past in *Edward II*," in *Marlowe's Empery: Expanding His Critical Contexts*, ed. Sara Munson Deats and Robert A. Logan, 164–87 (Newark: University of Delaware Press, 2002). More structuralist or thematic arguments tend to treat the play as a tragedy; see, for example, Sara Munson Deats, "Marlowe's Fearful Symmetry in *Edward II*," in *"A Poet and a Filthy Play-Maker": New Essays on Christopher Marlowe*, ed. Kenneth Friedenreich, Roma Gill, and Constance B. Kuriyama, 241–62 (New York: AMS, 1998), and David Bevington and James Shapiro, "'What Are Kings, When Regiment Is Gone?': The Decay of Ceremony in *Edward II*," in Friedenreich, Gill, and Kuriyama, *"A Poet and a Filthy Play-Maker,"* 263–78.

35. Most recently, Curtis Perry's work on the literature of favoritism takes up this line; see his *Literature and Favoritism in Early Modern England* (Cambridge: Cambridge University Press, 2006), as well as his earlier treatment of Marlowe's play in "The Politics of Access and Representations of the Sodomite King in Early Modern England," *Renaissance Quarterly* 53, no. 4 (2000): 1054–83. Marlowe's play was virtually rediscovered as what Wiggins and Lindsay call a "gay classic" after Alan Bray's pioneering work *Homosexuality in Renaissance England*, first published in 1982 (2nd ed., New York: Columbia University Press, 1995). On this subject, see also Emily Bartels, *Spectacles of Strangeness: Imperialism, Alienation, and Marlowe* (Philadelpha: University of Pennsylvania Press, 1993); Gregory Bredbeck, *Sodomy and Interpretation: Marlowe to Milton* (Ithaca: Cornell University Press, 1991); Jonathan Goldberg, "Sodomy and Society: The Case of Christopher Marlowe," in *Staging the Renaissance: Reinterpretations of Elizabethan and Jacobean Drama*, ed. David Scott Kastan and Peter Stallybrass, 75–82 (New York: Routledge, 1991); Jonathan Goldberg, "The Transvestite Stage: More on the Case of Christopher Marlowe," in *Sodometries: Renaissance Texts, Modern Sexualities* (Stanford, Calif.: Stanford University Press, 1992), 105–44; Mario DiGangi, "The Homoerotics of Favoritism in Tragedy," in *The Homoerotics of Early Modern Drama* (Cambridge: Cambridge University Press, 1997), 100–133; Stephen Orgel, "In the Eye of the Beholder," in *Impersonations: The Performance of Gender in Shakespeare's England* (Cambridge: Cambridge University Press, 1996), 31–52; Bruce R. Smith, "Masters and Minions," in *Homosexual Desire in Shakespeare's England: A Cultural Poetics* (Chicago: University of Chicago Press, 1991), 189–223; and Graham Hammill, *Sexuality and Form: Caravaggio, Marlowe, and Bacon* (Chicago: University of Chicago Press, 2000).

36. A stage direction original to the 1594 quarto. Charles Forker, the most recent textual editor of the play, argues that the quarto's source was in fact "Marlowe's fair copy (or a scribal transcript of this) sold to Pembroke's Men by the playwright and annotated in such a way as partially to guide a future copyist in the preparation of a promptbook." See Forker's introduction to the Revels edition of the play (Manchester, U.K.: Manchester University Press, 1994), 10.

37. See Jayne Elizabeth Lewis, ed., *The Trial of Mary Queen of Scots: A Brief History with Documents* (Boston: Bedford/St. Martin's, 1999); hereafter cited

parenthetically as *Trial*. See also Jayne Elizabeth Lewis, *Mary Queen of Scots: Romance and Nation* (London: Routledge, 1998); James Emerson Phillips, *Images of a Queen: Mary Stuart in Sixteenth-Century Literature* (Berkeley: University of California Press, 1964); and John Guy, *The True Life of Mary Stuart, Queen of Scots* (Boston: Houghton Mifflin, 2004). On the casket letters, see A. E. MacRobert, *Mary, Queen of Scots and the Casket Letters* (London: Tauris, 2002), and Clifford Bax, *Letters and Poems by Mary Stuart, Queen of Scots* (New York: Philosophical Library, 1947).

38. I draw here from Hannah Arendt's discussion of these traditions in *The Human Condition*, 2nd ed. (Chicago: University of Chicago Press, 1998).

39. See Guy, *True Life*, and MacRobert, *Casket Letters*.

40. See Kantorowicz, *The King's Two Bodies*, 411–12, on the origins of the cries "The king is dead . . . Long live the king!" first recorded in English usage at the death of Henry VII and the ascension of Henry VIII. While Kantorowicz traces this formula to its classical antecedents, it is worth pointing out that it also recalls part of the Catholic liturgy, assimilated by many reformers as the locus classicus articulation of the "mystery of faith": the assertion "Christ has died, Christ is risen, Christ will come again" that occurs in conjunction with the sacring.

41. The phrase is Etienne Balibar's; see his essay "Citizen Subject," in *Who Comes after the Subject?*, ed. Eduardo Cadava, Peter Connor, and Jean-Luc Nancy, 33–57 (New York: Routledge, 1991).

42. Bodin visited Elizabeth's court in 1581, attached to the court of the duc d'Alençon, as Marlowe (a probable opponent to the French match) may have known.

43. See Book I of Jean Bodin's *Six livres de la République*, first published in French in 1576, translated into Latin by the author in 1586, and translated into English in 1606 (see *On Sovereignty: Four Chapters from "The Six Books of the Commonwealth,"* trans. and ed. Julian H. Franklin [Cambridge: Cambridge University Press, 1992], 49–51; emphasis added). Though it is not certain that Marlowe read Bodin's work, Ribner speculates that his treatment of Tamburlaine owes something to Bodin's account (*EHP*, 64n67). On historical and legal precedents for Bodin's idea of the indivisibility of sovereignty, see Julian H. Franklin, *Jean Bodin and the Rise of Absolutist Theory* (Cambridge: Cambridge University Press, 1973), as well as John Neville Figgis's classic study, *The Divine Right of Kings*, first published in 1850 (New York: Harper and Row, 1965).

44. Reprinted in Lewis, *Trial*, 83; emphasis added.

45. Ibid., 98.

46. As evidenced by these excerpts from William Cobbett's *Parliamentary History*:

> She answered, That she was no subject, and rather would she die a thousand deaths than acknowledge herself a subject, considering that by such an acknowledgment she should both prejudice the height of regal majesty, and withal confess herself to be bound by all the laws of England, even in matters of religion. . . . She protested, that she was no subject of the queen's, but had been and was a free and absolute queen, and not to be constrained to appear before Commissioners, or any other Judge whatsoever, for any cause whatsoever, save before God alone the highest Judge. (Reprinted ibid., 96, 98).

47. Schmitt cites both Bodin and James I admiringly in his political works. In a brief monograph published in 1956, *Hamlet oder Hekuba: Der Einbruch der Zeit in das Spiel*, Schmitt belatedly responds to Benjamin's *Trauerspiel* book. Here Schmitt argues that the threat of history, in the form of James's possible succession (tainted by association with Mary Stuart), "interrupts" the aesthetic removal of Shakespeare's play. See Schmitt, *Hamlet or Hecuba*.

48. Marlowe paraphrases Holinshed very closely in both these scenes. See Raphael Holinshed, *Holinshed's Chronicles of England, Scotland, and Ireland* (New York: AMS Press, 1965), vol. 2 (England), 547, 549–50.

49. See Henry Ellis, ed., *The New Chronicles of England and France, in Two Parts; by Robert Fabyan . . . Reprinted from Pynson's Edition of 1516* (London, 1811), 420.

50. The crown as both metonymic and synedochic representation of the body politic is of course an ancient conceit, one Kantorowicz addresses as he retraces Maitland's footsteps. On the analogy between the crown and saints' halos, see Kantorowicz, *The King's Two Bodies*, 78–86. On the peculiarities of the English crown as legal fiction, see F. W. Maitland, "The Crown as Corporation" (1911), in *State, Trust and Corporation*, ed. David Runciman and Magnus Ryan, 32–51 (Cambridge: Cambridge University Press, 2003). See also Dale Hoak, "The Iconography of the Crown Imperial," in *Tudor Political Culture*, ed. Dale Hoak, 54–103 (Cambridge: Cambridge University Press, 1995).

51. I draw here from John Bossy's quadripart division of the communal bonds reinforced in the celebration of the Eucharist. Bossy argues that the Eucharistic community can be divided both vertically (living and dead) and horizontally (friends and enemies), echoing the cruciform scoring of the host. See his "The Mass as Social Institution, 1200–1700," *Past and Present* 100 (1983): 48–51.

52. Lupton, "The Denouement of Martyrdom," 66.

53. Literally, in terms of the cross that scores the host; see Bossy, "The Mass as Social Institution," 48–50, on the *fractio panis* (Breaking of Bread) along these lines, as well as Caroline Walker Bynum's discussion of the twelfth-century shift to imprinting the host with pictures of Christ rather than of the cross, in *Fragmentation and Redemption: Essays on Gender and the Human Body in Medieval Religion* (New York: Urzone, 1991), 127–28.

54. On this subject, see Francis Clark, S.J., *Eucharistic Sacrifice and the Reformation* (Oxford: Blackwell, 1967), and Lee Palmer Wandel, *The Eucharist in the Reformation: Incarnation and Liturgy* (Cambridge: Cambridge University Press, 2006).

55. See Miri Rubin, *Corpus Christi: The Eucharist in Late Medieval Culture* (Cambridge: Cambridge University Press, 1991), 131. On the elevation and sacring, see also Henri de Lubac, S.J., *Corpus Mysticum: The Eucharist and the Church in the Middle Ages,* trans. Gemma Simmons, C.J. (Notre Dame: University of Notre Dame Press, 2006)—a work Kantorowicz cites, in three earlier French printings (1939, 1940, 1949)—as well as Bossy, "The Mass as Social Institution," 29–61; Eamon Duffy, *The Stripping of the Altars*, 2nd ed. (New Haven: Yale University Press, 2005); William T. Cavanaugh, "Eucharistic Sacrifice and the Social Imagination in Early Modern Europe," *Journal of Medieval and Early Modern Studies* 31, no. 3 (2001): 585–605, and Bynum, *Fragmentation and Redemption.* Most recently, Jennifer R. Rust takes up Kantorowicz's debt to De

Lubac in *The Body in Mystery: The Political Theology of the* Corpus Mysticum *in the Literature of Reformation England* (Evanston, Ill: Northwestern University Press, 2014), 3–28.

56. See the articles "Of the Sacraments" and "Of the Lord's Supper" (London, 1563, 1571), reprinted in *Documents of the English Reformation*, ed. Gerald Bray (Minneapolis: Fortress, 1994), 298–303.

57. Matthew 27:37; Mark 15:18, 26; Luke 23:38; John 19:19–22. All biblical citations are taken from Robert Carroll and Stephen Prickett, eds., *The Bible: Authorized King James Version* (Oxford: Oxford University Press, 1997).

58. On "exscription" and the sacring, see Jean-Luc Nancy, *Corpus*, trans. Richard A. Rand (New York: Fordham University Press, 2008).

59. I focus on the Catholic doctrine in the preceding discussion because it is at this moment the supposed anti-Catholic bias of the play becomes more nuanced, less settled. Again, while I certainly don't think Marlowe was a crypto-Catholic, I do think his work needs to be read as taking Catholicism seriously and not simply dismissed as Protestant propaganda. For a far more thorough account of the ways *Edward II* draws on Catholic liturgy and iconography, see Patrick Ryan, "Marlowe's 'Edward II' and the Medieval Passion Play," *Comparative Drama* 32, no. 4 (1998/1999): 465–95.

60. See, in the *OED*, "runagate" (especially sense 2) and "renegade," as well as 19.85n. The term was commonly applied to those suspected of being recusant Catholics, or converts.

61. See Alain Boureau, *Kantorowicz: Stories of a Historian*, trans. Stephen G. Nichols and Gabrielle M. Spiegel (Baltimore: Johns Hopkins University Press, 2001), 1. Though Boureau does not note this, there is, in fact, an archive of some of Kantorowicz's papers and correspondence at the Leo Baeck Institute in New York (now jointly housed at the Center for Jewish Studies, also in New York).

62. See Cassirer, *The Myth of the State*, particularly chaps. 16 ("From Hero Worship to Race Worship") and 18 ("The Technique of the Modern Political Myths"), as well as Kahn, "Political Theology and Fiction."

63. Cassirer, *The Myth of the State*, 1.

64. See Walter Benjamin, "Theses on the Philosophy of History," in *Illuminations: Essays and Reflections*, trans. Harry Zohn, ed. Hannah Arendt (New York: Schocken, 1968), 257.

65. See Walter Benjamin, "Critique of Violence," trans. Edward Jephcott, in *Reflections: Essays, Aphorisms, Autobiographical Writings*, ed. Peter Demetz, 277–300 (New York: Schocken, 1978).

66. On the introduction of stage properties as a mark of separation between the "tragedy of fate" and *Trauerspiel*, see Benjamin, *Origin*, 132–34.

67. Lewis, *Romance and Nation*, 49.

68. On the curious conjunctions of history and royal portraiture, see Louis Marin, *Portrait of the King* (Minneapolis: University of Minnesota Press, 1988).

69. The portrait of Mary in captivity, though inscribed with the date 1578, was probably produced later. See Phillips, *Images of a Queen*, as well as Jayne Lewis's cogent reading of the portraits in *Romance and Nation*, 50–69. Elizabeth I's own colors were black and white, symbolizing constancy and virginity; see, by Roy Strong, *Gloriana: The Portraits of Queen Elizabeth I* (London: Pimlico, 2003),

21, and *The Cult of Elizabeth: Elizabethan Portraiture and Pageantry* (London: Pimlico, 1999), 71–75.

70. On the Continental reconstruction of Mary as a martyr, see Alexander S. Wilkinson, *Mary Queen of Scots and French Public Opinion, 1542–1600* (Houndmills, Basingstoke, U.K.: Palgrave Macmillan, 2004).

Chapter Two

1. See Richard Halpern, *Shakespeare among the Moderns* (Ithaca: Cornell University Press, 1997).

2. Ibid., 3.

3. The quotation is from Eliot's "Intimations of Mortality," first published in *Poems* (1920), reprinted in *Complete Poems and Plays, 1909–1950* (New York: Harcourt, Brace and World, 1962), 32–33.

4. See T. S. Eliot, *After Strange Gods: A Primer of Modern Heresy* (New York: Harcourt, Brace, 1934), the published version of a series of three lectures delivered in 1933 at the University of Virginia, which he never republished and later tried to suppress. The year 1934 also saw the appearance in England of Eliot's *Elizabethan Essays*, which he later returned to and edited afresh for the *Essays on Elizabethan Drama*, published in the United States in 1956. In *After Strange Gods* Eliot begins by lauding the purity of the South, contrasting it with his native New England, stating, "You are further from New York; you have been less industrialised and *less invaded by foreign races*, and you have more opulent soil" (16–17; emphasis added). He characterizes the lectures as a continuation of his by then famous essay "Tradition and the Individual Talent," from a *moral* rather than an aesthetic perspective. To this end, he argues, "It is not of advantage to us to indulge a sentimental attitude toward the past. For one thing, in even the very best living tradition there is always a mixture of good and bad, and much that deserves criticism. . . . *Nor should we cling to traditions as a way of asserting our superiority over less favoured peoples.* What we can do is to use our minds, remembering that a tradition without intelligence is not worth having, to discover what is the best life for us not as a political abstraction, but as a particular people in a particular place; what in the past is worth preserving and what should be rejected; and what conditions, within our power to bring about would foster the society that we desire. Stability is obviously necessary. You are hardly likely to develop tradition except where the bulk of the population is so well off where it is that it has no incentive or pressure to move about. *The population should be homogeneous; where two or more cultures exist in the same place they are likely either to be fiercely self-conscious or both to become adulterate. What is still more important is unity of religious background; and reasons of race and religion combine to make any large number of free-thinking Jews undesirable.* There must be a proper balance between urban and rural, industrial and agricultural development. *And a spirit of excessive tolerance is to be deprecated.* We must also remember that . . . the local community must always be the most permanent, and that the concept of the nation is by no means fixed and invariable. It is, so to speak, only one fluctuating circle of loyalties between the centre of the family and the local community, and the periphery of humanity entire" (19–21; emphasis added). Eliot tried to rehabilitate and distance himself from these sentiments for the rest of his life. See Peter Ackroyd, *T. S. Eliot: A Life* (New York: Simon and Schuster, 1984),

particularly 170–72 (on Eliot's interest in, and critique of, Fascism) and 201–2 (on Eliot's diatribe against American liberalism in general and "free-thinking Jews" in particular), as well as Anthony Julius, *T. S. Eliot: Anti-Semitism and Literary Form* (Cambridge: Cambridge University Press, 1996).

5. This is not to say that Halpern himself does not do this, throughout his book, just that—as one would expect—his focus on Shakespeare means that in his reading of Eliot, in particular, he pays more attention to the essays on Shakespeare than to those about Marston, Massinger, Ford, Jonson, Webster, Tourneur, and Marlowe. Divining a certain "primitivism" in Eliot's *Elizabethan Essays*, for example, Halpern argues that the essay on *Hamlet* is symptomatic of Eliot's atavistic formalism (Halpern, *Shakespeare among the Moderns*, 24–35).

6. One cannot—or at least I cannot—talk about "Hamlet's ghost" without citing Derrida's reading of the play in *Spectres of Marx: The State of the Debt, the Work of Mourning, and the New International*, trans. Peggy Kamuf (New York: Routledge, 1994). See especially 1–60.

7. See Brian Gibbons's introduction to the New Mermaids edition (New York: Norton, 1991), ix. Unless otherwise noted, all subsequent citations refer to this edition, which is based on a collation of the first two printings, the quartos of 1607 and 1608. For the sake of convenience, in the discussion that follows I adhere to the most recent attribution (to Middleton).

8. For a more thorough treatment of the question of authorship, see R. A. Foakes's account in his introduction to the Revels edition of the play (Manchester, U.K.: Manchester University Press, 1966), xlv–liv.

9. For background on Thorndike, I am indebted to John Kerrigan's preface to *Revenge Tragedy: Aeschylus to Armageddon* (Oxford: Oxford University Press, 1996), viii. See also Aristotle, *Poetics*, trans. Stephen Halliwell (Cambridge, Mass.: Harvard University Press, 1995).

10. See John W. Cunliffe, *The Influence of Seneca on Elizabethan Tragedy* (New York: Gordon Press, 1974), first published 1893; F. L. Lucas, *Seneca and Elizabethan Tragedy* (New York: Gordon Press, 1973), originally published in 1922; and, by T. S. Eliot, "Seneca in Elizabethan Translation" (1927), in *Essays on Elizabethan Drama*, 3–55, and "Shakespeare and the Stoicism of Seneca," in *Elizabethan Essays* (London: Faber and Faber, 1934), 33–54.

11. Ronald Broude, in "Revenge and Revenge Tragedy in Renaissance England," *Renaissance Quarterly* 28 (1975): 35–58, contests the Senecan genealogy to a certain extent, claiming that "as a critical term, [revenge tragedy] depends upon the modern meaning of *revenge*," identifying it with "extralegal retaliation" (38). Broude argues that the Renaissance nuances of the term align it more closely to our modern sense of "retribution," suggesting that "revenge tragedy may in some sense be understood as a form of response to the basic questions of crime and punishment posed by [Tudor and Stuart] transformations in sociolegal thought and practice" (39). (Thus his argument does, in some ways, return to the post-Romantic characterization of the revenger he initially refutes: the one who defines the limits of moral and social law by operating outside them.)

12. On this subject, see William Empson, *Some Versions of Pastoral* (Norfolk, Conn.: Loughlin, 1960), 25–84, especially 46–50.

13. See Fredson Bowers, *Elizabethan Revenge Tragedy, 1587–1642* (Princeton: Princeton University Press, 1940), 132. T. S. Eliot had already argued that "even

the philosophical basis, the general attitude toward life of the Elizabethans, is one of anarchism, of dissolution, of decay. It is in fact exactly parallel and indeed one and the same thing with their artistic greediness, their desire for every sort of effect together, their unwillingness to accept any limitation and abide by it. The Elizabethans are in fact a part of *the movement of progress or deterioration which has culminated in Sir Arthur Pinero and in the present regimen of Europe*" ("Four Elizabethan Dramatists," in *Elizabethan Essays*, 18; emphasis added).

14. See Halpern, *Shakespeare among the Moderns*, 27.

15. See Jonathan Dollimore, *Radical Tragedy: Religion, Ideology, and Power in the Drama of Shakespeare and His Contemporaries* (Durham, N.C.: Duke University Press, 1993); Katharine Eisaman Maus's introduction to the Oxford World's Classics edition of *Four Revenge Tragedies* (Oxford: Oxford University Press, 1995); Kerrigan, *Revenge Tragedy*; Stanley Cavell, "Hamlet's Burden of Proof," in *Disowning Knowledge in Six Plays of Shakespeare* (Cambridge: Cambridge University Press, 1987), 179–91; as well as the essays on various individual revenge dramas collected in David Scott Kastan and Peter Stallybrass, eds., *Staging the Renaissance: Reinterpretations of Elizabethan and Jacobean Drama* (New York: Routledge, 1991).

16. Bowers, *Elizabethan Revenge Tragedy*, 138.

17. Ibid., 136.

18. See T. S. Eliot, "Cyril Tourneur," in *Essays on Elizabethan Drama*, 114.

19. Ibid., 120.

20. Notably *Prufrock and Other Observations*, one of the press's first publications, in 1917.

21. See Kerrigan, *Revenge Tragedy*, 5–8.

22. Foakes preserves Collins's speech heading "Junior Brother," while Gibbons prefers "Younger Son." In the subsequent discussion, I follow Foakes's designation, since "Junior Brother" is more commonly mentioned in the criticism.

23. "Quant à moy, en la justice misme, tout ce qui est au delà de la mort simple me semble pure cruauté, et notamment à nous qui devrions avoir respect d'en envoyer les ames en bon estat; ce qui ne se peut, les ayant agitées et desesperées par tourmens insupportables." See Michel de Montaigne, "De la cruauté," in *Essais*, ed. Maurice Rat (Paris: Garnier, 1962), 473; all subsequent quotations in French refer to this edition, hereafter cited parenthetically. For the English translation used in the preceding paragraph, see Florio's 1603 edition of "On Cruelty" in the *Essais* (Menston, U.K.: Scolar Press, 1969), 248; emphasis in original. Montaigne repeats this statement nearly verbatim in "Cowardize the Mother of Cruelty": "Whatsoever is beyond a simple death, seemeth to mee meere crueltie" (403, in Florio's translation).

24. "Of Revenge," in *The Essays, or Counsels Civil and Moral*, ed. Brian Vickers (Oxford: Oxford University Press, 1999), 10.

25. See Michel Foucault, *The History of Sexuality, Volume 1*, trans. Robert Hurley (New York: Random House, 1978).

26. See Bacon, *Essays*, appendix 3, 154.

27. See *decido* in Lewis and Short, *A Latin Dictionary* (A Latin Dictionary. Founded on Andrews' edition of Freund's Latin dictionary. revised, enlarged, and in great part rewritten by. Charlton T. Lewis, Ph.D. and. Charles Short, LL.D. Oxford: Clarendon Press, 1879).

28. See "The Taboo of the Queen," in Carl Schmitt, *Hamlet or Hecuba: The Intrusion of Time into the Play*, trans. David Pan and Jennifer R. Rust, 11–18 (New York: Telos, 2009).

29. I borrow Eric Santner's term here, though without its specific context in German-Jewish thought.

30. "Ceux qui ont à la combatre la volupté usent volontiers de cet argument, pour montrer qu'elle est toute vitieuse et desraisonnable: que lors qu'elle est en son plus grand effort, elle nous maistrise de façon que la raison n'y peut avoir accez; et aleguent l'experience que nous en sentons en l'accointance des femmes,

> cùm jam proesagit gaudia corpus,
> Atque in eo est venus ut muliebria conserat arva

où il leur semble que la plaisir nous transporte si fort hors de nous que nostre discours ne sçauroit alors faire son office, tout perclus et ravi en la volupté" (Montaigne, "De la cruauté," 471–72). See "On Cruelty," in *The Complete Essays*, trans. and ed. M. A. Screech (Harmondsworth, U.K.: Penguin, 1987). Unless otherwise noted (e.g., in the earlier references to Florio), all subsequent English quotations will be taken from this modern edition, hereafter cited parenthetically.

31. Compare "On Some Lines of Virgil," 947–1016, in Screech's edition.

32. "Je sçay qu'il en peut aller autrement, et qu'on arrivera par fois, si on veut, à rejetter l'ame sur ce mesme instant à autres pensemens. Mais il la faut tendre et roidir d'aguet. Je sçay qu'on peut gourmander l'effort de ce plaisir; et m'y cognoy bien; et si n'ay point trouvé Venus si imperieuse Deesse que plusieurs et plus chastes que moy la tesmoignent" (472).

33. "Je hay, entre autres vices, cruellement la cruauté, et par nature et par jugement, comme l'extreme de tous les vices" (471).

34. "Les premieres crautez s'exercent pour elles mesmes: de là s'engendre la crainte d'une juste revanche, qui produit après une enfilure de nouvelles cruautez pour les estouffer les unes par les autres. Philippus Roy de Macedoine, celuy qui eut tant de fusées à demesler avec le peuple Romain, agité de l'horreur des meurtres commis par son en divers temps offensées, print party de se saisir de tous les enfants de ceux qu'il avoit faict tuer, pour, de jour en jour, les perdre l'un apres l'autre, et ainsi establir son repos" (103).

35. "Qui rend les Tyrans si sanguinaires? c'est le soing de leur seurté, et que leur lache coeur ne leur fournit d'autres moyens de s'asseurer qu'en exterminant ceux qui les peuvent offencer, jusques aux femmes" (103).

36. On the play's talky moralizing and frequent use of sententiae, see Foakes's introduction to the Revels edition of the play, in which he likens Middleton's seemingly hollowed-out morals to Donne's reworking of the classical genre of the satire. Foakes remarks, "The originality and splendour of [the play's] poetry have often been remarked upon, yet the finest flights are liable to end in a thumping *sententia* or a sequence of generalizing couplets. . . . Only the bastard, Spurio, who openly parades his viciousness and has the courage and attractiveness of a character with convictions, believes in his own evil. The others screen what they do as a rule behind a facade of commonplaces; and Vindice, who is always self-conscious, and thinks he knows himself, satirically exploits the distances between what the courtiers profess and what they do" (xxvii–xxviii).

37. See Michael Neill, "Bastardy, Counterfeiting, and Misogyny in *The Revenger's Tragedy*," *SEL* 36, no. 2 (1996): 397–416.

38. Northrop Frye would perhaps classify this play as "the less authentic version of tragedy that we call melodrama," which he characterizes as follows: "Melodrama leans to the moral and conceptual, and tries to identify us with a heroism we admire and separate us from a villainy we detest. Melodrama thus tends to find its emotional tragic focus in the punishment of the villain . . . thus [it] appeals to emotions akin to those aroused in watching a public execution" (*Fools of Time: Studies in Shakespearean Tragedy* [Toronto: University of Toronto Press, 1967], 77).

39. In this he becomes an example of what Benjamin calls the "intriguer" (*Intrigant*) (*Origin* 95).

40. See, for the most sustained reading of the this dynamic, Steven Mullaney, "Mourning and Misogyny: *Hamlet*, *The Revenger's Tragedy*, and the Final Progress of Elizabeth I, 1600–1607," *Shakespeare Quarterly* 45, no. 2 (1994): 139–62.

41. My own reading here owes much to Peter Stallybrass's brilliant argument, which traces how Vindice simultaneously celebrates Gloriana's removal from the marketplace and reinjects her dead body into it when he instrumentalizes her skull in the Duke's murder. See his "Reading the Body: *The Revenger's Tragedy* and the Jacobean Theater of Consumption," in *Renaissance Drama: Essays on Sexuality, Influence, and Performance*, ed. Mary Beth Rose, 121–48 (Evanston, Ill.: Northwestern University Press, 1987).

42. See Eric L. Santner, *On Creaturely Life: Rilke, Benjamin, Sebald* (Chicago: University of Chicago Press, 2006). In his careful analysis of Benjamin's slippery use of the terms "natural history" and "nature-history," Santner writes,

> In Benjamin's parlance, *Naturgeshichte* has to do with what Pippin referred to as the breakdown and reification of the normative structures of human life and mindedness. It refers, that is, not to the fact that nature also has a history but to the fact that the artifacts of human history tend to acquire an aspect of mute, natural being at the point where they begin to lose their place in a viable form of life (think of the process whereby architectural ruins are reclaimed by nature). . . . Natural history is born out of the dual possibilities that life can persist beyond the death of the symbolic forms that gave it meaning and that the symbolic forms can persist beyond the death of the form of life that gave them human vitality. *Natural history transpires against the background of this space between real and symbolic death, this space of the "undead."* (16–17; emphasis added)

This space perhaps corresponds with Freud's *unheimlich*, or with Bataille's remarks concerning corpses, things that have become less than things.

43. See William Shakespeare, *Othello*, ed. Edward Pechter (New York: Norton, 2004), I.i.394–95.

44. Both Stallybrass and Mullaney also note this. See Stallybrass, "Reading the Body," 130–32, Mullaney, "Mourning and Misogyny," 159–61.

45. Drawing on Freud to demonstrate the ambiguity of the kiss, "the imagined vanishing point of the body," Stallybrass argues, "In this play, the reordering of social boundaries and the construction of genealogies through marriage is displaced by the ordering/disordering of eating and of the kiss. Into the physical

gesture of the kiss are condensed the contradictory readings of the body that the play presents" ("Reading the Body," 133). See also Sigmund Freud, *On Sexuality: Three Essays on the Theory of Sexuality and Other Works*, trans. James Strachey, ed. Angela Richards (Harmondsworth, U.K.: Penguin, 1977), 62–64.

46. Gibbons notes, "Presumably the author changed the character's name to 'Hippolito' in the course of composition, but forgot to cancel it here" (9n107).

47. Benjamin remarks on the spectral time of *Trauerspiel* (*Origin* 134–35), something Middleton's play continually emphasizes. The day/night transversals repeat throughout the play: compare Vindice's lines at II.iii, "Night, thou that look'st like funeral herald's fees / Torn down betimes in the morning, thou hang'st fitly / To grace those sins that have no grace at all" (132–34). The "unnatural" conversion of night into day is repeated when Vindice engineers Lussorioso's attempt to surprise Spurio and the Duchess in bed (which culminates in Lussorioso's attempt to kill the Duke, thinking he is Spurio). Spurio's "Is the day out o'the socket, / That it is noon at midnight, the Court up?" (II.iii.44–45) echoes the earlier lines, while the Duke's murder occurs in an "unsunned lodge / Wherein 'tis night at noon" (III.v.18–19); the temporal exchange is again paralleled in the revengers' final masque.

48. In his astute reading of the doubled imagery of counterfeit coin and adultery that seams the play, Michael Neill remarks, "The female body, once it surrenders the 'close' condition of virginity (I.iii.137), constitutes a dangerous kind of opening in the otherwise impermeable edifice of patriarchal power and property-holding, a conduit of pollution, debasement, and usurpation that requires constant regulation. For, as the fates of Gloriana and Antonio's wife reveal, ultimately only death can preserve the closeness of virginity against the voracious 'moths' that 'lust to eat / Into [the proprietor's] wearing' (I.iv.33–34)" ("Bastardy," 407).

49. The "tomb of pearl" perhaps suggests Elizabeth I, both because of her appropriation of the pearl as a symbol of chastity (see, e.g., the Armada portrait) and because of her infamous resolution, "And in the end this shall be sufficient: that a marble stone shall declare that a queen, having reigned such a time, lived and died a virgin" (first speech before Parliament, February 10, 1559). See *Elizabeth I: Collected Works*, ed. Leah S. Marcus, Janel Mueller, and Mary Beth Rose (Chicago: University of Chicago Press, 2000), 58. Louis Montrose argues that the pearl ornament placed directly over the queen's sex in the Armada portrait both calls attention to and iconographically seals off her virginity. See his "The Elizabethan Subject and the Spenserian Text," in *Literary Theory/Renaissance Texts*, ed. Patricia Parker and David Quint, 303–40 (Baltimore: Johns Hopkins University Press, 1986); see also Andrew Belsey and Catherine Belsey, "Icons of Divinity: Portraits of Elizabeth I," in *Renaissance Bodies: The Human Figure in English Culture c. 1540–1660*, ed. Lucy Gent and Nigel Llewellyn, 11–35 (London: Reaktion Books, 1990).

50. On Mary's and Elizabeth's tombs, see Arthur Penrhyn Stanley, *Historical Memorials of Westminster Abbey, Volume 1* (New York: Anson D. F. Randolph and Company, 1882), 209–15. Of Mary Stuart's tomb, Stanley writes, "Over [the coffin] was raised a monument 'like to that of Elizabeth,' but on a grander scale, as if to indicate the superiority of the mother to the predecessor [Elizabeth I], of the victim to the vanquisher" (214). Stanley goes on to record that Mary's tomb

was "revered by devout Scots as the shrine of a canonised saint," speculating that it is "the last instance of a miracle-working tomb in England" (214). See also Nigel Llewellyn, "The Royal Body: Monuments to the Dead, for the Living," in Gent and Llewellyn, *Renaissance Bodies*, 224–28, as well as Julia M. Walker, "Reading the Tombs of Elizabeth I," *ELR* 26, no. 3 (1996): 510–30. On James's monumental rehabilitation of his mother's memory, see also Jonathan Goldberg, *James I and the Politics of Literature: Jonson, Shakespeare, Donne, and Their Contemporaries* (Stanford, Calif.: Stanford University Press, 1993), 14.

51. See James's epistle "To the Reader" in the *Basilikon Doron*, which was completed in 1598 and privately printed and distributed in 1599. Reprinted in *King James VI and I: Political Writings*, ed. Johann P. Sommerville (Cambridge: Cambridge University Press, 1994), 3–12.

52. See, in the *OED*, "confection," which records only a single use of the latter sense—in the anti-Catholic cleric Thomas Becon's diatribe against "the popish mass" as the "sink of all iniquities." See John Ayre, ed., *Prayers and Other Pieces of Thomas Becon* (New York: Johnson Reprint, 1968), 498.

53. Catherine Winiarski persuasively argues that the analogy between idolatry and adultery pervades Renaissance drama. See her "Adulterers, Idolators, and Emperors: The Politics of Iconoclasm in English Renaissance Drama" (Ph.D. diss., University of California, Irvine, 2007). On early modern constructions of "turning to Mahomet," see Daniel Vitkus, *Turning Turk: English Theater and the Multicultural Mediterranean, 1570–1630* (New York: Palgrave Macmillan, 2003). Vitkus notes, "Given the conventional association made by European Christians between Islam and promiscuity, it is not surprising that the English expression 'to turn Turk' carried a sexual connotation," citing *The Revenger's Tragedy* passage on maids "turn[ing] to Mahomet" as an example (88). See also Jonathan Burton, *Traffic and Turning: Islam and English Drama, 1579–1624* (Newark: University of Delaware Press, 2005), and Benedict S. Robinson, *Islam and Early Modern English Literature: The Politics of Romance from Spenser to Milton* (New York: Palgrave Macmillan, 2007).

54. Though other critics have disagreed, Northrop Frye among them. Attributing this play to Tourneur and contrasting it with Middleton's *The Changeling* (1622), Frye remarks, "Middleton is more restrained than Ford and Tourneur, who are particularly fond of putting up signs reading 'Danger—God at work' in the course of the action. . . . In both of Tourneur's plays there is a muttering roll of thunder when the villainy really has gone too far. The religious dimension, in both Ford and Tourneur, goes with a moral interest that leads them to call their characters by allegorical names, like the Lussorioso and Vindice of *The Revenger's Tragedy*." See Frye, *Fools of Time*, 80.

55. Whereas some critics (such as Frye) take the play's self-consciously theatrical treatment of religious symbology straightforwardly, more recent treatments have tended to argue that the metatheatrical moments in the play render any call for religious meaning ironic. See, for example, Jonathan Dollimore, "*The Revenger's Tragedy*: Providence, Parody and Black Camp," in *Radical Tragedy: Religion, Ideology and Power in the Drama of Shakespeare and His Contemporaries*, 2nd ed. (Durham, N.C.: Duke University Press, 1993), 139–52; reprinted in Stevie Simkin, ed., *Revenge Tragedy*, 107–20 (Houndmills, Basingstoke, U.K.: Palgrave Macmillan, 2001).

56. See Stallybrass, "Reading the Body," 134–36.

57. On female incontinence both sexual and physiological, see Gail Kern Paster, *The Body Embarrassed: Drama and the Disciplines of Shame in Early Modern England* (Ithaca: Cornell University Press, 1993), chap. 1, as well as Stallybrass, "Reading the Body," and Mullaney, "Mourning and Misogyny."

58. See George Schwab's discussion of *Die Diktatur* and Schmitt's reading of Article 48 of the Weimar constitution in his introduction to Schmitt, *Political Theology*, xlv–xlix. Schwab notes, "Schmitt published a comprehensive study of dictatorship shortly before the appearance of *Political Theology*. There he traced the history of dictatorship and concluded that it can be categorized into two forms: commissarial and sovereign. *A sovereign dictatorship utilizes a crisis to abrogate the existing constitution in order to bring about a 'condition whereby a constitution [that the sovereign dictator] considers to be a true constitution will become possible,' whereas a commissarial dictatorship endeavors to restore order so that the existing constitution can be revived and allowed to function normally*" (xlv; emphasis added).

59. See Joseph de Maistre, *The Pope: Considered in His Relation with the Church, Temporal Sovereignties, Separated Churches, and the Cause of Civilization*, trans. Rev. Aeneas McD. Dawson (1850; repr., New York: Fertig, 1975), 1, cited parenthetically hereafter.

60. De Maistre spent part of his exile in Russia and was deeply concerned with the contrasts between Roman Catholicism and Orthodoxy, which he tends to align with the "national religions" of Reformed Europe. In an extraordinary passage that exemplifies the notion of the Catholic Church's universality and infallibility, de Maistre writes, "France, after the horrible revolution it experienced, remained Catholic; in other words, whatever has not continued Catholic is nothing. Such is the force of truth when subjected to the most terrible ordeal. *Men*, doubtless, may have been changed by this ordeal, but not doctrine; because it is essentially unchangeable. It is quite the reverse with all false religions. As soon as ignorance has ceased to maintain their forms, and they are attacked by philosophical opinions, they fall into a state of dissolution, and hasten on with obviously accelerated motion to utter annihilation. And, as the putrefaction of large bodies produces innumerable *sects* of miry reptiles, national religions, when putrefied, produce in like manner a multitude of religious *insects*, which drag out on the same soil the remains of a divided, imperfect, and disgusting existence. This may be observed on all sides, and by this may England and Russia, particularly, account for the number and inexhaustible fecundity of the sects which pullulate within their immense territories. These *sects* are born of the putrefaction of a great body. Such is the order of nature" (*The Pope* IV.iii.308).

61. Hobbes was, of course, one of Schmitt's favorite political thinkers. See his highly contentious reading of Hobbes in *The Leviathan in the State Theory of Thomas Hobbes: Meaning and Failure of a Political Symbol*, trans. George Schwab and Erna Hilfstein (Westport, Conn.: Greenwood Press, 1996), which he himself claimed was a response to Benjamin. See, also, Horst Bredekamp's analysis of both Benjamin's and Schmitt's concepts of "exceptional time" ("From Walter Benjamin to Carl Schmitt," 261). Bredekamp argues that the figure of the Leviathan becomes a sort of ghost in both the *Trauerspiel* book and the "Critique of Violence" and thus that "Benjamin occupies a middle ground between Hobbes and Schmitt" (259).

62. See Carl Schmitt, *Roman Catholicism and Political Form*, trans. G. L. Ulmen (Westport, Conn.: Greenwood Press, 1996); hereafter cited parenthetically as *RCPF*. In decrying the "economic" ideology that propels modern capitalism, Schmitt ends up in some ways curiously close to Arendt's critique of the rise of the social—both valorize sovereign states and a coherent political order, but whereas Arendt finds her primary example in the Greek polis, Schmitt locates his model in the Church. For further points of connection between Schmitt and Arendt, see two articles in *Telos* 142 (2008): Christian J. Emden, "Carl Schmitt, Hannah Arendt, and the Limits of Liberalism" (110–34), and Hans Sluga, "The Pluralism of the Political: From Carl Schmitt to Hannah Arendt" (91–109), though neither mentions *Roman Catholicism and Political Form*. Julia Reinhard Lupton also analyzes the occasional conjunctions between the two in the opening pages of her application of Schmitt's categories of the friend and the enemy to *Hamlet*. See her "Hamlet, Prince," in *Alternative Shakespeares 3*, ed. Diana Henderson (Routledge, 2007), 181–203, as well as a later iteration of the argument, "The Hamlet Elections," in *Thinking with Shakespeare* (Chicago: University of Chicago Press, 2011), 69–95.

63. Several recent works of criticism have noted the ways Schmitt's anti-Freudianism ends up being curiously Freudian. Eric Santner likens Schmitt's narrative of decisionist sovereignty to Freud's myth of the slaughter of the primal father in, especially, its earliest redactions in *Totem and Taboo* (first published between 1912 and 1913). See Sigmund Freud, *Totem and Taboo: Some Points of Agreement between the Mental Lives of Savages and Neurotics*, trans. and ed. James Strachey (New York: Norton, 1950), and Santner, *On Creaturely Life*, 69–75. Johannes Türk, in a reading of *Hamlet oder Hekuba*, analyses this tension in detail, arguing that "it is Freud whose interpretation of *Hamlet* secretly informs Schmitt's reading." See his "The Intrusion: Carl Schmitt's Non-Mimetic Logic of Art," *Telos* 142 (2008): 79. Julia Lupton, again, brings this conjunction to bear on Shakespeare studies; see her "Invitation to a Totem Meal: Hans Kelsen, Carl Schmitt, and Political Theology," in *The Return of Theory in Early Modern English Studies: Tarrying with the Subjunctive*, eds. Paul Cefalu and Bryan Reynolds (Houndmills, Basingstoke, U.K.: Palgrave MacMillan, 2011), 121-41.

64. See Türk ("The Intrusion") and Bredekamp ("From Walter Benjamin to Carl Schmitt") on ideas of representation in Schmitt and Benjamin.

65. See Carl Schmitt, *The Concept of the Political*, trans. George Schwab (Chicago: University of Chicago Press, 1996), especially 25–27. In his introduction, Schwab notes that "the thesis of this didactic essay appeared originally in 1927 under the title 'Der Begriff des Politischen' in *Archiv für Sozialwissenschaft und Sozialpolitik*, Vol. 58, No. 1, 1–33. This essay was further elaborated and published in 1932 under the same title by Duncker & Humblot, Munich" (5).

66. See also Jacob Taubes's discussion of this moment in Schmitt's work in *The Political Theology of Paul*, trans. Dana Hollander (Stanford, Calif.: Stanford University Press, 2004), 64–70.

67. This "interim" (to use Schmitt's term) or moment of delay, of suspension of the decision between life and death, finds a certain analogue in Kantorowicz's reading of the "period between the periods" in the declaration "The king is dead . . . Long live the king!" This moment, the literal interregnum, also rests on a moment of decision and provides an example of a space in which the vox populi

overwhelms the sovereign decree. Here, and perhaps only here, the sovereign becomes subject to *decisio* in the primary sense, "to die," for here the people pronounce the decision on him.

68. "Alle prägnanten Begriffe der modernen Staatslehre sind säkularisierte theologische Begriffe. Nicht nur ihrer historischen Entwicklung nach, weil sie aus der Theologie auf die Staatslehe übertragen wurden, indem zum Beispiel der allmächtige Gott zum omnipotenten Gesetzgeber wurde, sondern auch in ihrer systematischen Struktur, deren Erkenntnis notwendig ist für eine soziologishe Betrachtung dieser Begriffe. Der Ausnahmezustand hat für die Jurisprudenz eine analoge Bedeutung wie das Wunder für die Theologie" (*PT* 37).

69. See appendix 2 in *Hamlet or Hecuba*, "On the Barbarian Character of Shakespearean Drama: A Response to Walter Benjamin on *The Origin of German Tragic Drama*," 59–65. The "primitivism" Schmitt remarks on in this appendix recalls Eliot's essays from the 1930s.

70. O. K. Werckmeister notes that in both of his descriptions of Klee's painting, "Benjamin has invested Klee's image with aggressive and destructive traits absent in the original," and that "the pictorial field of the watercolor offers no suggestion of a 'catastrophe which keeps piling wreckage upon wreckage and hurls it in front of his feet,' as in the thesis" ("Walter Benjamin's Angel of History, or the Transfiguration of the Revolutionary into the Historian," *Criticial Inquiry* 22, no. 2 [1996]: 245).

71. See Virginia Woolf, *Orlando: A Biography*, ed. Brenda Lyons (Harmondsworth, U.K.: Penguin, 1993). Woolf writes, "The age was Elizabethan; their morals were not ours; nor their poets; nor their climate; nor their vegetables even. Everything was different. The weather itself, the heat and cold of summer and winter, was, we may believe, of another temper altogether. The brilliant amorous day was divided sheerly from the night as land from water. Sunsets were redder and more intense; dawns were whiter and more auroral. Of our crepuscular half-lights and lingering twilights they knew nothing. The rain fell vehemently, or not at all. The sun blazed or there was darkness. Translating this to the spiritual regions as their wont is, the poets sang beautifully how roses fade and petals fall. The moment is brief they sang; the moment is over; one long night is then to be slept by all. As for using the artifices of the greenhouse or conservatory to prolong or preserve these fresh pinks and roses, that was not their way. The withered intricacies and ambiguities of our more gradual and doubtful age were unknown to them. Violence was all. The flower bloomed and faded. The sun rose and sank. The lover loved and went. And what the poets said in rhyme, the young translated into practice" (19–20).

72. On Benjamin's polyvalent concept of history, see Santner, *On Creaturely Life*; Werckmeister, "Walter Benjamin's Angel of History"; Joseph Mali, *Mythistory: The Making of a Modern Historiography* (Chicago: University of Chicago Press, 2003), 228–83; and Beatrice Hanssen, *Walter Benjamin's Other History: Of Stones, Animals, Human Beings, and Angels* (Berkeley: University of California Press, 1998).

73. See, for example, *Roman Catholicism and Political Form*, 9–11. Despite his insistence that a Hegelian (though, perhaps, more Lockean) "dichotomy between a rationalistic-mechanistic world of human labor and a romantic virginal state of nature is totally foreign to the Roman Catholic concept of nature," Schmitt's

idealized portrait of Catholic workers essentially wedded to the feminized, fruitful soil in a symbolic and a symbiotic marriage does not so much refute the dichotomy as reify it.

74. See chap. 3, "Allegory and *Trauerspiel*," in Benjamin, *Origin*. All quotations in English refer to this edition. For the German, see *Ursprung des deutschen Trauerspiels* (Frankfurt: Suhrkamp, 1963), hereafter cited parenthetically as *UDT*.

75. "Wenn mit dem Trauerspiel die Geschichte in den Schauplatz hineinwandert, so tut sie es als Schrift. Auf dem Antlitz der Natur steht 'Geschichte' in der Zeichenschrift der Vergängnis. Die allegorische Physiognomie der Natur-Geschichte, die auf der Bühne durch das Trauerspiel gestellt wird, ist wirklich gegenwärtig als Ruine. Mit ihr hat sinnlich die Geschichte in den Schauplatz sich verzogen. Und zwar prägt, so gestaltet, die Geschichte nicht als Prozeß eines ewigen Lebens, vielmehr als Vorgang unaufhaltsamen Verfalls sich aus. Damit bekennt die Allegorie sich jenseits von Schönheit. Allegorien sind im Reiche der Gedanken was Ruinen im Reiche der Dinge. . . . Was da in Trümmern abgeschlagen liegt, das hochbedeutende Fragment, das Bruchstück: es ist die edelste Materie der barocken Schöpfung. Denn jenen Dichtungen ist es gemein, ohne strenge Vorstellung eines Ziels Bruchstücke ganz unausgesetzt zu häufen und in der unablässigen Erwartung eines Wunders Stereotypien für Steigerung zu nehmen. Als ein Wunder in diesem Sinne müssen die barocken Literaten das Kunstwerk betrachtet haben" (*Ursprung* 197–98).

76. Benjamin speaks about the macabre humor of the intriguer in *Origin* 227. Compare Nicholas Brooke's short but influential analysis in *Horrid Laughter in Jacobean Tragedy* (New York: Barnes and Noble, 1979). In *The Revenger's Tragedy*, the farcical intrigues of Supervacuo and Ambitioso that result in the death of the brother they had planned to save and the release of the brother they had planned to kill perhaps best demonstrate this dynamic (III.iv and III.vi).

77. See Benjamin again: "One might say [that] nature remained the great teacher for the writers of this period. However, nature was not seen by them in bud and bloom, but in the over-ripeness and decay of her creations. In nature they saw eternal transience, and here alone did the saturnine vision of this generation recognize history. Its monuments, ruins, are, according to Agrippa von Nettesheim, the home of the saturnine beasts. In the process of decay, and in it alone, the events of history shrivel up and become absorbed in the setting. The quintessence of these decaying objects is the polar opposite to the idea of transfigured nature as conceived by the early renaissance" (*Origin* 180).

78. Compare Hanssen, *Walter Benjamin's Other History*, 99–102; Santner, *On Creaturely Life*, 16–21.

79. Victoria Silver notes that the quaint/acquaint puns in this play are linked with Horatian decorum (unpublished lecture, University of California, Irvine, August 2005).

80. Compare the later exchange between Lussorioso and Vindice: "Thy name? I have forgot it. / Vindice, my lord. / 'Tis a good name, that. / Ay, a revenger" (IV. ii.172–73).

81. See Eliot, "Cyril Tourneur," 114–15.

82. "Gerade eine Philosophie des konkreten Lebens darf sich vor der Ausnahme und vor dem extremen Falle nicht zurückziehen, sondern muß sich im höchsten Maße für ihn interessieren. Ihr kann die Ausnahme wichtiger sein als

die Regel, nicht aus einer romantischen Ironie für das Paradoxe, sondern mit dem ganzen Ernst einer Einsicht, die tiefergeht als die klaren Generalisationen des durchschnittlich sich Wiederholenden. Die Ausnahme ist interessanter als der Normalfall. Das Normale beweist nichts, die Ausnahme beweist alles; sie bestätigt nicht nur die Regel, die Regel lebt überhaupt nur von der Ausnahme. In der Ausnahme durchbricht die Kraft des wirklichen Lebens die Kruste einer in Wiederholung erstarrten Mechanik" (*PT* 15).

Chapter Three

1. "ek toutōn oun phaneron hoti tōn phusei hē polis esti, kai hoti ho anthrōpos phusei politikon zōon, kai ho apolis dia phusin kai ou dia tukhēn ētoi phaulos estin, ē kreittōn ē anthrōpos: hōsper 5 kai ho huph' Homērou loidorētheis 'aphrētōr athemistos anestios': (Hom. Il. 9.63) hama gar phusei toioutos kai polemou epithumētēs[.]" See the Loeb parallel text edition of Aristotle, *Politics*, trans. H. Rackham (Cambridge, Mass.: Harvard University Press, 1932), hereafter cited parenthetically. The translation I cite earlier is Jonathan Barnes's for the Bollingen *Complete Aristotle*, excerpted in *"The Politics" and "The Constitution of Athens,"* ed. Stephen Everson (Cambridge: Cambridge University Press, 1996), 13.

2. Unless otherwise noted, all citations of the play refer to Lee Bliss's New Cambridge Shakespeare edition (Cambridge: Cambridge University Press, 2000), hereafter cited parenthetically.

3. See, by Andrew Hadfield, "Tarquin's Everlasting Banishment: Republicanism and Constitutionalism in *The Rape of Lucrece* and *Titus Andronicus*," *Parergon: Journal of the Australian and New Zealand Association for Medieval and Early Modern Studies* 19, no. 1 (2002): 77–104; "Shakespeare and Republicanism: History and Cultural Materialism," *Textual Practice* 17, no. 3 (2003): 461–83; and *Shakespeare and Republicanism* (Cambridge: Cambridge University Press, 2005), 1–3, 13–14. Hadfield mentions *Coriolanus* only in passing in this book, while his *Shakespeare and Renaissance Politics* (London: Thomson, 2004) contains a more extensive treatment. In the latter work—which, curiously, considers the play in the context of "Alternative Forms of Government" rather than "Republicanism and Constitutionalism"—Hadfield cautiously argues against a critical consensus that he diagnoses as "conservative" or "authoritarian" (179–80).

4. See A. C. Bradley, "Coriolanus," British Academy: Second Annual Shakespeare Lecture (New York: Oxford University Press, 1912), 4. I would not go quite so far as Bradley's later claim, "I think we should feel it extremely hazardous to ascribe to [Shakespeare] any political feelings at all," but I'm back with him by the end of the sentence: "and ridiculous to pretend to certainty on the subject" (5).

5. See Ineke Murakami, "The 'Bond and Privilege of Nature' in *Coriolanus*," *Religion and Literature* 38, no. 3 (2006): 128.

6. A critical survey of the most influential arguments in this vein would take into account James Emerson Phillips Jr., "Violation of Order and Degree in *Coriolanus*," in *The State in Shakespeare's Greek and Roman Plays* (Folcroft, Penn.: Folcroft Press, 1940), and the last two chapters of Clifford Huffman, *"Coriolanus" in Context* (Lewisburg, Penn.: Bucknell University Press, 1971). Huffman argues that "there was a Jacobean parallel to the Roman political situation of

Coriolanus" and focuses on the English sense of the threat posed by the idea of absolute monarchy and the "cross-currents of ideas urgent in European Counter-Reformation civilization" (171). Ultimately, Huffman claims, Shakespeare offers up what Anne Barton calls "an apology for Jacobean absolutism"; see her "Livy, Machiavelli, and Shakespeare's *Coriolanus*," in *Shakespeare and Politics*, ed. Catherine M. S. Alexander (Cambridge: Cambridge University Press, 2004), 88. Barton herself, while skeptical of Huffman's reading, offers no definite opinion of her own on this question, though she closes by emphasizing the ways Shakespeare's treatment of his sources plays up "hopeful, communal, and progressive" elements" (88–89). Annabel Patterson reads the play as a proto-Republican commentary on Jacobean politics; see her chapter "'Speak, speak!': The Popular Voice and the Jacobean State," in *Shakespeare and the Popular Voice* (Oxford: Blackwell, 1989), 120–53. James Kuzner refutes Patterson's reading in particular in his "Unbuilding the City: *Coriolanus* and the Birth of Republican Rome," *Shakespeare Quarterly* 58, no. 2 (2007): 174–99; see, especially, 174, 177–79, as well as the revised argument in "Unbuilding the City: *Coriolanus, Titus Andronicus*, and the Forms of Openness," Chap. 3 of *Open Subjects* (84–124). Stanley Cavell's elegant reading draws together what he sees as the two most persuasive strands of critical thought on the play, "political" and "psychoanalytic"; see his "*Coriolanus* and Interpretations of Politics: ('Who does the wolf love?')," in *Disowning Knowledge in Six Plays of Shakespeare* (Cambridge: Cambridge University Press, 1987), 143–77. For Cavell, Menenius's parable of the belly functions as a synecdochic commentary on the entire play, with its focus on the cycling of nourishment and abjection as a figure for political representation (the latter in turn synecdochically represented by the citizens' "voices"). For other recent arguments centering on Shakespeare's often ambivalent inheritance of the ideals of Republican Rome, see Rita Bannerjee, "The Common Good and the Necessity of War: Emergent Republican Ideals in Shakespeare's *Henry V* and *Coriolanus*," *Comparative Drama* 40, no. 1 (2006): 29–49; John Michael Archer, "Tragedy: What Rome?," in *Citizen Shakespeare: Freemen and Aliens in the Language of the Plays* (New York: Palgrave Macmillan, 2005), 120–91; and Coppélia Kahn, "Roman Virtue on English Stages," in *Roman Shakespeare: Warriors, Wounds, and Women* (London: Routledge, 1997), 1–26.

7. The opening stage direction's call for a "Company" of Citizens deserves special notice, recalling as it does the players' companies.

8. See, for example, Hadfield, *Shakespeare and Renaissance Politics*: "The opening scenes of the play foreground political issues in a manner which also resembles the first act of *Othello*. The angry citizens enter as a large group, but unlike the mobs represented in *Julius Caesar* and *2 Henry VI*, they are concerned with political questions rather than violent revenge" (171).

9. See Huffman, *"Coriolanus" in Context*, and William Hazlitt, *Characters of Shakespeare's Plays and Lectures on the English Poets* (London: Macmillan, 1920). Huffman's final words on the play will illustrate: "A play put on at the Globe and Blackfriars theaters by the King's Men would necessarily oppose political innovation; it would be conservative in tendency, to the despair of generations of later audiences" (222).

10. See Agamben, *HS*. For examples of arguments that take up Agamben's designation in relation to the play, see Kuzner, "Unbuilding the City"; Rebecca

Lemon, "Arms and Laws in Shakespeare's *Coriolanus*," in *The Law in Shakespeare*, ed. Constance Jordan and Karen Cunningham (Houndmills, Basingstoke, U.K.: Palgrave Macmillan, 2007), 233–34; and Murakami, "The 'Bond and Privilege of Nature.' "

11. See Murakami, "The 'Bond and Privilege of Nature,' " 130.

12. See Jonathan Goldberg, *Sodometries: Renaissance Texts, Modern Sexualities* (Stanford, Calif.: Stanford University Press, 1992).

13. See Kuzner, "Unbuilding the City," 175, 177, 179–84, 193–99.

14. See Lemon, "Arms and the Law," 244–46.

15. See *HS* on the sovereign ban as the "threshold" or "limit concept" of the law: "What is captured in the sovereign ban is a human victim who may be killed but not sacrificed: *homo sacer*" (83). See, further, Giorgio Agamben, *State of Exception*, trans. Kevin Attell (Chicago: University of Chicago Press, 2005).

16. Agamben argues that "the exception is situated in a symmetrical position with respect to the example, with which it forms a system. Exception and example constitute the two modes by which a set tries to found and maintain its own coherence. But while the exception is . . . an *inclusive exclusion* (which thus serves to include what is excluded), the example instead functions as an *exclusive inclusion*" (*HS* 21).

17. See Walter Benjamin, "Critique of Violence," trans. Edmund Jephcott, in *Reflections: Essays, Aphorisms, Autobiographical Writings*, ed. Peter Demetz, 277–300 (New York: Schocken, 1978); hereafter cited parenthetically as *CV*. Quotations in German are taken from "Zur Kritik der Gewalt," in *Gesammelte Schriften*, II.i (Frankfurt: Suhrkamp, 1977); hereafter cited as KG. Cassell's German dictionary defines *bloß* as "bare, naked, nude, uncovered, unprotected, deprived (of); destitute; pure, mere, sole." For the sake of convenience I preserve here Jephcott's translation of Benjamin's phrase as "mere life," carefully bearing in mind these other senses, particularly those of deprivation or destitution, which convey the sense of an originary *having* or *location* that has been stripped away.

18. All citations of Plutarch refer to the Loeb parallel text edition of the *Lives*, vol. 4. Unless otherwise noted, quotations in English are taken from Bernadette Perrin's translation (Cambridge, Mass.: Harvard University Press, 1916).

19. For historical background on military life in Elizabethan England, see Lindsay Boynton, *The Elizabethan Militia 1558–1638* (London: Routledge and Kegan Paul, 1967), as well as C. G. Cruickshank, *Elizabeth's Army*, 2nd ed. (Oxford: Clarendon Press, 1966). For the most comprehensive treatment of military themes in Shakespeare, see Paul A. Jorgensen, *Shakespeare's Military World* (Berkeley: University of California Press, 1956); for a thoughtful treatment of the conflict between military and civic *virtù* in this play, see Bannerjee, "The Common Good and the Necessity of War." For general background on Shakespeare's Roman plays, see also Marjorie Garber, "A Rome of One's Own," in *Shakespeare's Ghost Writers: Literature as Uncanny Causality* (New York: Routledge, 1987), 52–73; Coppélia Kahn, *Roman Shakespeare: Warriors, Wounds, and Women* (New York: Routledge, 1997); Paul A. Cantor, *Shakespeare's Rome: Republic and Empire* (Ithaca: Cornell University Press, 1976); W. A. MacCallum, *Shakespeare's Roman Plays and Their Background* (1910; repr., New York: Russell and Russell, 1967); and Geoffrey Miles, *Shakespeare and the Constant Romans* (Oxford: Oxford University Press, 1996).

20. See. in the *OED*, "no man's land," especially senses 1 and 4.

21. See Jacques Derrida, *The Gift of Death*, trans. David Wills (Chicago: University of Chicago Press, 1996). In a reading of Jan Patočka's *Heretical Essays on the Philosophy of History* that turns on an interpretation of Heidegger's *Sein und Zeit*, Derrida argues that for Heidegger, death epitomizes the impossibility of the gift, as well as the gift of the impossible: "I can give my whole life for another, I can offer my death to the other, but in doing this I will only be replacing or saving something partial in a particular situation (there will be a nonexhaustive exchange or sacrifice, an economy of sacrifice). I know on absolute grounds and in an absolutely certain manner that I will never deliver the other from his death, from the death that affects his whole being. . . . **Death's dative (dying *for* the other, giving one's life *to* the other) does not signify a substitution (*for* is not *pro* in the sense of "in place of the other")**. If something radically impossible is to be conceived of—and everything derives its sense from this impossibility—it is indeed dying *for the other* in the sense of dying *in place of* the other. **I can indeed give the other everything except immortality, except this *dying for her* to the extent of dying in place of her and so freeing her from her own death.** I can die for the other in a situation where my death gives him a little longer to live, I can save someone by throwing myself in the water or fire in order to temporarily snatch him from the jaws of death, I can give her my heart in the literal or figurative sense in order to assure her of a certain longevity. But I cannot die in her place, I cannot give her my life in exchange for her death" (43; emphases in bold added).

22. I borrow this formulation from Julia Lupton's reading of *Othello*. See her "Othello Circumcised," in *Citizen-Saints: Shakespeare and Political Theology* (Chicago: University of Chicago Press, 2005), 103–24, as well as an earlier incarnation of the argument, "*Othello* Circumcised: Shakespeare and the Pauline Discourse of Nations," *Representations* 57 (1997): 73–89.

23. See J. G. A. Pocock, *The Machiavellian Moment: Florentine Political Thought and the Atlantic Republican Tradition* (Princeton: Princeton University Press, 1975), particularly chaps. 7–9, pp. 183–332. See also Huffman's discussion of Shakespeare's possible Italian sources and influences in *"Coriolanus" in Context*, 97–136.

24. Menenius's "parable of the belly" provides, of course, one of the locus classicus articulations of the body politic. For a brief yet cogent reading of this element in Shakespeare's play and its resonances in Jacobean England, see Andrew Gurr, "'Coriolanus' and the Body Politic," *Shakespeare Survey* 28 (1975): 63–69; for more extensive readings, see also Zvi Jagendorf, "*Coriolanus*: Body Politic and Private Parts," in *"Coriolanus": Critical Essays*, ed. David Wheeler, 229–50 (New York: Garland, 1977), and T. Motohashi, "Body Politic and Political Body in *Coriolanus*," *Forum for Modern Language Studies* 30, no. 2 (April 1994): 97–112. In "Fables of the Belly in Early Modern England," Michael Schoenfeldt places Menenius's fable in the context of early modern anatomical medicine; see his essay in *The Body in Parts: Fantasies of Corporeality in Early Modern Europe*, ed. David Hillman and Carla Mazzio, 242–61 (New York: Routledge, 1997).

25. Unless otherwise noted, all quotations in English are taken from Neal Wood's translation of Machiavelli's *The Art of War* (Cambridge, Mass.: Da Capo, 1965), hereafter cited parenthetically in the body of the argument. Citations in

Italian are taken from the online Progetto Machiavelli, ed. Giuseppe Bonghi (1997), which reproduces the text of Machiavelli's *Complete Works*, ed. Mario Martelli (Florence: Sansoni, 1971), http://www.lastoria.org/progetto/.

26. See Neal Wood's introduction to Machiavelli's *The Art of War*, lxxxiv. See also Whitehorne's translation, *The arte of warre, written first in Italia[n] by Nicholas Machiauell, and set forthe in Englishe by Peter Whitehorne, studient at Graies Inne* (London, 1562), and Huffman, *"Coriolanus" in Context*, though Huffman focuses mainly on the *Discorsi* and *Il principe* and does not mention the *Arte della guerra*. Similarly, Anne Barton makes no mention of the *Arte* in her fine analysis; see her "Livy, Machiavelli, and Shakespeare's *Coriolanus*," 67–90.

27. Many critics have made this point. See, in particular, Paul A. Jorgensen's treatment of the conflict between military and civilian life in *Shakespeare's Military World* (Berkeley: University of California Press, 1956), especially chaps. 5 and 6, "War and Peace" and "The Soldier in Society: From Casque to Cushion," 169–314; and Cathy Shrank, "Civility and the City in *Coriolanus*," *Shakespeare Quarterly* 54, no. 4 (2003): 406–23.

28. In a well-known passage, Clausewitz claims that "war is not merely a political act, but also a real political instrument, a continuation of political commerce, a carrying out of the same by other means." See Carl von Clausewitz, *On War* (Harmondsworth, U.K.: Penguin, 1982), 119.

29. Machiavelli's designation oscillates between the "art" (*arte*) and "exercise" (*esercizio*) of warfare, a distinction that should not go unremarked. While the first term, as Pocock notes, "signifies both the 'art' of war in the sense of the creative skill of generalship, and the 'profession' of war, in the sense in which the principal skilled occupations of Florence were organized into greater and lesser *arti* or guilds," the second does not carry the same sense of civic affiliation but suggests more the practice of warfare for its own sake (*The Machiavellian Moment*, 199–200).

30. Jorgensen discusses the Elizabethan view of returning soldiers as both a political threat and an economic burden who were granted little provision other than special limited licenses to beg and not be jailed as vagabonds; as he notes, for common soldiers in particular "the shocking truth was that Elizabethan warfare, with its dysentery, famine, and crude surgery, allowed conscripts relatively little reason for anxiety about a postwar future on earth" (*Shakespeare's Military World*, 209–10, 212).

31. For this assertion, compare Cicero's discussion of military decorum in *De officiis*, trans. Walter Miller (Cambridge, Mass.: Harvard University Press, 1913).

32. For background on the history of the republic and the functions of the magistrates I have relied most heavily upon Cicero's *De re publica* and *De legibus*, in Clinton W. Keyes's Loeb parallel text edition (Cambridge, Mass.: Harvard University Press, 1928), and the selection of Polybius's *Histories* in *The Rise of the Roman Empire*, trans. Ian Scott-Kilvert, ed. F. W. Walbank (Harmondsworth, U.K.: Penguin, 1979), as well as Andrew Lintott, *The Constitution of the Roman Republic* (Oxford: Clarendon Press, 1999), particularly chaps. 7–12; hereafter cited as *CRR*. For briefer, introductory treatments, I have also consulted Stephen P. Oakley, "The Early Republic," and T. Corey Brennan, "Power and Process under the Republican 'Constitution,'" both in *The Cambridge Companion to the Roman Republic*, ed. Harriet I. Flower, 15–65 (Cambridge: Cambridge University

Press, 2004), and John A. North, "The Constitution of the Roman Republic," in *A Companion to the Roman Republic*, ed. Nathan Rosenstein and Robert Morstein-Marx, 256–77 (Oxford: Blackwell, 2006). For discussions of the tribunes in Shakespeare's play, see, in particular, MacCallum, *Shakespeare's Roman Plays*, chap. 3, "The Grand Contract: Shakespeare's Conception of the Situation in Rome," 518–48, and Cantor, *Shakespeare's Rome*, 88–89. For background on the *iustitium* or temporary suspension of law peculiar to the Republic, as well as a careful distinction between the concepts of *auctoritas* and *potestas*, see also Agamben, *State of Exception*, particularly chaps. 3 and 5, pp. 41–51, 74–88.

33. See Cicero, *"De re publica" and "De legibus,"* trans. Clinton Walker Keyes (Cambridge, Mass.: Harvard University Press, 1961). Parenthetical citations refer to the book, paragraph, and page numbers in this edition.

34. The view that Shakespeare also intended topical references to the series of protests (in Northamptonshire, Leicestershire, and his native Warwickshire) against enclosure in 1607 collectively known as the Midland Revolt is now widely accepted. See, for example, E. C. Pettet, "Coriolanus and the Midlands Insurrection of 1607," *Shakespeare Survey* 3 (1950): 34–42, and Lee Bliss, "Introduction," in *Coriolanus* (Cambridge: Cambridge University Press, 2000), 17–27.

35. See Polybius, *The Rise of the Roman Empire*, as well as Lintott, *CRR*, on the origins, developments, and functions of the tribunate. Since the tribunes were considered sacrosanct (touching them was taboo), their power of veto could extend to physically barring the way to assemblies or votes that they expected to go against them.

36. See Polybius, "On the Roman Constitution at Its Prime," in *The Rise of the Roman Empire*, 311–18.

37. Unless otherwise noted, all citations in Italian refer to Niccolò Machiavelli, *Discorsi sopra la prima Deca di Tito Livio* (Torino: Einaudi, 1983). The English translations are taken from *Discourses on Livy*, trans. Julia Conaway Bondanella and Peter Bondanella (Oxford: Oxford University Press, 1997); parenthetical citations refer to the book, chapter, and page number in the Bondanellas' edition.

38. Lintott notes that "magistrates with imperium could act in a judicial capacity, whether this was *iuris dictio*—the definition and ratification of a civil lawsuit performed in the city by the *praetor urbanus* or *peregrinus* before the actual hearing of the case—or the actual investigation (*quaerere*, *cognoscere*) of a crime or a delict against administrative law. In practice, in Rome and Italy consuls only undertook criminal trials of special cases, while in civil matters we only know of them being assigned jurisdiction over lawsuits concerning the possession of land" (*CRR* 96).

39. Plutarch's account: "A reconciliation followed [Menenius Agrippa's parable of the belly], after the people had asked and obtained from the senate the privilege of electing five men as protectors of those who needed succour, the officers now called tribunes of the people. And the first whom they chose to this office were Junius Brutus and Sicinius Vellutus, who had been their leaders in the secession. When the city was thus united, the common people at once offered themselves as soldiers, and the consuls found them ready and eager for service in the war. As for Marcius, though he was displeased himself to have the people increase in power at the expense of the aristocracy, and though he saw that many of the patricians were of the same mind, he nevertheless exhorted them not to fall behind the common

people in contending for their country's welfare, but to show that they were superior to them in valour rather than in political power" (VII.1–2.132–33).

40. Lee Bliss makes something of a similar observation when he writes that "Shakespeare makes his version of Plutarch available for consideration in this light [constitutional questions that are larger than the immediate question of franchise or election] by devoting the middle of the play to the political process whose breakdown is the catalyst for the protagonist's personal tragedy" ("Introduction," 32). The only thing that I would quibble with in this statement is the notion that the tribunes' intervention is, in fact, a "breakdown" of the electoral process; in fact, the rescinding of the popular election constitutes the essence of this new form of Republican political process.

41. This passage only is taken from Cicero, *"On the Commonwealth" and "On the Laws,"* ed. James E. G. Zetzel (Cambridge: Cambridge University Press, 1999), 27–28; other references to these works are to the Loeb parallel text edition.

42. "Perché le ferite ed ogni altro male che l'uomo si fa da sé spontaneamente e per elezione, dolgano di gran lunga meno che quelle che ti sono fatte da altrui" (135). The Bondanellas' translation of the phrase *per elezione* is "voluntarily."

43. For a particularly perceptive treatment of this identification, see Cynthia Marshall, "Wound Man: *Coriolanus*, Gender, and the Theatrical Construction of Interiority," in *Feminist Readings of Early Modern Culture: Emerging Subjects*, ed. Valerie Traub, M. Lindsay Kaplan, and Dympna Callaghan, 93–118 (Cambridge: Cambridge University Press, 1996).

44. See Kermode's introductions to *Coriolanus* and *Timon* in *The Riverside Shakespeare*, ed. G. Blakemore Evans et al. (Boston: Houghton Mifflin, 1974), 1392, 1444.

45. See Ken Jackson, "'One Wish' or the Possibility of the Impossible: Derrida, the Gift, and God in *Timon of Athens*," *Shakespeare Quarterly* 52, no. 1 (2001): 34–66.

46. I draw this phrase from Benjamin, "Critique of Violence," which I will address more fully in the second half of this chapter.

47. See Jacques Derrida, *Given Time I: Counterfeit Money*, trans. Peggy Kamuf (Chicago: University of Chicago Press, 1992).

48. See Marcel Mauss, *The Gift: The Form and Reason for Exchange in Archaic Societies*, trans. W. D. Halls (New York: Norton, 1990), 13.

49. This tension is formally evident in the Folio's ordering of the names ("Martius Caius Coriolanus" rather than "Caius Martius Coriolanus," as in Plutarch—Martius is the patronymic). See Bliss's "Textual Analysis," 277–78.

50. In this context, the common period sexual double entendres of both "thing" and "nothing" must also be noted.

51. See Mauss, *The Gift*, 12.

52. "The Old High German word *thing* means a gathering, and specifically a gathering to deliberate on a matter under discussion, a contested matter. In consequence, the Old German words *thing* and *dinc* become the names for an affair or matter of pertinence. They denote anything that in any way bears upon men, concerns them, and that accordingly is a matter for discourse. The Romans called a matter for discourse *res*. The Greek *eiro* (*rhetos*, *rhetra*, *rhema*) means to speak about something, to deliberate on it. *Res publica* means, not the state, but that which, known to everyone, concerns everybody and is therefore deliberated

in public. . . . The Roman word *res* designates that which concerns somebody, a contested matter, a case at law. The Romans also use for it the word *causa* . . . [which] means the case and hence also that which is the case, in the sense that something comes to pass and becomes due." See Martin Heidegger, "The Thing," in *Poetry, Language, Thought*, trans. Albert Hofstadter (New York: Harper and Row, 1971), 174–75.

53. See *xaris*, especially sense 3, and *xarisma*, in Henry George Liddell and Robert Scott, *An Intermediate Greek-English Lexicon* (Oxford: Oxford University Press, 1994). All the senses quoted are taken from this dictionary.

54. In the comparison of Coriolanus and Alcibiades, Plutarch uses *xaris* to describe Coriolanus's concession to his mother's embassy. See the *Lives*, IV.iv.229.

55. See *xenos* and *philos* in Liddell and Scott, *Greek-English Lexicon.*

56. See *exceptio* and *eligo* in Lewis and Short, *Latin Dictionary* (Oxford: Clarendon Press, 1879).

57. This evocative scene has attracted much critical attention, particularly in some of the excellent feminist psychoanalytic readings of the play. See, for example, Janet Adelman, "Escaping the Matrix: The Construction of Masculinity in *Macbeth* and *Coriolanus*," in *Suffocating Mothers: Fantasies of Maternal Origin in Shakespeare's Plays, "Hamlet" to "The Tempest"* (New York: Routledge, 1992), 130–64. Coppélia Kahn's analysis in "The Milking Babe and the Bloody Man in *Coriolanus* and *Macbeth*" is, in turn, indebted to Adelman's; see Coppélia Kahn, *Man's Estate: Masculine Identity in Shakespeare* (Berkeley: University of California Press, 1981), 151–92. In "Annihilating Intimacy in *Coriolanus*," Madelon (Gohlke) Sprengnether examines the gendered inflections of the play through the lens of object relations theory; see her essay in *"Coriolanus": Critical Essays*, ed. David Wheeler, 179–202 (New York: Garland, 1977). Other readings that focus on Coriolanus and Volumnia include Marilyn L. Williamson, "Violence and Gender Ideology in *Coriolanus* and *Macbeth*," in *Shakespeare Left and Right*, ed. Ivo Kamps, 147–66 (New York: Routledge, 1998), and Bernard J. Paris, *Character as a Subversive Force in Shakespeare: The History and Roman Plays* (Rutherford, N.J.: Fairleigh Dickinson University Press, 1991), 165–207. Cavell, "*Coriolanus* and Interpretations of Politics," and Williamson, "Violence and Gender Ideology in *Coriolanus* and *Macbeth*," also draw on Adelman's arguments. See also Motohashi, "Body Politic and Political Body in *Coriolanus*,"; Jagendorf, "*Coriolanus*"; and Marshall, "Wound Man." Though the readings cited here certainly draw from Freud even when they depart from him, it is important to note that even pre-Freudian commentators paid attention to Plutarch's claim that Coriolanus's values rested not on his own interpretation of the patrician code of manly honor (Roman *virtus*) but on his mother's ideas of the patrician code. For influential examples of this line of argument, see Bradley, "Coriolanus"; MacCallum, *Shakespeare's Roman Plays*, chap. 4, "The Kinsfolk and Friends of Coriolanus," 549–70; and J. Middleton Murray's discussion of Virgilia in relation to Volumnia in "A Neglected Heroine of Shakespeare," in *Countries of the Mind: Essays in Literary Criticism* (London: Collins, 1922), 31–50; and even G. Wilson Knight, "The Royal Occupation: An Essay on *Coriolanus*," in *The Imperial Theme* (1931; repr., London: Methuen, 1965), 154–98 (though neither of the latter texts are "pre-Freudian," they are more in line with pre-Freudian character analyses than many subsequent critics).

58. See Karl Marx, *Capital: A Critique of Political Economy, Volume 1* (1867), trans. Ben Fowkes (New York: Vintage, 1977). Marx defines the two terms as follows: "The usefulness of a thing makes it a use-value. But this usefulness does not dangle in mid-air. It is conditioned by the physical properties of the commodity, and has no existence apart from the latter. It is therefore the physical body of the commodity itself, for instance iron, corn, a diamond, which is the use-value or useful thing. This property of a commodity is independent of the amount of labour required to appropriate its useful qualities. . . . Use-values are only realized [*verwirklicht*] in use or in consumption. They constitute the material content of wealth, whatever its social form may be. In the form of society to be considered here they are also the material bearers [*Traeger*] of . . . exchange-value. . . . Exchange-value appears first of all as the quantitative relation, the proportion, in which use-values of one kind exchange for use-values of another kind. This relation changes constantly with time and place. Hence exchange-value appears to be something accidental and purely relative, and consequently an intrinsic value, i.e. an exchange-value that is inseparably connected with the commodity, inherent in it, seems a contradiction in terms" (126).

59. Ibid., 164.

60. See *sumbolon* in Liddell and Scott, *Greek-English Lexicon*; all the senses quoted are taken from this dictionary.

61. Much critical commentary focuses on the citizens' "voices" within the play. In his chapter on *Coriolanus* in *Shakespeare's Language* (New York: Farrar, Straus and Giroux, 2000), Frank Kermode notes that "the words 'voice' and 'voices' occur forty-eight times in the play, thirty-two times in this scene; such battering of the audience is unparalleled in the canon. 'Voices' remains a synecdoche for citizens, for 'poor people' " (250). See also Annabel Patterson's argument in *Shakespeare and the Popular Voice*.

62. Both "will" as in "ability to complete an action," that is, "can give our voices," and "will" as in "desire, want," that is, "desire our voices to be given." On Third Citizen's play on the dual meaning of power, Bliss notes, "Third Citizen's punning distinction is important; it contrasts 'power' in the sense of legal ability or capacity with 'power' as the moral right to exercise that ability" (169, II.iii.n.4–5). The play on "will" returns in IV.vi, when Third Citizen claims "though we willingly consented to his banishment, yet it was against our will" (148–49).

63. An allusion that Stanley Cavell also notes, although he does not mention this passage. See Cavell, "*Coriolanus* and Interpretations of Politics."

64. See Agamben, *HS*.

65. See Jean-Luc Nancy, *The Ground of the Image*, trans. Jeff Fort (New York: Fordham University Press, 2005), 1–2.

66. This short and exceptionally dense, or, as Derrida would have it, "slippery" text, has received a great deal of attention. Among the most important readings would be Hannah Arendt's separation of violence and state power in *On Violence* (New York: Harcourt Brace, 1970), which implicitly rewrites Benjamin's "Critique," and Derrida, "Force of Law: The 'Mystical Foundation of Authority,' " trans. Mary Quaintance, *Cordozo Law Review* 11 (1990): 920–1045, reprinted with additional material translated in *Acts of Religion*, ed. Gil Anidjar, 228–98 (London: Routledge, 2002). Derrida's argument has, in turn, generated

many responses and counter-readings. These include Drucilla Cornell, "The Violence of the Masquerade: Law Dressed Up as Justice," and Dominic LaCapra, "Violence, Justice, and the Force of Law," both in the same issue of the *Cordozo Law Review* as the translation of Derrida's essay (1047–64 and 1065–77, respectively), as well as Beatrice Hanssen, "On the Politics of Pure Means: Benjamin, Arendt, Foucault," in *Violence, Identity, and Self-Determination*, ed. Hent de Vries and Samuel Weber, 236–52 (Stanford, Calif.: Stanford University Press, 1997). In de Vries and Sullivan, *Political Theologies*, see de Wilde "Violence in the State of Exception," and Judith Butler, "Critique, Coercion, and Sacred Life in Benjamin's 'Critique of Violence,' " 201–19. Finally, Slavoj Žižek takes up Benjamin's critique in *Violence* (New York: Picador, 2008).

67. In employing the phrase "creaturely life" I deliberately invoke Benjamin's remarks in *The Origin of German Tragic Drama*, which collapses sovereignty into the always subjected realm of the created: "The level of the state of creation, the terrain on which the *Trauerspiel* is enacted, also unmistakably exercises a determining influence on the sovereign. However highly he is enthroned over subject and state, his status is confined to the world of creation; he is the lord of creatures, but he remains a creature" (*Origin* 85).

68. Derrida takes this division between "mythic" or foundational violence and "divine" or annihilating violence to imply a corresponding distinction between Greek and Jewish "meanings" (see, e.g., "Force of Law," 981, 1026–35)—a distinction Judith Butler and others contest, or at least seek to nuance. In her recent essay on the "Critique of Violence," Butler writes, "It is important to tread carefully here, since it would be a mistake to say this essay constitutes a 'Jewish critique,' even though a strand of Jewish theology runs through it, and certainly it makes no sense to call this a 'Jewish critique' because Benjamin was a Jew. If the critique can justifiably be called 'Jewish,' that is only as a result of some of the critical resources Benjamin brings to bear" ("Critique, Coercion," 205). Carefully sidestepping the issue of whether or not the essay constitutes a "Jewish critique" (something I don't think Derrida claims either, at least not in that way), I would still agree with Derrida that the Torah, and specifically Genesis and Leviticus, constitute a significant though perhaps not overt intertext in Benjamin's treatment of divine violence, as I hope to demonstrate in what follows.

69. "Ist die mythische Gewalt rechtsetzend, so die göttliche rechtsvernichtend, setzt jene Grenzen, so venichtet diese grezenlos, ist die mythische verschuldend und sühnend zugleich, so die göttliche entsühnend, ist jene drohend, so diese schlagend, jene blutig, so diese auf unblutige Weise letal" (*KG* 199).

70. All biblical citations are taken from Robert Carroll and Stephen Prickett, eds., *The Bible: Authorized King James Version* (Oxford: Oxford University Press, 1997).

71. "Die Auslösung der Rechtsgewalt geht nun, wie hier nicht genauer dargelegt werden kann, auf die Verschuldung des bloßen natürlichen Lebens zurück, welche den Lebenden unschuldig und unglücklich der Sühne überantwortet, die seine Verschuldung "sühnt"—und auch wohl den Schuldigen entsühnt, nicht aber von einer, sondern vom Recht. Denn mit dem bloßen Leben hört die Herrschaft des Rechts über den Lebendigen auf. Die mythische Gewalt ist Blutgewalt über das bloße Leben um ihrer selbst, die göttliche reine Gewalt über alles Leben um des Lebendigen willen. Die erste fordert Opfer, die zweite nimmt sie an" (*KG* 199–200).

72. In a particularly beautiful, and particularly chilling, reading of this difficult passage, Butler writes, "Divine power is described as lethal without spilling blood. It strikes at the legal shackles by which the body is petrified and forced into endless sorrow, but it does not strike, in Benjamin's view, at the soul of the living. . . . By distinguishing the soul of the living from 'life' itself, Benjamin asks us to consider what value life has once the soul has been destroyed" ("Critique, Coercion," 210).

73. See Derrida, "Force of Law," 1990.

74. Though he does not address the idea of "guilt" in his reading, Derrida argues that in his equivocal remarks on the sacredness of the life of man Benjamin attempts to capture "the potential, the possibility of justice, the yet-to-come [*avenir*] of justice, the yet-to-come of his being-just, of his having-to-be-just. What is sacred in his life is not his life but the justice of his life" ("Force of Law," 1029).

75. Genesis 4:16–17.

76. See Benjamin, *Origin,* 85. Of the melancholic tyrant, Benjamin writes "*er ist der Herr der Kreaturen, aber et bleibt Kreatur*" (*Ursprung*, 79).

77. "*Die göttliche Gewalt, welche Insignium und Siegel, niemals Mittel heiliger Vollstreckung ist, mag die waltende heißen*" (*KG* 203).

78. Derrida reads this last sentence as a "signature" that allows Benjamin to play on his own name, Walter, in its proximity to *waltende* while still allowing "God, the Wholly Other," the last word.

79. While I would not dispute this distinction as it appears in the writings of Aristotle, from which Agamben derives the main part of his claim, it should be noted that for Herodotus *zoê* does indicate "a way of life" proper to individuals or groups.

80. This essential distinction between "sacred" and "religious" orders that is exemplified by the paradox of "life that can be killed, *yet not sacrificed*," is one that some recent commentaries on the play fail to take into account. In her astute reading of the tension between an archaic notion of heroic martial *virtus* necessarily crumbling in the face of a new juridical order, Rebecca Lemon argues that Coriolanus in effect becomes *homo sacer*, simultaneously sovereign and exile. With this I would certainly agree. Yet in reading Coriolanus's death as "sacrificial demise," Lemon departs from Agamben's distinction, returning Coriolanus to a religious order that is itself always also a civic order. See her "Arms and Laws in Shakespeare's *Coriolanus*," 233–48.

81. Agamben notes that "the most ancient recorded forms of capital punishment (the terrible *poena cullei*, in which the condemned man, with his head covered in a wolf-skin, was put in a sack with serpents, a dog and a rooster, and then thrown into water, or defenestration from the Tarpean rock) are actually purification rites and not death penalties in the modern sense: the *neque fas est eum immolari* served precisely to distinguish the killing of *homo sacer* from ritual purifications, and decisively excluded *sacratio* from the religious sphere in the strict sense" (*HS* 81). On capital punishment in Republican Rome, see O. F. Robinson, *Penal Practice and Penal Policy in Ancient Rome* (London: Routledge, 2007), particularly chap. 8, pp. 184–93; Richard A. Bauman, *Crime and Punishment in Ancient Rome* (London: Routledge, 1996), especially chaps. 1–4, 12; and Lintott, *CRR*.

82. In Plutarch's account the trial (*krisis*) scene encapsulates the political crisis of the Conflict of the Orders, a showdown between the tribunes' demands for Marcius's death and the patricians' defense of one of their own (XIX.3.162–65). Plutarch notes that division occurs even within the patricians: the younger men, many of whom had fought with Marcius, support him absolutely, while "the oldest senators, and those most inclined to favour the people, maintained that it [i.e., the people] would not be rendered harsh or severe by its exercise of this power, but mild and humane; for since it did not despise the senate, but rather thought itself despised by that body, the prerogative of trying a senator would be a solace to its feelings and a mark of honour, so that as soon as it proceeded to vote it would lay aside its wrath" (XIX.3.164–65). The latter argument, though in favor of the *demos*, casts the Senate as both victims and pacifiers of the plebeian rabble and this initiatory popular verdict as a definitive civic bond that will quell a potential plebian uprising. In this *krisis*, then, Marcius and his not-yet-specified crime are almost unnecessary accessories but become expiatory sacrifices to a greater political good.

> Marcius, therefore, seeing that the senate was in suspense between its kindly feelings towards him and its fear of the people, asked the tribunes what the accusations against him were, and on what charge he would be tried if they led him before the people. They replied that the charge against him was usurpation [*turannis*], and that they would prove him guilty of planning a usurpation of the government. Thereupon he rose of his own accord and said he was going at once before the people to make his defence, and would deprecate no manner of trial, nor, should he be found guilty, any form of punishment; "Only," said he, "see that ye confine yourselves to the charge mentioned, and do not play false with the senate." The tribunes agreed to this, and on these terms the trial was held. (XX.i.164–67)

Yet in the event, the *krisis* goes awry when the agreed-upon charge of tyranny (*turannos*) is changed in the course of the trial, and the tribunes change the method of voting so that the tribes rather than the centuries cast ballots; thus the common people rather than the patricians hold the majority.

Plutarch's account of the trial is as follows: "But when the people were come together, in the first place, the tribunes insisted that the votes be cast not by centuries, but by tribes, thus making the indigent and officious rabble, which had no thought of honour, superior in voting power to the wealthy and well-known citizens of the military class. In the second place, abandoning the charge of usurpation, which could not be proven, they dwelt again upon the speech which Marcius had previously made in the senate, when he protested against the lowering of the market-price of grain, and urged them to take the tribunate away from the people. They also added a fresh charge against him, namely, his distribution of the spoils which he had taken from the country of Antium; these, they said, he had not turned into the public treasury, but had distributed them among those who made the campaign with him. By this accusation Marcius is said to have been more disturbed than by all the rest. For he had not expected it, and was not ready at once with an answer which would satisfy the people, but began to praise those who had made the campaign, whereupon he was clamorously interrupted by those who had not made it, and they were the more numerous. In the end, therefore, the vote was taken in tribes, and a majority of three condemned him. The penalty assigned was perpetual banishment" (XX.4.166–69).

Regarding the first sentence in the excerpted account, in the Loeb edition, Bernadette Perrin notes that "out of the 193 centuries, the richest class alone had 98, against 95 of all the other five classes put together" (167).

83. See *krisis* in Liddell and Scott, *Greek-English Lexicon*, especially "I. a separating, power of distinguishing; choice, selection. II. a decision, judgment. 2) in legal sense, a *trial*; *the result of a trial, condemnation*; 3) *a trial* of skill; 4) *a dispute*; III. *the event or issue* of a thing."

84. See Kuzner, "Unbuilding the City," 180–84, 196–99.

85. A detail not present in Plutarch's very brief account of Coriolanus's death (XXXIX.5.216–17).

86. In describing divine grace as "the only gift possible"—that is, the only gift that exceeds or transcends an economy of exchange—I draw, once again, on Derrida, as well as on Georges Bataille, *Theory of Religion*, trans. Robert Hurley (New York: Urzone, 1989) and *The Accursed Share*, Vols. I and III, trans. Robert Hurley (New York: Urzone, 1991), especially Part I of Vol. III, "*Sovereignty*," 197–257.

87. See G. W. F. Hegel, *Reason in History*, trans. Robert S. Hartman (New York: Macmillan, 1953), 34–43.

Chapter Four

1. See Giorgio Agamben, *The Time That Remains: A Commentary on the Letter to the Romans*, trans. Patricia Dailey (Stanford, Calif.: Stanford University Press, 2005); hereafter cited parenthetically.

2. On the question of the unrepresentable, see also Jacques Rancière, *The Future of the Image*, trans. Gregory Elliot (London: Verso, 2007), 108–38, particularly 113–18.

3. Weil, letter to her parents, August 4, 1943, from *Simone Weil: Seventy Letters*, trans. Richard Rees (Oxford: Oxford University Press, 1965), 199–201. Her "London Notebook" of 1943 also contains a brief mention of *Lear*, in conjunction with the *lama sabachthani*. Weil's interest in the English poets and playwrights of the sixteenth and seventeenth centuries (particularly the metaphysical poets) has been remarked upon before; famously, her first visionary experience occurred while repeating a verse of George Herbert's (see Weil's "Spiritual Autobiography," in *Waiting for God*, trans. Emma Craufurd [New York: Putnam, 1951], 26–27, as well as Francine du Plessix Gray, *Simone Weil* [London: Weidenfeld and Nicolson, 2001], 124–27). And it was to Charles Bell, the Oxford undergraduate whom she met in Solesmes in 1938 and who introduced her to the seventeenth-century poets, that she seems to have written her first letter on *Lear* and affliction (see "To an Oxford Poet" [1938], in *Seventy Letters*, 102–5).

4. Weil's "fools" seems to me to refer to the Fool himself, Cordelia, and Lear. Given the possible doubling of Cordelia and the Fool in early performances and the famously uncertain referent of Lear's lament that "[his] poor fool is hanged," Weil's remark acquires yet more pathos. See John Kerrigan, "Revision, Adaptation, and the Fool in *King Lear*," in *The Division of the Kingdom: Shakespeare's Two Versions of "King Lear*," ed. Gary Taylor and Michael Warren, 195–246 (Oxford: Oxford University Press, 1983).

5. Simone Weil, "Gravity and Grace," in *Gravity and Grace*, trans. Arthur Wills (Lincoln: University of Nebraska Press, 1997), 45. Essays from this collection hereafter cited parenthetically.

6. In relation to her meditations on *Lear* in the 1938 letter "To an Oxford Poet," Weil writes,

> The nobleness of suffering is not to be spoken of lightly or too often; it can too easily become mere literature in the mouth of people who have not suffered pain that can break the very soul. Do you realise there are millions and millions of people on earth who suffer nearly always, from birth to death? It is a pity they have not learned expression; they would say the truth about suffering. Yet they have sometimes expressed themselves—through anonymous melodies, songs, legends, religions—and then they have sometimes, as I think, surpassed the greatest geniuses. (104)

While Weil's mention of the "millions and millions . . .who suffer always . . . [who] have not learned expression" amounts to a certain primitivism, her interest here in getting at "the truth about suffering," characteristically, does not amount to the equation *of* truth and suffering. In the "First Notebook" of 1933, Weil wrote in the margins of the opening pages, "Value of suffering—I believe in the value of suffering, so long as one makes every [legitimate] effort to escape it"; in the last (London) notebook (1943), she moves between Aeschylus and Paul on *tô pathê mathos* (3, 344).

7. Simone Weil, "Affliction," in *Gravity and Grace*, 132; emphasis added. See also *Seventy Letters*, particularly Weil's reflections on suffering and Greek tragedy in the context of a discussion of Nietzsche's *The Birth of Tragedy* (with which she profoundly disagreed) in a 1940 letter "To A. W." (122–26), as well as *The Notebooks of Simone Weil*, trans. Arthur Wills, 2 vols. (London: Routledge and Kegan Pauul, 1956), hereafter cited as *Notebooks* 1 and 2.

8. Meeks translates Paul's *kharisma* as "free gift," e.g. in Romans 6:20–23.

9. See Jonathan Gil Harris, *Untimely Matter in the Time of Shakespeare* (Philadelphia: University of Pennsylvania Press, 2009), particularly the introduction (1–25) and chap. 6 (169–88).

10. See, for example, Joseph Wittreich, *"Image of that Horror": History, Prophecy, and Apocalypse in "King Lear"* (San Marino, Calif.: Huntington Library, 1984), and Paul Fiddes, *The Promised End: Eschatology in Theology and Literature* (Oxford: Blackwell, 2000), particularly chap. 3. Even Frank Kermode, in *The Sense of an Ending* (Oxford: Oxford University Press, 1966), engages with apocalyptic readings, to a certain extent, though Kermode's point is that in the perpetual sense of crisis that characterizes modernity we have lost the true sense of apocalypse.

11. On the subject of exceeding representation, see Terry Eagleton, *William Shakespeare* (Oxford: Blackwell, 1986), 76–89. Eagleton claims that "the paradox which *King Lear* explores is that it is 'natural' for the human animal to transcend its own limits, yet this creative tendency to exceed oneself is also the source of destructiveness" (81).

12. Compare Emmanuel Lévinas, *Time and the Other*, trans. Richard A. Cohen (Pittsburgh: Duquesne University Press, 1987).

13. On the perverse aesthetic appeal of bodies in pain, see Susan Sontag, *Regarding the Pain of Others* (New York: Picador, 2003).

14. See Saint Augustine, *Confessions*, trans. Henry Chadwick (Oxford: Oxford University Press, 1991), 231.

15. Unless otherwise noted, all Folio citations refer to R. A. Foakes's Arden edition (London: Thomson, 1997); Quarto citations are taken from Stanley Wells's Oxford edition, from the text prepared by Gary Taylor (Oxford: Oxford University Press, 2000). For various reflections on the textual differences, see Gary Taylor and Michael Warren, eds., *The Division of the Kingdoms: Shakespeare's Two Versions of "King Lear"* (Oxford: Oxford University Press, 1983).

16. In the Quarto, Albany's line is "Who, man? Speak" (24.220).

17. Guy Story Brown argues that Edmund's appeal to legitimacy means that "it will all have been done in the name of Goneril's authority, an authority she may long have assumed, as eldest daughter or crown princess" (*Shakespeare's Philosopher King: Reading "The Tragedy of King Lear"* [Macon, Ga.: Mercer University Press, 2010], 332). I don't find this a convincing argument—Goneril and Regan both act with at least the appearance of the imprimatur of their husbands' authority.

18. William R. Elton's influential, but I think dismissive, reading of Kent as a Stoic notwithstanding. See *"King Lear" and the Gods* (San Marino, Calif.: Huntington Library, 1966).

19. For particularly brilliant readings of the Cerasi conversion, see Matthew Ancell, "*Credo Ergo Sum:* Pictorial Logic and Blindness in Caravaggio," *Oxford Art Journal* 37, no. 2 (June 2014): 193–210. Jacques Derrida, *Memoirs of the Blind: The Self-Portrait and Other Ruins*, trans. Pascale-Anne Brault and Michael Naas (Chicago: Univeristy of Chicago Press, 1993); Leo Bersani and Ulysse Dutoit, *Caravaggio's Secrets* (Cambridge, Mass.: MIT Press, 1998); Graham Hammill, *Sexuality and Form: Caravaggio, Marlowe, and Bacon* (Chicago: University of Chicago Press, 2000); and Jonathan Goldberg's introduction to *The Seeds of All Things: Theorizing Sexuality and Materiality in Renaissance Representations* (New York: Fordham University Press, 2009). Although they focus on a different painting, I find Hammill's discussion of voice or calling (he likens the voice to Lacan's *objet a*) and Goldberg's insistence on grace (11–12) to be immensely relevant to my own reading. For Hammill, "Caravaggio's painting arrests Paul in the very moment of embodying his question 'What am I to do?' . . . [The] pose resuscitates the flesh that Paul relinquishes (Gal. 1:16), and it resuscitates it in the psychic space of spectatorship," which is something akin to what I will be saying about Lear bearing the body of Cordelia in the last section of this chapter. I am grateful to Matthew Ancell for sharing the draft of his article on Caravaggio with me and for bringing Derrida's reading of the painting to my attention.

20. See Alain Badiou, *Saint Paul: The Foundation of Universalism*, trans. Ray Brassier (Stanford, Calif.: Stanford University Press, 2003).

21. The phrase is Walter Friedlaender's; see *Caravaggio Studies* (New York: Schocken, 1972), 18.

22. On blindness and conversion, see Ancell, "*Credo Ergo Sum*," and Derrida, *Memoirs of the Blind.*

23. Unless otherwise noted, English citations of Paul refer to the Revised Standard Version, as reprinted in *The Writings of St. Paul*, ed. Wayne A. Meeks (New York: Norton, 1972). Greek text is taken from *The New Testament in the Original Greek*, revised by Brooke Foss Westcott, D.D., and Fenton John Anthony Hort, D.D. (New York: Harper and Brothers, 1885); online at perseus.tufts.edu. Both texts are hereafter cited parenthetically. The first of the two translations given at p. 124 is from George Ricker Berry's *Interlinear Greek-English New Testament (King James Version)* (Grand Rapids, Mich.: Baker Book House, 1984 [Hinds and Nobel, 1897]). On the iconographic tradition Caravaggio drew on for his depictions of the horse, see Walter Friedlaender, "The Conversion of St. Paul," in *Caravaggio Studies*, 3–28 (though Friedlaender focuses more on the Cerasi painting).

24. See Bersani and Dutoit, *Caravaggio's Secrets*.

25. See *ektrōma*, *trauma* (Dor. *trōma*) in Henry George Liddell and Robert Scott, *An Intermediate Greek-English Lexicon* (Oxford: Oxford University Press, 1994).

26. Agamben also notes the double movement and the paradoxical prefix (*The Time That Remains: A Commentary on the Letter to the Romans*, trans. Patricia Dailey [Stanford, Calif.: Stanford University Press, 2005], 78).

27. Compare, on the Pauline split subject, Badiou, *Saint Paul*, and Slavoj Žižek, "Paul and the Truth Event," in *Paul's New Moment: Continental Philosophy and the Future of Christian Theology*, ed. John Milbank, Slavoj Žižek, and Creston Davis, 74–99 (Grand Rapids, Mich.: Brazos Press, 2010).

28. See Agamben, *The Time That Remains*, 63. Frank Kermode, in *The Sense of an Ending*, helpfully summarizes some of the scholarship on this distinction, including James Barr's critique thereof. Kermode himself links "reality" with *chronos* (mechanistic time); "fiction" with *kairos*—in a sense, the "season" of *kairos* allows an "escape" from the pressures of mechanistic time (44–52). Kermode's insistence that as readers "we still need the fullness of it, the *pleroma*" to derive a sense of pleasure in narrative in some ways anticipates, though in a literary-critical rather than a political-theological mode, Agamben's reading of Paul.

29. See *sustellô* in Liddell and Scott, *Greek-English Lexicon.*

30. 1 Corinthians 14:20; my translation.

31. Compare Kent's attack on Oswald in scene 7 in the Quarto and 2.2 in the Folio. Oswald's bewildered "Why dost thou use me thus? I know thee not" . . . "What dost thou know me for?" (Q 7.10, 12; F 2.2.11, 13) reiterates Lear's own skeptical dilemma in savagely comic terms, and Kent's invective catalogue provides another index for Lear's cursing. In Lear's case, as in Job's or Philoctetes's, we witness the irony underlying the formal curse: rhetorical hyperbole proceeding from absolute corporeal deprivation. Kent's case is different, as is his mode of address—yet he too exemplifies the "superflux" of cursing, most obviously in yet another moment of textual difference. In the Quarto, his answer to Oswald's "What dost thou know me for?" includes, "a whoreson, glass-gazing, *superfinical* rogue . . . whom I will beat into clamorous whining if thou deny the least syllable of the addition" (16–17, 20–22; emphasis added). In the Folio, the line is "whoreson, glass-gazing, *super-serviceable, finical* rogue . . . *one* whom I will beat into clamorous whining if thou deniest the least syllable of thy addition"

(2.2.17–18, 22–23; emphasis added). While the Quarto text precedes the Folio's, thus one could hardly make a temporal argument here, its apparent collapse of "super-serviceable finical" into "superfinical"—with the happily attendant sense of "superficial" in this context—performs something of the same double movement I'm suggesting Lear's prayer does.

32. See Weil, "Affliction," in *Gravity and Grace*, 133.

33. On "supernatural intervention," see Weil, "Gravity and Grace," 45; on "supernatural help," see Simone Weil, "Void and Compensation," in *Gravity and Grace*, 49–56. This conceptual shift from "intervention" to "help" should not go unremarked—while "intervention" implies a coming-between the self (a perhaps violent excision from one's own ego, comparable to the Pauline split subject), "help" seemingly offers an alternative, in which the subject first *decides* to evacuate the ego. "Help" in this context thus seems closer to Weil's brief remarks on the extinction of desire according to Buddhism (e.g., in "Detachment," *Gravity and Grace*, 58, *Waiting for God*,) than her arguments about the privileged place of suffering in Christianity.

34. Simone Weil, "The Love of God and Affliction," in *Waiting for God*, 68. See also Maurice Blanchot's remarkable reading of Weil's focus on "attention and affliction" in "Affirmation, Desire, Affliction," in *The Infinite Conversation*, trans. Susan Hanson (Minneapolis: University of Minnesota Press, 1993); see especially 120–22. Blanchot notes, too, both attention's and affliction's relations to time, for Weil, and his remarks on Weil's "attention" lead us back to her thoughts on grace (116, 121).

35. On the links between the bestial and the feminine, see Jacques Derrida, *The Beast and the Sovereign*, trans. Geoffrey Bennington, 2 vols. (Chicago: University of Chicago Press, 2009); Laurie Shannon, "Poor, Bare, Forked: Animal Sovereignty, Human Negative Exceptionalism, and the Natural History of *King Lear*," *Shakespeare Quarterly* 60, no. 2 (2009): 168–96; and James Tink, "'Expose Thyself to What Wretches Feel': The Figure of Bare Life in *King Lear* and *Timon of Athens*," *Shakespeare Studies* 43 (2005): 37–61.

36. See Simone Weil, "Love of the Order of the World," in *Waiting for God*, 99–117; "Beauty," in *Gravity and Grace*, 204–8; and *First and Last Notebooks*, 75, 138–40.

37. "Logizomai gar hoti ouk axia ta pathēmata tou nun kairou pros tēn mellousan doxan apokaluphthēnai eis hēmas . . . [22] oidamen gar hoti pasa hē ktisis sunstenazei kai sunōdinei akhri tou nun" (Romans 8:18, 8:22; my translation).

38. See *hupomonê* (a remaining behind, a holding out, patient endurance) and *apekdekhomai* (to exepect anxiously, to look for, await) in Liddell and Scott, *Greek-English Lexicon.*

39. See *huiothesian*, *tithêmi* (ibid).

40. Though even Badiou concedes, at the end, that differences matter. See, for example, *Saint Paul*: "That every truth procedure collapses differences, infinitely deploying a purely generic multiplicity, does not permit us to lose sight of the fact that, in the situation (call it: the world), *there are differences*. One can even maintain that there is nothing else" (98).

41. It is impossible not to wonder if Weil had this passage in mind when she speculates, in 1942, about the subject of "Sons of adoption, adoptive children of God," and asks, "What does that mean?" (*First and Last Notebooks*, 332).

42. On this subject, see Kermode, *The Sense of an Ending*; Stephen Booth, *"King Lear," "Macbeth," Indefinition, and Tragedy* (New Haven: Yale University Press, 1983); Jan Kott, *Shakespeare Our Contemporary*, trans. Bolesław Taborski (New York: Doubleday, 1966); and Fiddes, *The Promised End*. Kermode writes, "In *King Lear* everything tends toward a conclusion that does not occur; even personal death, for Lear, is terribly delayed. Beyond the apparent worst there is a worse suffering, and when the end comes it is not only more appalling than anybody expected, but a mere image of that horror, not the thing itself. The end is now a matter of immanence; tragedy assumes the figurations of apocalypse, of death and judgment, heaven and hell; but the world goes forward in the hands of exhausted survivors. Edgar haplessly assumes the dignity; only the king's natural body is at rest. This is the tragedy of sempiternity; apocalypse is translated out of time into the *aevum*" (82).

43. F 5.3.261–62; Q 24.259–60.

44. See Stanley Cavell's treatment of skepticism in the play, in *Disowning Knowledge in Six Plays of Shakespeare* (Cambridge: Cambridge University Press, 1987). See, also, Richard Strier, "Shakespeare and the Skeptics," *Religion and Literature* 32, no. 2 (2000): 171–96, and *The Unrepentent Renaissance: From Petrarch to Shakespeare to Milton* (Chicago: University of Chicago Press, 2011), 48–53, and Claire McEachern, "Figures of Fidelity: Believing in *King Lear*," *Modern Philology* 98, no. 2 (2000): 211–30.

45. See, especially, the following works by Jacques Rancière: *The Politics of Aesthetics: The Distribution of the Sensible*, ed. and trans. Gabriel Rockhill (New York: Continuum, 2004); *The Future of the Image*; *Aesthetics and Its Discontents*, trans. Steven Corcoran (Cambridge: Polity, 2009); *The Aesthetic Unconscious*, trans. Debra Keats and James Swenson (Cambridge: Polity, 2009); and *Dissensus: On Politics and Aesthetics*, ed. and trans. Steven Corcoran (London: Continuum, 2010). It's worth noting, if only in passing, that Rancière's notion of aesthetics as "carr[ying] a politics, or micro-politics, within it," implicitly also carries a political theology within it, or at least a response to political theology—particularly when it comes to his critique of Lyotard's reading of the sublime (*Aesthetics and Its Discontents*, 20–21).

46. On this point, see Rancière, *Aesthetics and Its Discontents*, 23–26 (the quotation is on p. 26). In a more recent work, *The Politics of Literature* (Cambridge: Polity, 2011), Rancière extends this notion of a "special relationship" between politics and theatre to literature.

47. For an influential example of the former, see especially T. S. Eliot's preface to Simone Weil, *The Need for Roots: Prelude to a Declaration of Duties towards Mankind*, trans. Arthur Wills (London: Routledge, 1952). Eliot writes that in order to avoid being "distracted" by agreement or disagreement with the content of Weil's thought, "we must simply expose ourselves to the personality of a woman of genius, of a kind of genius akin to that of the saints" (viii). Susan Sontag, who could hardly be further from Eliot in many respects, nevertheless echoes this appraisal: "Some lives are exemplary, others not; and of exemplary lives, there are those which invite us to imitate them, and those which we regard from a distance with a mixture of revulsion, pity, and reverence. It is, roughly, the difference between the hero and the saint (if one may use the latter term in an aesthetic, rather than a religious sense). Such a life, absurd in its exaggerations and

degrees of self-mutilation—like Kleist's, like Kierkegaard's—was Simone Weil's." See Sontag's brief essay, "Simone Weil," in *Against Interpretation, and Other Essays* (New York: Picador, 2001), 49–51 (the quotation is on p. 51).

48. Recall Hannah Arendt's helpful gloss on the correlation of privacy and privation in *The Human Condition* (see prologue for a fuller treatement of this conjunction).

49. This despite a critical tendency to focus on Weil's "asexual" persona, or at least her sublation of any erotic energy into religious "fanaticism" (seemingly the preferred term, in this context).

50. Hence Benjamin's almost parenthetical remarks on the "particularity" of *Trauerspielen* centering on women (*Origin*, 73–74).

51. See Julia Reinhard Lupton, "Deformations of Fellowship in Marlowe's *Jew of Malta*," in *Citizen-Saints: Shakespeare and Political Theology* (Chicago: University of Chicago Press, 2005), 63, as well as a shorter version of the essay in *The Cambridge Companion to Christopher Marlowe*, ed. Patrick Cheney, 144–57 (Cambridge: Cambridge University Press, 2004).

52. Most prominently, perhaps, Paul Giniewski, *Simone Weil: Ou la haine de soi* (Paris: Berg, 1978). Emmanuel Lévinas's brief discussion, "Simone Weil against the Bible," offers a thoughtful treatment; see his *Difficult Freedom: Essays on Judaism*, trans. Seán Hand (Baltimore: Johns Hopkins University Press, 1990), 133–41. It is certainly true that Weil overtly repudiated her Jewish heritage, both professionally and politically, for example in her claims to the Vichy authorities in France that her intellectual background derived primarily from traditions of Classical and Englightenment thinkers. Politically, she went even further; her writings on this point can be overtly antisemitic, expressing a desire for a Christian society freed from a dissenting Jewish minority. See, for discussion, Mary G. Dietz, *Between the Human and the Divine: The Political Thought of Simone Weil* (Totowa, N.J.: Rowman and Littlefield, 1988), which ultimately argues for "a modified Platonism" that Dietz terms "an antipolitics of spirituality." Compare Alexander Irwin, *Saints of the Impossible: Bataille, Weil, and the Politics of the Sacred* (Minneapolis: University of Minnesota Press, 2002). Irwin concludes that "for these figures, sacrality names an intellectual style, a pattern of self-positioning in political spaces. Sainthood as practiced by Weil and Bataille is a systematically critical orientation to society and politics, always operating from a stance of heterogeneity and risk. Sacrality is the performative assertion of alterity and unmasterability" (221). While both Dietz and Irwin treat Weil's overt hostility to Judaism, their conclusions sidestep, to a certain extent, "the Jewish question" rather than confronting it, as Weil herself did. See also Robert Coles, *Simone Weil: A Modern Pilgrimage* (Reading, Mass.: Merloyd Lawrence, 1987), chap. 3, as well as Rachel Feldhay Brenner's arguments concerning Weil and Stein and their differing approaches to Judaism and conversion in *Writing as Resistance: Four Women Confronting the Holocaust: Edith Stein, Simone Weil, Anne Frank, Etty Hillesum* (University Park: Pennsylvania State University Press, 1997).

53. Hence some feminist critiques of both Weil and Arendt, and particularly the focus on Weil's "sexlessness." See Rachel Feldhay Brenner, "Simone Weil: Philosopher, Socialist and Christian Mystic—a Jew and a Woman Despite Herself," in *The Netherlands and Nazi Genocide: Papers of the 21st Annual Scholars' Conference* (Lewiston, N.Y.: Mellen Press, 1971), 259–75.

54. While Weil herself wrote that she could never be baptized as a Catholic, some claim she was secretly baptized on her deathbed.

55. See Cavell, *Disowning Knowledge*; Strier, "Shakespeare and the Skeptics"; McEachern, "Figures of Fidelity."

56. On tears, particularly female tears, see Janet Adelman, *Suffocating Mothers: Fantasies of Maternal Origin in Shakespeare's Plays, "Hamlet" to "The Tempest"* (New York: Routledge, 1992); Gary Kuchar, *The Poetry of Religious Sorrow in Early Modern England* (Cambridge: Cambridge University Press, 2008); Gail Kern Paster, *Humoring the Body: Emotions and the Shakespearean Stage* (Chicago: University of Chicago Press, 2004).

57. Many feminist readings of the play have focused on Lear's "mother." See, for example, Adelman, *Suffocating Mothers*; Barbara Bono, "'The Chief Knot of All the Discourse': The Maternal Subtext Tying Sidney's *Arcadia* to Shakespeare's *King Lear*," in *Gloriana's Face: Women, Public and Private, in the English Renaissance*, ed. S. P. Cerasano and Marion Wynne-Davies, 105–28 (Detroit: Wayne State University Press, 1992); and Claire McEachern, "Fathering Herself: A Source Study of Shakespeare's Feminism," *Shakespeare Quarterly* 39, no. 3 (1988): 269–90.

58. Compare Strier's reading of this passage, "Shakespeare and the Skeptics," 185–87.

59. I am more inclined toward Daniel Boyarin's reading of Paul's gender politics in *A Radical Jew: Paul and the Politics of Identity* (Berkeley: University of California Press, 1994).

60. The play's farcical trappings have often been noted, but it's worth pausing for a moment to connect this moment of false witnessing to other scenes of witnessing: Edgar, hiding behind the tree, or, most obviously of course, the mock trial scene in the Folio.

61. On this distinction, see Jacob Taubes, *The Political Theology of Paul*, trans. Dana Hollander (Stanford, Calif.: Stanford University Press, 2004), 13–15; Badiou, *Saint Paul*, 45; Agamben, *The Time That Remains*, 23–29. The political-theological status of calling forms the burden of my final chapter.

62. See, for example, his argument in *Aesthetics and Its Discontents*: "Schiller's *Juno Ludovisi* . . . belong[s] to a different regime, which I call the aesthetic regime of art. In this regime, the statue of Juno does not draw its property of being an artwork from the conformity of the sculptor's work to an adequate idea or to the canons of representation. It draws it from its belonging to a specific sensorium. The property of being art refers back not to a distinction between the modes of doing, but to a distinction between modes of being. This is what 'aesthetics' means: in the aesthetic regime of art, the property of being art is no longer given by the criteria of technical perfection but is ascribed to a specific form of sensory apprehension. The statue is a 'free appearance.' It stands thus as a twofold contrast to its representative status: it is not an appearance drawn from a reality that would serve as its model. Nor is it an active form imposed on passive matter. As a sensory form, it is heterogeneous to the ordinary forms of sensory experience that these dualities inform. *It is given in a specific experience, which suspends the ordinary connections not only between appearance and reality, but also between form and matter, activity and passivity, understanding and sensibility*" (29–30).

63. See Jacques Rancière, "Are Some Things Unrepresentable?," in *The Future of the Image*, 109–38. Here Rancière notes that "the preferred site of representation is the theatre, a space of exhibition entirely given over to presence, but held by this very presence to a double restraint: the restraint of the visible under the sayable and of meanings and affects under the power of action—an action whose reality is identical to its unreality . . . if there are things which cannot be represented, it is precisely in this [representative] regime" (116–17).

64. By "prop" I meant a property of the staging, one that physically weighs Lear down—remember, he's supposed to be over eighty!—"the oldest have borne most," indeed. See Peter Stallybrass's brief but elegant treatment of this dynamic in "The Mystery of Walking," *Journal of Medieval and Early Modern Studies* 32, no. 3 (2002): 571–80.

65. Rancière, *The Future of the Image*, 120; see Kermode on the *fictive* aspect of *kairos*, in *The Sense of an Ending*, 46–47.

66. The responses of two priests who rejected the work, quoted in Friedlaender, *Caravaggio Studies*, 195.

67. See, especially, Bersani and Dutoit, *Caravaggio's Secrets*, 30–33, as well as Pamela Askew's detailed study *Caravaggio's Death of the Virgin* (Princeton: Princeton University Press, 1990), especially chap. 8, "The Virgin: Vessel of the Incarnation, Vehicle of Ascent," 108–32.

68. See Emmanuel Lévinas, *Time and the Other and Additional Essays*, trans. Richard A. Cohen (Pittsburgh: Duquesne University Press, 1987), 69.

69. See Terry Eagleton, *Sweet Violence: The Idea of the Tragic* (Oxford: Blackwell, 2003).

70. Weil, *Gravity and Grace*, 206.

Chapter Five

1. As critics from G. Wilson Knight to Janet Adelman have noted. See G. Wilson Knight, "*Cymbeline*," in *The Crown of Life: Essays in Interpretation of Shakespeare's Final Plays* (New York: Barnes and Noble, 1966), 129–202, and Janet Adelman, "The Return to Origins in the Romances," in *Suffocating Mothers: Fantasies of Maternal Origin in Shakespeare's Plays, "Hamlet" to "The Tempest"* (New York : Routledge, 1992), 200–20. All citations of the play refer to Roger Warren's Oxford edition of *Cymbeline* (Oxford: Oxford University Press, 1998); hereafter cited parenthetically.

2. See "*Cymbeline*," in *Shakespeare's Holinshed*, ed. Richard Hosley (New York: Capricorn, 1968), 4.

3. See, for example, Robin Moffet, "*Cymbeline* and the Nativity," *Shakespeare Quarterly* 13, no. 2 (1962): 207–18; Maurice Hunt, "Dismemberment, Corporal Reconstitution, and the Body Politic in *Cymbeline*," *Studies in Philology* 99, no. 4 (2002). 404–31; and Marjorie Garber, "*Cymbeline* and the Languages of Myth," *Mosaic* 10, no. 3 (1977): 105–15. Hunt's most recent treatment of the play, "Syncretistic Religion in Shakespeare's Late Romances," *South Central Review* 28, no. 2 (2011): 57–79, places *Cymbeline*'s recombinant strands of pagan, Judaic, Protestant, and Catholic elements in the context of Renaissance humanism's valorization of the classics, particularly Greek traditions and texts. In this he follows Northrop Frye's genealogy, which begins with Hellenistic romance, though he does not cite Frye in this article. See Frye's influential work,

The Secular Scripture: A Study of the Structure of Romance (Cambridge, Mass.: Harvard University Press, 1976).

4. From Forman's diary, quoted in Warren, *Cymbeline*, 4.

5. Wilson Knight's influential argument that *Cymbeline* is a "national" play has many recent reinterpreters, particularly in the aftermath of Benedict Anderson's argument positing nationalism as a form of "imagined community." See, for example, Jodi Mikalachki, "The Masculine Romance of Roman Britain: *Cymbeline* and Early Modern English Nationalism," *Shakespeare Quarterly* 46, no. 3 (1995): 301–22; Paul Innes, "*Cymbeline* and Empire," *Critical Survey* 19, no. 2 (2007): 1–18; Andrew Escobedo, "From Britannia to England: *Cymbeline* and the Beginning of Nations," *Shakespeare Quarterly* 59, no. 1 (2008): 60–87, and Hunt, "Dismemberment, Corporal Reconstitution." Graham Hammill's treatment of *Cymbeline* in the context of Mosaic law and Baruch Spinoza's 1670 *Theological-Political Treatise*, which invokes Carl Schmitt's conception of the *ius publicam europaeum*, stands as both example of and exception to this critical trend. I am grateful to Graham for sharing his unpublished essay "The Spirit of Europe: Political Theology from Shakespeare to Spinoza," which he contributed to a 2011 SAA seminar on Shakespeare and Political Theology I co-organized with Jennifer Rust. See Baruch Spinoza, *Theological-Political Treatise*, trans. Samuel Shirley, 2nd ed. (Indianapolis: Hackett, 1998), and Carl Schmitt, *The Nomos of the Earth in the International Law of the Jus Publicum Europaeum*, trans. G. L. Ulmen (New York: Telos, 2006).

6. See Max Weber, "The Profession and Vocation of Politics," in *Political Writings*, ed. Peter Lassman and Ronald Speirs, 309–69 (Cambridge: Cambridge University Press, 1994); hereafter cited parenthetically as PVP.

7. Compare Hunt, "Dismemberment, Corporal Reconstitution," which begins by treating the Pauline metaphor of the body politic in Romans 12:1–8 and 1 Corinthians 12:4–13. My own argument, while touching on ideas of the body politic, is more focused on Paul's conception of bodies, letters, and laws.

8. Though perhaps this is an unfair claim to make given my own focus more on residual Catholic strands of political-theological thought than on the twinned rise of Protestant theologies and capitalist economies.

9. Unless otherwise noted, references to Paul in English are to Wayne A. Meeks and John T. Fitzgerald, eds., *The Writings of St. Paul*, 2nd ed. (New York: Norton, 2007), though I will have occasion to cite other translations, including Meeks's own first edition (Norton, 1972). While the second edition uses Today's New International Version, Meeks's first edition uses the Revised Standard Version. When referring to the Meeks editions, I cite them hereafter as Meeks 1st ed. and Meeks 2nd ed.

10. Both the 1560 Geneva Bible and the King James Bible render the verse "Let such an one think this, that, such as we are in word by letters when we are absent, such *will we be* also in deed when we are present" (emphasis in originals). One might expect the Catholic Douay-Rheims to translate *ergô* as "works," as it is elsewhere, but it is "let him thinke that is such a one, that such a we are in word by epistles, absent: such also we are in deede, present" (*The New Testament of Jesus Christ, translated faithfully into English . . . at the English College of Rheims* [Rheims, 1582], 487). Other translations include the Revised Standard's

"Let such people understand that what we say by letter when absent, we do when present" (Meeks 1st ed.) and Today's New International's "Such people should realize that what we are in our letters when we are absent, we will be in our actions when we are present" (Meeks 2nd ed.).

11. The Latin Vulgate is "*hoc cogitet qui eiusmodi est quia quales sumus verbo per epistulas absentes tales et praesentes in facto*" (http://www.perseus.tufts.edu/hopper/text).

12. All my remarks concerning absence and the letter have Jacques Derrida behind them. See Jacques Derrida, "Signature Event Context," trans. Samuel Weber and Jeffrey Mehlman, *Glyph* 1 (1977), reprinted in *Limited Inc* (Evanston, Ill.: Northwestern University Press, 1988), 1–24, especially 4–10. I take my second epigraph from the first of two hypotheses governing Derrida's analysis of speech act theory: "Since every sign, whether in the 'language of action' or in articulated language (before even the intervention of writing in the classical sense), presupposes a certain absence (to be determined), *the absence within the particular field of writing will have to be of an original type if one intends to grant any specificity whatsoever to the written sign*" (7; emphasis added). I am suggesting that it is the *corporeality* of letters, emerging in this strange conjunction with *work*, that must paradoxically be considered the "original type" of absence in Paul's account.

13. For example, 2 Corinthians 12:9; 1 Corinthians 2:4. For more extended readings, see Agamben, *The Time that Remains*, as well as Richard Kearney, "Paul's Notion of *Dunamis*: Between the Possible and the Impossible," in *St. Paul among the Philosophers*, ed. John D. Caputo and Linda Martín Alcoff, 142–59 (Bloomington: Indiana University Press, 2009).

14. I am grateful to Alex Gottesman, my colleague in the Department of Greek and Roman Classics, for vetting this section and for pointing out that Paul's final *kai* adds emphasis. Any errors and exigencies of translation and interpretation are my own.

15. See Max Weber, *The Protestant Ethic and the "Spirit" of Capitalism*, ed. and trans. Peter Baehr and Gordon C. Wells (Harmondsworth, U.K.: Penguin, 2002), 28–36, on the Lutheran translation and significance of *Beruf*, as well as Giorgio Agamben, *The Time That Remains: A Commentary on the Letter to the Romans*, trans. Patricia Dailey (Stanford, Calif.: Stanford University Press, 2005). Agamben's treatment of Weber and the connection between *klêsis* and *Beruf* occurs on pp. 19–23.

16. See the *OED*'s etymological note on "clown," as well as "clod" (n) and "clot" (n). Compare Margreta de Grazia's argument concerning the pseudo-Latin etymology of "clown" in her discussion of the graveyard scene in *Hamlet*: "By a spurious etymology cited by Holinshed, *clown* was derived from the Latin *colonus*, 'a tiller of the soil.' Like its synonym *rustic*, from the Latin *rus*, and *peasant*, from the French *païs*, the name linked a man to the land which was his sustenance" (*"Hamlet" without Hamlet* [Cambridge: Cambridge University Press, 2007], 132.)

17. Marjorie Garber is an exception; see her discussion of Cloten and sacrifice in "The Languages of Myth," 111–15.

18. See, for example, 1 Corinthians 15:53–54; Romans 13:12; Galatians 3:27.

19. Compare Desdemona's handkerchief and sheets—Janet Adelman also makes this connection.

20. Graham Hammill argues that "this substitution, Fidele for Euriphile, implies two claims. First, Euriphile must be thought of as Fidele, so that faith becomes the grounds for building European unity. Second, though, since both Fidele and Euriphile are dead, the weird, seeming death of faith is the very reason that Euriphile cannot be resurrected" ("The Spirit of Europe," 15).

21. On sacrifice in the play, see Garber, "The Languages of Myth," as well as William Barry Thorne, "*Cymbeline*: 'Lopp'd Branches' and the Concept of Regeneration," *Shakespeare Quarterly* 20, no. 2 (1969): 143–59.

22. I am grateful to my former student Benjamin Satlow for pointing out the link between Orpheus and Cloten. Hunt, "Dismemberment, Corporal Reconstitution," 419–20, also makes this point, citing previous critics who have made the connection (420, n28).

23. See Julia Lupton, "Creature Caliban," in *Citizen-Saints: Shakespeare and Political Theology* (Chicago: University of Chicago Press, 2005), 159–80.

24. Visually exemplified in V.i, when Prospero appears "aloft" to guide as well as witness the metatheatrical scenes he conjures. Prospero's *removal*—or, we might say, his *absence*—constitutes one facet of art, whether it relates to his abdication of ducal responsibilities or, in the final twist, to his abjuration of "this rough magic."

25. "Hē epistolē hēmōn humeis este, engegrammenē en tais kardiais hēmōn, ginōskomenē kai anaginōskomenē hupo pantōn anthrōpōn: phaneroumenoi hoti este epistolē Khristou diakonētheisa huph' hēmōn, 'engegrammenē' ou melani alla pneumati theou zōntos, ouk en 'plaxin lithinais' all' en 'plaxin kardiais' sarkinais." Emphasis added and translation slightly modified; Meeks, 2nd ed., has "on tablets of human hearts."

26. Graham Hammill's analysis of the play's treatment of grafting in connection with the language of prophecy in "The Spirit of Europe" informs my own argument.

27. See, for example, emblems 24 and 42 in Alciatus, *Emblemata* (1631), available online at http://www.mun.ca/alciato/ltext.html.

28. Regarding the phrase "stinking elder," Warren notes, "This phrase is hyphenated in F, which suggests that it may reflect rural usage, though OED does not include it among the many plant-names beginning 'stinking-'. The elder gained its evil reputation from its pungent smell, and from the tradition that Judas Iscariot hanged himself on one after betraying Christ" (4.2.l. 61n).

29. See, in the *OED*, "spur," senses 5 and 6.

30. As, again, the *OED* notes; see "spur," sense 9.

31. As Derrida, again, reminds us. See Jacques Derrida, *Dissemination*, trans. Barbara Johnson (Chicago: University of Chicago Press, 1981).

32. Hammill connects this scene with "the divisive coupling of faith and violence [that] looks forward to the divisions and crisis through which early modern Europe takes shape" ("The Spirit of Europe," 19).

33. I have in mind Jean-Luc Nancy's reading of this episode and its iconography in *"Noli me tangere": On the Raising of the Body*, trans. Sarah Clift, Pascale-Anne Brault, and Michael Naas (New York: Fordham, 2008), which focuses so intently on the image. See also Northrop Frye's discussion of suffering

femininity: "With the rise of the romantic ethos, heroism comes increasingly to be thought of in terms of suffering, endurance, and patience, which can coexist with such weakness, whatever other kinds of patience it may require. This is also the ethos of the Christian myth, where the heroism of Christ takes the form of enduring the Passion. Such a change in the conception of heroism largely accounts for the prominence of female figures in romance" (*Secular Scripture*, 88). Here Frye comes close to Benjamin's observations about women in *Trauerspielen*.

34. See Daniel Boyarin's astute analysis of Paul's treatment of gender in *A Radical Jew: Paul and the Politics of Identity* (Berkeley: University of California Press, 1994).

35. Compare the opening scene of Webster's *Duchess of Malfi*.

36. In a Girardian reading of the play (though he does not cite Girard), William Thorne notes, "It seems quite clear that, as in *Romeo and Juliet*, the relation between the two lovers has a bearing upon the community and the relation of the King to his people, for a potentially destructive situation is resolved through the actions of the lovers. The young must suffer in this play, for it seems their sacrifice insures the well-being of the community. . . . Clearly, the young in *Cymbeline* are significant participants and even scapegoats to a degree; their agony provides the basis for a regeneration of the kingdom and the spiritually sterile king" ("'Lopp'd Branches,'" 153). Yet the "regeneration" Thorne detects is, as I hope to demonstrate, never complete—it is the sense of messianic *potential*, always allusively but never fully present, that drives the play's treatment of suffering.

37. On perilous grafts, compare Marvell's "The Garden" and the Mower poems, as well as the *Duchess of Malfi*, II.i, when "grafted" apricocks confirm the Duchess's pregnancy to the scheming Bosola.

38. See, in the *OED*, "graft" (n), sense 1.

39. Derrida's concept of autoimmunity and Roberto Esposito's works on the "potentiality" of biopolitics are relevant in this context. See Esposito's *Immunitas: The Protection and Negation of Life* (Cambridge: Polity, 2011).

40. Here I invoke Freud but avoid an overtly Freudian reading, as so many remarkable critics have already taken this route. See Adelman, *Suffocating Mothers*, as well as Garber's "Languages of Myth" and *Shakespeare After All* (New York: Random House, 2004), 802–26

41. Moffet makes this point; see his "*Cymbeline* and the Nativity," 217

42. See Hunt, "Dismemberment, Corporal Reconstitution," for a thorough discussion of the metaphor of the body politic in the play.

43. See Sarah Beckwith's reading of this scene in *Shakespeare and the Grammar of Forgiveness* (Ithaca: Cornell University Press, 2011), 106–10. Beckwith astutely teases out the connections between confessional practice and Posthumous's economic vocabulary.

44. Though "theme" derives from the Greek *tithenai* (to set, place, or put), it also points us toward *themistos* (law). See, in the *OED*, "theme" (n); Henry George Liddell and Robert Scott, *An Intermediate Greek-English Lexicon* (Oxford: Oxford University Press, 1994), *tithenai*, *themistos*.

45. On the politics of physical proximity to the monarch, see Curtis Perry, *Literature and Favoritism in Early Modern Europe*.

46. Though, formally, the archaic "fourteeners" of the ghosts' speech do act as a form of literary recollection.

47. See Adelman, *Suffocating Mothers*, and Mikalachki, "The Masculine Romance of Roman Britain."

48. The full passage, from the original printing of Weber's *Politik als Beruf* (Munich: Duncker and Humblot, 1919): "Es gibt der inneren Rechtfertigungen, also: der *Legitimitäts*gründe einer Herrschaft—um mit ihnen zu beginnen—im Prinzip drei. Einmal die Autorität des ‚ewig Gestrigen': der durch unvordenkliche Geltung und gewohnheitsmäßige Einstellung auf ihre Innehaltung geheiligten *Sitte*: ‚traditionale' Herrschaft, wie sie der Patriarch und der Patrimonialfürst alten Schlages übten. Dann: die Autorität der außeralltäglichen persönlichen *Gnadengabe* (Charisma), die ganz persönliche Hingabe und das persönliche Vertrauen zu Offenbarungen, Heldentum oder anderen Führereigenschaften eines einzelnen: ‚charismatische' Herrschaft, wie sie der Prophet oder—auf dem Gebiet des Politischen—der gekorene Kriegsfürst oder der plebiszitäre Herrscher, der große Demagoge und politische Parteiführer ausüben. Endlich: Herrschaft kraft ‚Legalität', kraft des Glaubens an die Geltung legaler *Satzung* und der durch rational geschaffene Regeln begründeten sachlichen ‚Kompetenz', also: der Einstellung auf Gehorsam in der Erfüllung satzungsmäßiger Pflichten: eine Herrschaft, wie sie der moderne ‚Staatsdiener' und alle jene Träger von Macht ausüben, die ihm in dieser Hinsicht ähneln.—Es versteht sich, daß in der Realität höchst massive Motive der Furcht und der Hoffnung—Furcht vor der Rache magischer Mächte oder des Machthabers, Hoffnung auf jenseitigen oder diesseitigen Lohn—und daneben Interessen verschiedenster Art die Fügsamkeit bedingen. Davon sogleich. Aber wenn man nach den ‚Legitimitäts' gründen dieser Fügsamkeit fragt, dann allerdings stößt man auf diese drei ‚reinen' Typen. Und diese Legitimitätsvorstellungen und ihre innere Begründung sind für die Struktur der Herrschaft von sehr erheblicher Bedeutung. Die reinen Typen finden sich freilich in der Wirklichkeit selten. Aber es kann heute auf die höchst verwickelten Abwandlungen, Übergänge und Kombinationen dieser reinen Typen nicht eingegangen werden: das gehört zu dem Problem der ‚allgemeinen Staatslehre'. *Uns interessiert hier vor allem der zweite von jenen Typen: die Herrschaft kraft Hingabe der Gehorchenden an das rein persönliche ‚Charisma' des ‚Führers'. Denn hier wurzelt der Gedanke des Berufs in seiner höchsten Ausprägung*" (http://de.wikisource.org/wiki/Politik_als_Beruf, seiten 5–6; emphasis added).

49. For a compelling study of Weber's conception of charisma in conjunction with early modern drama, see Raphael Falco, *Charismatic Authority in Early Modern English Tragedy* (Baltimore: Johns Hopkins University Press, 2000).

50. "Es wäre ja schön, wenn die Sache so wäre, daß dann Shakespeares 102. Sonett gelten würde: Damals war Lenz und unsere Liebe grün,

> Da grüßt' ich täglich sie mit meinem Sang,
> So schlägt die Nachtigall in Sommers Blühn—
> Und schweigt den Ton in reifrer Tage Gang.

Aber so ist die Sache nicht. Nicht das Blühen des Sommers liegt vor uns, sondern zunächst eine Polarnacht von eisiger Finsternis und Härte, mag äußerlich jetzt siegen welche Gruppe auch immer. Denn: wo nichts ist, da hat nicht nur der Kaiser, sondern auch der Proletarier sein Recht verloren" (*Politik als Beruf*, http://de.wikisource.org/wiki/Politik_als_Beruf, seite 66).

51. From Colin Burrows's 2002 Oxford edition.

52. "Die Politik bedeutet ein starkes langsames Bohren von harten Brettern mit Leidenschaft und Augenmaß zugleich. Es ist ja durchaus richtig, und alle geschichtliche Erfahrung bestätigt es, daß man das Mögliche nicht erreichte, wenn nicht immer wieder in der Welt nach dem Unmöglichen gegriffen worden wäre. Aber der, der das tun kann, muß ein Führer und nicht nur das, sondern auch—in einem sehr schlichten Wortsinn—ein Held sein. Und auch die, welche beides nicht sind, müssen sich wappnen mit jener Festigkeit des Herzens, die auch dem Scheitern aller Hoffnungen gewachsen ist, jetzt schon, sonst werden sie nicht imstande sein, auch nur durchzusetzen, was heute möglich ist. Nur wer sicher ist, daß er daran nicht zerbricht, wenn die Welt, von seinem Standpunkt aus gesehen, zu dumm oder zu gemein ist für das, was er ihr bieten will, daß er all dem gegenüber: ‚dennoch!' zu sagen vermag, nur der hat den ‚Beruf' zur Politik" (*Politik als Beruf*, http://de.wikisource.org/wiki/Politik_als_Beruf, seiten 66–67).

53. For an in-depth treatment of Weber's political thought and its connections to Schmitt's and Arendt's later works, see Andreas Kalyvas, *Democracy and the Politics of the Extraordinary: Max Weber, Carl Schmitt, and Hannah Arendt* (Cambridge: Cambridge University Press, 2008).

54. Again, compare Hegel's "world historical individual."

55. Perhaps, in these lines, Weber refers to the George circle, and the poet-mystic Stefan George in particular. Like Kantorowicz, who attended Weber's lectures and later associated with George, Weber had been a peripheral member of the group, embarking on a correspondence with George himself as well as with his disciple Friedrich Gundolf in 1910. George's poem "Der Krieg," critical of the war, was published in 1917, two years before Weber's lecture; *Das neue Reich* (which included "Secret Germany," George's vision of a mystic political order) appeared in 1928. George dedicated the latter work to Berthold von Stauffenberg, who, along with his brother Claus, would later become a member of the German resistance. Claus von Stauffenberg attempted to assassinate Hitler in the 20 July Plot of 1944. The fullest treatment of the subject is Robert Norton, *Secret Germany: Stefan George and His Circle* (Ithaca: Cornell University Press, 2002); see, especially, 475–81, where Norton discusses Weber's connections with the group. See also Bryan S. Turner, *Max Weber: From History to Modernity* (London: Routledge, 1992).

56. Remembering that Paul's journeys, as described in Acts, might also be read as a form of romance. On this point, see Randall Martin's essay "Pauline Cartography, Missionary Nationalism, and *The Tempest*," in *Shakespeare/Adaptation/Modern Drama: Essays in Honour of Jill J. Levenson*, ed. Randall Martin and Katherine Schiel, 198–217 (Toronto: University of Toronto Press, 2011).

57. I am heavily indebted to Frye's *The Secular Scripture* for this reading.

58. In particular, her closing reference to "Lud's town with rejoicing fires bright"—though she does not speak overtly of sacrifice, it's a reasonable conjecture. Jodi Mikalachki's reading of the Queen's link to ancient British warrior women such as Boudicca is particularly fine.

59. As Hunt, again, notes. See also Sarah Beckwith's reading of the scene in *Shakespeare and the Grammar of Forgiveness*.

60. As briefly discussed in chapter 4. See Alain Badiou, *Saint Paul: The Foundation of Universalism*, trans. Ray Brassier (Stanford, Calif.: Stanford University Press, 2003).

Epilogue

1. All citations are taken from Anthony B. Dawson and Gretchen E. Minton's Arden edition of the play (London: Cengage, 2008).

2. Recall that Alcibiades is also the beautiful boy who so captured Socrates in Plato's *Symposium* and elsewhere, so he's posed as a potential distraction to the life of the mind.

INDEX

Page numbers in **bold** refer to illustrations.